*W*orldwide websites of

 The New Life Mission

Please find your vernacular websites below.
You can download Christian e-books and request Christian books for free.
Feel free to visit our websites below right now!

A
- www.nlmafghanistan.com
- www.nlmafrikaans.com
- www.nlmalbania.com
- www.nlmamharic.com
- www.nlmangola.com
- www.nlmarabemirates.com
- www.nlmarabic.com
- www.nlmargentina.com
- www.nlmarmenia.com
- www.nlmaruba.com
- www.nlmaustralia.com
- www.nlmaustria.com

B
- www.nlmbahamas.com
- www.nlmbahrain.com
- www.nlmbangladesh.com
- www.nlmbelarus.com
- www.nlmbelgium.com
- www.nlmbengali.com
- www.nlmbenin.com
- www.nlmbhutan.com
- www.nlmbolivia.com
- www.nlmbotswana.com
- www.nlmbrasil.com
- www.nlmbriton.com
- www.nlmbrunei.com
- www.nlmbulgalia.com
- www.nlmburkinafaso.com
- www.nlmburundi.com

C
- www.nlmcameroon.com
- www.nlmcanada.com
- www.nlmcebuano.com
- www.nlmchichewa.com
- www.nlmchile.com
- www.nlmchin.com

- www.nlmchina.com
- www.nlmcolombia.com
- www.nlmcongo.com
- www.nlmcostarica.com
- www.nlmcotedivoire.com
- www.nlmcroatia.com
- www.nlmczech.com

D
- www.nlmdenmark.com
- www.nlmdioula.com
- www.nlmdominica.com
- www.nlmdutch.com

E
- www.nlmecuador.com
- www.nlmegypt.com
- www.nlmelsalvador.com
- www.nlmequatorialguinea.com
- www.nlmethiopia.com

F
- www.nlmfinland.com
- www.nlmfrance.com
- www.nlmfrench.com

G
- www.nlmgabon.com
- www.nlmgeorgian.com
- www.nlmgerman.com
- www.nlmgermany.com
- www.nlmghana.com
- www.nlmgreek.com
- www.nlmgrenada.com
- www.nlmguatemala.com
- www.nlmgujarati.com

H
- www.nlmhaiti.com
- www.nlmhindi.com
- www.nlmholland.com
- www.nlmhonduras.com
- www.nlmhungary.com

Turn over

© Some of these websites may not work because they are still under construction.

Worldwide websites of

 The New Life Mission

I
www.nlm-india.com
www.nlmindonesia.com
www.nlmiran.com
www.nlmiraq.com
www.nlmisrael.com
www.nlmitaly.com

J
www.nlmjamaica.com
www.nlmjapan.com
www.nlmjavanese.com

K
www.nlmkannada.com
www.nlmkazakhstan.com
www.nlmkenya.com
www.nlmkhmer.com
www.nlmkirghiz.com
www.nlmkirundi.com
www.nlmkorea.com

L
www.nlmlatvia.com
www.nlmluganda.com
www.nlmluo.com

M
www.nlmmadi.com
www.nlmmalagasy.com
www.nlmmalayalam.com
www.nlmmalaysia.com
www.nlmmarathi.com
www.nlmmauritius.com
www.nlmmexico.com
www.nlmmindat.com
www.nlmmizo.com
www.nlmmoldova.com
www.nlmmongolia.com
www.nlmmyanmar.com

N
www.nlmnepal.com
www.nlmnewzealand.com
www.nlmnigeria.com
www.nlmnorthkorea.com
www.nlmnorway.com

P
www.nlmpakistan.com
www.nlmpanama.com
www.nlmperu.com
www.nlmphilippines.com
www.nlmpoland.com

www.nlmportugal.com
www.nlmportuguese.com
www.nlmprcongo.com

Q
www.nlmqatar.com

R
www.nlmromania.com
www.nlmrussia.com

S
www.nlmsaudiarabia.com
www.nlmserbian.com
www.nlmshona.com
www.nlmsingapore.com
www.nlmslovakia.com
www.nlmslovene.com
www.nlmsolomon.com
www.nlmsouthafrica.com
www.nlmspain.com
www.nlmspanish.com
www.nlmsrilanka.com
www.nlmsuriname.com
www.nlmswahili.com
www.nlmswaziland.com
www.nlmsweden.com
www.nlmswiss.com

T
www.nlmtagalog.com
www.nlmtaiwan.com
www.nlmtamil.com
www.nlmtanzania.com
www.nlmtelugu.com
www.nlmthailand.com
www.nlmtogo.com
www.nlmtonga.com
www.nlmturkey.com

U
www.nlmuganda.com
www.nlmukraine.com
www.nlmurdu.com
www.nlmusa.com

V
www.nlmvenezuela.com
www.nlmvietnam.com

Z
www.nlmzambia.com
www.nlmzimbabwe.com
www.nlmzou.com

The Righteousness of God that is revealed in Romans

Our LORD
Who Becomes the
Righteousness
of God
(I)

Dear Readers of This Book:

The New Life Mission has been sending out Free Christian Books of Rev. Paul C. Jong through the homepage (www.nlmission.com or www.bjnewlife.org) in order to preach the gospel of the water and the Spirit throughout the entire world. We have been advertising our website on well known web search engines, such as, Google and Yahoo, which is on a cost-per-click pricing basis so that many more people can come to know the gospel of the water and the Spirit. However, this method of advertising has resulted in an increase of costs for us in order to preach this genuine gospel to more souls. Moreover, the current global economic crisis has become an obstacle for our gospel ministry.

Therefore, we, the staff members of The New Life Mission, are requesting you to give our homepage address (www.nlmission.com or www.bjnewlife.org) to many people around you and bookmark our homepage on your computer so that you can access it easily while allowing us to save on these high advertising costs and still be able to preach the genuine gospel to many more souls. Your immediate cooperation will be highly appreciated as this will enable us to send out many more Free Christian Books to thirsty souls. This will be your first step in participating in this beautiful gospel ministry.

Our LORD
Who Becomes the
Righteousness
of God
(I)

PAUL C. JONG

Hephzibah Publishing House

A Ministry of THE NEW LIFE MISSION
SEOUL, KOREA

Our LORD Who Becomes the Righteousness of God (I)
Copyright © 2002 by Hephzibah Publishing House
Scripture quotations are from *the New King James Version.*

ISBN 89-8314-197-2
Cover Art by Min-soo Kim
Illustration by Young-ae Kim
Printed in Korea

Hephzibah Publishing House
A Ministry of THE NEW LIFE MISSION
P.O. Box 18 Yang-Cheon Post Office
Yang-Cheon Gu, Seoul, Korea

♠ Website: http://www.nlmission.com
          http://www.bjnewlife.org
          http://www.nlmbookcafe.com
♠ E-mail: newlife@bjnewlife.org

Words of Gratitude

Words are inadequate to express my heartfelt gratitude to our Lord Jesus. He always provides me with enough of His words to preach the gospel of the water and the Spirit worldwide, and has encouraged me to write this book according to His will.

I would like to thank all of the individuals involved in this publication. First of all, I owe a debt of gratitude that cannot be repaid to all the members of The New Life Mission. They have been praying for and supporting this task with all their hearts.

I express my special gratitude to my fellow workers Rev. John Shin and Rev. Sangchan Lee, who have been in charge of this publication. I cannot thank Sangmin Lee enough for editing, Yoonhee Hwang for translating, and Suzanne Lee for her faithful proofreading.

I owe all the glory to our Lord God who has made us His children through the riches of His righteousness.

Hallelujah!

PAUL C. JONG

CONTENTS

CONTENTS

CHAPTER 3

CHAPTER 4

CHAPTER 5

CHAPTER 6

You can download Rev. Paul C. Jong's Christian Books on iPhone, iPad, or Blackberry by going to Amazon's Kindle e-bookstore (www.amazon.com).

Preface

If the Doctrine of Justification or the Doctrine of Sanctification that prevails in Christianity nowadays were really true, a lot of people throughout the world would have already been saved from their sins. However, the reality of it is that this is not the case and as a result, no one has been able to obtain deliverance from all his or her sins through the doctrines.

To witness this reality is truly tantalizing. Even though people are able to be saved from all their sins by simply believing in the gospel of the water and the Spirit written in the Bible, they are neither willing to hear nor to believe in this truth, therefore they are on the verge of destruction not knowing God's free gift contained in this truth. It becomes clear that the reason for this phenomenon is due to the preachers, clergymen, and leaders of today's Christianity.

God tells us to get rid of the false prophets. It is deplorable to see that though it is certainly true that there are too many false prophets nowadays, most Christians do not perceive the prophets' false teachings as something false. However, regardless of whom God raises and uses, He raises the servants of the gospel of the water and the Spirit and they shout it out. How many people in this world indeed are willing to listen to those who shout out the gospel of the water and the Holy Spirit, which God acknowledges?

The time has now arrived and God has revealed the truth of the water and the Spirit to the thirsty spirits all over the world through His servants who are bearing witness to it. I hope that you will be able to rebuild your faith, which has been ruined by the false teachers, by believing in the true gospel after rooting out and throwing down the false doctrines in Christianity today. We should be very thankful that there are true servants of God during these last days.

Those who possess the righteousness of God are now shouting out the truth of the water and the Holy Spirit. This truth will be spread to every part of this world, where it has not reached until now. *"For there is nothing hidden which will not be revealed, nor has anything been kept secret but that it should come to light" (Mark 4:22).* The gospel of the water and the Spirit, together with God's righteousness, will bear witness to the only truth that allows all the people in this world to receive the remission of sin.

Therefore, even though every believer in God's righteousness receive salvation from the judgment and punishment of sin, those who don't believe in it will receive the fatal condemnation of eternal death, which God sends down to sinners.

The time has arrived for you to decide whether you will believe in the false doctrines on justification or sanctification instead of believing in God's righteousness, which lies inside the gospel of the water and the Spirit. It is totally up to you whether you believe in this truth or not.

However, it is you who will be bound to the results of the decision. You should not forget that God gave you His righteousness as a gift together with the gospel of the water and the Spirit. It is not too late for you to believe in the true righteousness of God. Only then will you be able to obtain the eternal righteousness inside God and live happily for an eternity.

In Romans, God's righteousness is thought of as most important and is preciously born witness to. Therefore, we should learn about God's righteousness through Romans since the gospel containing God's righteousness brings this righteousness to us.

Now is the time for Christianity to discard the false gospel, which does not contain God's righteousness, and return to His righteousness. In order to do so, we need to learn what God's righteousness really is and recover the true faith. The time has arrived for us to know about God's righteousness through Romans.

Luther, one of the greatest religious reformers, was in need of God's righteousness. He realized that one could not wash away one's sins through virtuous deeds regardless of whether one believed in God's righteousness or not. God's righteousness, which is talked about in the Bible, is not so called 'the righteousness acquired by faith' that can be obtained by a doctrinal and incomplete faith and most Christians are supporting.

People are trying to build up the moral righteousness of human deeds in a state in which they have not truly realized what God's righteousness really is. Therefore, innumerable Christians have fallen into an ethical faith of Christianity. In fact, we can nowadays often witness that Christians compete with one another while trying to show off their own virtuous deeds.

Though there are many who say that they have obtained the remission of their sins by believing in Jesus, there are rarely those who truly know the righteousness of God and believe in it. Many people believe in the Doctrine of Justification or the Doctrine of Sanctification, which are the pivotal doctrines in today's Christianity, and have fallen into 'self-conceit' of their faith while not knowing God's righteousness. They brag about themselves with their absurd and false faiths saying, "I will go to Heaven even though I have sin, because I believe in Jesus!"

Can one truly go to Heaven when he/she possesses sin just because he/she believes in Jesus somehow?

Reconsider this question with your conscience. It is arrogant for one to believe that one can go to Heaven even though one has sin by believing in Jesus somehow. This is a self-justified faith that has sprung out from religion. We should discard the false faith that says that one can go to Heaven even when there is sin by only believing in Jesus. Isn't God holy? Does God acknowledge one just because he/she believes in the Doctrine of Justification that says that he/she has received salvation from his/her own sins even though he/she has sin in his/her heart? Can one obtain the righteousness of the true God by believing in forged doctrines on justification or sanctification? Certainly not.

How could a person say that he/she is sinless though there is evidently sin inside his/her heart? Without knowing and believing in the righteousness of God written in His words, one cannot say that he/she is actually sinless in his/her conscience. The reason some people can say recklessly that they are able to go to Heaven is because they believe in the forged doctrines on justification or sanctification that prevail in today's Christianity. Did your sins really disappear when you relied on these kinds of doctrines? Is it possible? Only one who discovers and believes in God's righteousness by believing in the words of the gospel of the water and the Spirit can say that he/she surely is sinless.

However, one who has faith in the Doctrine of Justification, which is one of the principal Christian doctrines, believes that he/she is sinless only due to the reason that he/she believes in Jesus somehow, though in truth he/she has sin. You should know that the faiths of these kinds of people are just like the tower of Babel, built by a human plot against God's word. It is not hard to realize that it is impossible for one to escape from all sins by doctrinal faith. The Lord Jesus revealed God's righteousness through the baptism He received from John, His blood on the Cross, and His resurrection. He gave it to all those who believe in Him. Therefore, Paul said clearly that in the gospel God's righteousness is revealed from faith to faith (Romans 1:17).

There are many Christian leaders who are outstanding in their ethical and moral standards. However, they teach their followers to pursue the human righteousness inside Christianity stirring up the human ethics and morals of Christians. They don't even have the slightest idea about the gospel of the water and the Spirit containing God's righteousness.

Therefore, they can't teach their followers about the righteousness of God. This is the reason why the true gospel in which God's righteousness is revealed cannot be found inside the doctrines and teachings of Christianity nowadays. Christianity has not spread God's righteousness, which is revealed inside the gospel of the water and the Spirit and is considered the most important by God, until now. Therefore, no one is able to soundly encounter God's righteousness with Christian doctrines.

Then where can God's righteousness be found? It is revealed where one can obtain salvation from all sin by discovering and believing in God's righteousness inside the baptism Jesus received and His blood on the Cross. The Bible explains God's righteousness through the gospel of the water and the Spirit. The faith believing in the baptism Jesus Christ received from John the Baptist, His bloodshed on the Cross, and the resurrection leads us to know about God's righteousness.

If we wish to own the righteousness of God, we should believe in the words of the gospel of the water and the Spirit. God's righteousness is abundantly revealed inside the gospel of the water and the Spirit God has given. Therefore, anyone who makes up his/her mind to believe in God's righteousness can find and believe in it right now.

What I want to tell you brethren is that one cannot know about God's righteousness by a doctrinal faith that still prevails inside Christianity. I tell you that this is only possible by believing in the words of the water and the Holy Spirit, which contains God's righteousness. However, most believers and theologians of today's Christianity do not even wish to know about God's righteousness. Rather, they are not able to know it. The reality is that they fear that the doctrinal faiths they had until now would be deteriorated.

However, God's righteousness only can actually bring the remission of sin to all sinners. The reason these people are not able to accept the words containing God's righteousness is that they have been fed with ethical and moral teachings until now. Satan has turned the attention of people elsewhere so that they would not know about the righteousness God has given to them.

What Christian believers need at this time is not the ethical righteousness of religion, but to have faith in God's righteousness. Presently, most people who say that they believe in Jesus as their Savior have not been able to equip themselves with the faith in God's righteousness and are therefore on the verge of spiritual death. Therefore, today's Christian believers should be clothed with God's righteousness in their hearts.

This righteousness of God can only be obtained when our souls believe in the gospel of the water and the Spirit. In order to do that, we need to first discard the doctrinal faiths based on human logic and the false teachings on salvation. Moreover, we should be most concerned with the salvation of our own souls. One can get clothed with God's righteousness only after one's soul has obtained eternal redemption from all the sins of his/her whole life.

Right now, Christianity has departed itself from God and is running on a carriage of theoretical doctrines toward complete darkness. The doctrinal faiths that theologians have forged gave birth to human-centered religious faiths. Now, Christianity might at this moment seem to have obtained great success based on worldly standards, but we see that there isn't the slightest bit of God's righteousness inside it. Rather we can find only human righteousness inside Christianity, and it is human righteousness that blocks God's blessings.

Right now, most Christian souls are about to go to hell after death due to their spiritual starvation and sins. They should realize and believe that only the abundance of God's righteousness can save them from hell. Therefore, we should deliver the abundant truth of God's righteousness to all the sinners who still do not know about it.

Now we will learn and come to know what God's righteousness is. If we don't believe in His righteousness, even though we know about it, we will receive eternal destruction, but we will surely enjoy the spiritual blessings of Heaven if we do believe in it.

Christianity today has degraded itself into a worldly religion due to the Doctrine of Justification and the Doctrine of Sanctification. This religion is like 'the great harlot' in the Bible. The Doctrine of Justification and the Doctrine of Sanctification that theologians have invented inside Christianity are causing a favorable reaction among people, though they are nothing more than the religious doctrines that have been concocted by human thought. There is not a single person whose sins were perfectly eliminated by believing in these doctrines!

The Doctrine of Sanctification is the same as the doctrine that worldly religions teach on virtuous deeds. It is impossible to obtain the righteousness of God, which is talked about in the Bible, with these kinds of doctrinal faiths. Most Christians regard the doctrinal righteousness in the same light with God's righteousness, and that is a false teaching from Satan. One who blocks people from believing in God's righteousness will remain as a great enemy to God. Therefore, God can't allow people to obtain His righteousness inside worldly religions because it has only been allowed by the gospel of the water and the Spirit.

All of those who eagerly long for God's righteousness! I hope you will obtain the remission of sin and eternal life by believing that Jesus Christ came to this world, took over your sins by the baptism He received from John, died on the Cross, and resurrected on the third day. God's righteousness will bring eternal life and the blessing of becoming God's children to all those who believe in His righteousness. God's righteousness is different from the human righteousness that can be obtained by keeping the law. God's righteousness allows the eternal remission of sin to all sinners at once.

Nothing in heaven or on earth can separate those who possess the faith in God's righteousness from God's love that is revealed inside Jesus Christ. The faith in God's righteousness is true and should be appreciated inside Christianity. God's righteousness can be obtained only by believing in the gospel of the water and the Spirit.

Paul asserted that even the Israelites would receive salvation from sin in the last days by believing in God's righteousness. He believed that since God did not break the promise that He would save the Israelites from sin, God would work in the last days and save them from sin. God always works consistently according to His will. He wants to save all humankind. There is no one from any historical time period who has been left out from the blessing that can be obtained by believing in God's righteousness, just because he/she was not a Jew.

It is really unfortunate that there are people who reject the gospel of the water and the Spirit without knowing that God's love and His righteousness are hidden inside it. We should remember and keep in our hearts the fact that there is only human righteousness remaining for those who say that they believe in Jesus without knowing the abundance of God's righteousness. The salvation from sin God has given to mankind can only be acquired by believing in the righteousness of God.

In conclusion, a person gets saved from sin not by his/her own efforts, but by believing in the abundance of God's righteousness that is revealed inside the gospel of the water and the Spirit. God did not abandon the Jews or leave out the Gentiles from the blessing of being clothed with His righteousness. God allowed His righteousness, which can be obtained by the faith in Jesus' baptism and His blood of the Cross, to be given to both the Israelites and the Gentiles.

Iniquities are prevailing in the present generation we live in. Therefore, we can only receive the remission of sin by believing in God's righteousness right now. Paul the Apostle said, *"In it (the gospel of Christ) the righteousness of God is revealed from faith to faith" (Romans 1:17)*. Now is the time we all should believe in the abundance of God's righteousness.

We should all obtain the abundance of His righteousness that He has given to all humanity by believing in the words of the gospel of the water and the Spirit. God blessed us so that we could praise Him for eternity by believing in His righteousness, which never changes.

I am sure that this book will be "the bunker-buster" to Christianity's false teachers and their followers in today's world. They are the perpetrators of Satan who have made deep caves of Christian doctrines and dwelt in them. They are so well adapted to the dark caves of Satan that they are unable to see God's life-giving light, unless the bunkers were to be blown out. When these sinners lose their old habitats through this "bunker-buster," they will be blessed abundantly with the righteousness of God.

Let us give thanks and praise to the Holy Triune God—God the Father, Jesus Christ the Son, and the Holy Spirit who has saved us from all the sins in this world through His righteousness. ⊠

CHAPTER

1

You can download Rev. Paul C. Jong's Christian Books on iPhone, iPad, or Blackberry by going to Amazon's Kindle e-bookstore (www.amazon.com).

Introduction to Romans Chapter 1

"The Epistle of Paul the Apostle to the Romans" can be referred to as the treasure of the Bible. It mainly deals with how one can obtain God's righteousness by believing in the gospel of the water and the Spirit. Comparing Romans to the Epistle of James, someone defined the former as 'the word of treasures' and the latter as 'the words of straw.' However, James is the word of God just as Romans is. The only difference is that Romans is precious because it provides a general overview of the Bible, whereas James is precious for it is the word that makes the righteous live by God's will.

Who is the man, Paul?

Let's read Romans 1:1-7 first. *"Paul, a bondservant of Jesus Christ, called to be an Apostle, separated to the gospel of God which He promised before through His prophets in the Holy Scriptures, concerning His Son Jesus Christ our Lord, who was born of the seed of David according to the flesh, and declared to be the Son of God with power according to the Spirit of holiness, by the resurrection from the dead. Through Him we have received grace and Apostleship for obedience to the faith among all nations for His name, among whom you also are the called of Jesus Christ: To all who are in Rome, beloved of God, called to be saints: Grace to you and peace from God our Father and the Lord Jesus Christ."*

These passages may be counted for "Paul's greetings to Christians in Rome." Paul greets them as a bondservant of Jesus Christ, who becomes the righteousness of God.

Verse 1 talks about the question 'Who is Paul?' He was a Jew who met the resurrected Lord on the road to Damascus, and who was a chosen vessel of the Lord (Acts 9:15) to spread the gospel to the Gentiles.

Paul spread the true gospel based on the sacrificial system and the prophecies of the Old Testament

In verse 2, Paul the Apostle was spreading the gospel based on the words of the Old Testament. He defined *"the gospel of God"* as *"which He promised before through His prophets in the Holy Scriptures."* Through this verse, we can see that Paul the Apostle preached the gospel of the water and the Spirit based on the sacrificial system in the Old Testament. Moreover, verse 2 indicates that Paul was chosen to do the work of the gospel.

The phrase *'through His prophets in the Holy Scriptures'* implies God's promises to send Jesus Christ, who appears in the sacrificial system or the prophecies in the Old Testament. All of the prophets of the Old Testament, including Moses, Isaiah, Ezekiel, Jeremiah and Daniel, bore witness to the fact that Jesus Christ would come into this world and die on the Cross after taking over the sins of the world.

What is the gospel that Paul the Apostle delivered like? He preached the gospel of the water and the Spirit that spoke about the Son of God, Jesus Christ.

Some people say that the words of the Old Testament have already ended, and others insist on the same point, providing the words of Matthew 11:13 as evidence. Some well-known evangelists even ignore the entire part of the Old Testament.

However, God made a promise to us through the Old Testament and He has fulfilled this promise through Jesus Christ in the New Testament. Therefore, in the world of faith, the New Testament cannot exist without the Old Testament, and in the same way, the words of the Old Testament cannot be fulfilled without the words of the New Testament.

Paul the Apostle was chosen for God's gospel. Well then, the question is, "What kind of gospel did he preach?" He preached the fact that Jesus Christ came to this world and saved us from all our sins through the gospel of the water and the Spirit, based on the Old Testament. Therefore, whenever we are preaching the gospel of the water and the Spirit, we should do so based on the prophecies and the sacrificial system of the Old Testament. Only then will people come to believe that the gospel of the water and the Spirit is the truth, and that the New Testament is the fulfillment of the words of promise of the Old Testament.

From the beginning of the New Testament, we can find that an emphasis was put on the baptism Jesus received from John and His blood on the Cross. While in the kernel of the Old Testament, there was the sacrificial system, which was the redeeming way for a sinner. He/she had to pass over his/her sin by laying his/her hands on the head of a sin offering and making it bleed to death in order to be forgiven for the sin.

Then, if there were the laying on of hands and the blood of the sacrificial animals for the remission of sin in the Old Testament, what was there in the New Testament? There was the baptism Jesus received and His blood on the Cross.

Moreover, the High Priest mentioned in the Old Testament (Leviticus 16:21) was equivalent to John the Baptist in the New Testament.

Verses 3 and 4 talk about the question, "What kind of a Person was Jesus?" The verses explain His generic character. Jesus Christ was physically born of David's family and by the Spirit of holiness, he was recognized as the Son of God by His power of resurrection from the dead. Therefore, He became the Savior by giving the water and the blood to those who believed in Him. Jesus Christ became the God of salvation, the King of kings, and eternal High Priest of Heaven to those who believed.

In some Christian theologies, the divinity of Jesus has been denied. These theologies say, "He was just an outstanding youth." Moreover, according to the New Theology, "There is salvation in all religions." Therefore, in liberal seminaries, people insist that they have to accept exorcism, Buddhism, Catholicism and all the other religions in this world. This so-called Liberal Theology or the New Theology says that everything should be paid respect to, and therefore, all humans have to unite and become 'one'.

However, it was clearly said in the Bible that in the beginning, God created the heavens and the earth. Then, who's this God? It is Jesus Christ. The name 'Christ' means having been anointed with oil. In the Old Testament, a king or a prophet was anointed on their heads from the High Priest. Therefore, Jesus is referred to as the King of kings. A person who denies Jesus as God is not a believer in God.

Nowadays, the faiths of the people throughout the world are turning back to the Ecumenicalism based on religious pluralism. They praise and give worship while combining all kinds of elements from heathenish religions such as Buddhism and Confucianism. At certain times, the congregation worships a Buddhist way, and at other times they do it in a Christian way. Well, there may be a delicious fusion of food. However, when it comes to faith, the purer the better.

Therefore, the answer to the question in verses 3 and 4, 'Who is Jesus?' is that He is the one who has been acknowledged as the Son of God by His power of resurrection from the dead. Christ became the Lord and Savior to us.

Verses 5 and 6 talk about how Paul became an Apostle through God. He became a witness to preach the gospel to the Gentiles so that they could receive salvation by believing in Jesus Christ.

What kind of authority did Paul the Apostle have?

As it is written in verse 7, Paul the Apostle had the authority to bless believers in Jesus by God's name. The authority of an Apostle means the spiritual power of being able to bless all the people by the name of Jesus Christ.

Therefore, Paul could say, *"Grace to you and peace from God our Father and the Lord Jesus Christ."*

Here, I would like to think a little bit more about this benediction. It seemed that Paul the Apostle had the authority to make benedictions for people, and whenever we end worship services on Sundays, we close up with benedictions. "God wishes to give out this kind of blessing to the saints." The original words of blessing are as follows.

Let's start with Numbers 6:22. *"And the Lord spoke to Moses, saying: 'Speak to Aaron and his sons, saying, 'This is the way you shall bless the children of Israel. Say to them: The Lord bless you and keep you; the Lord make His face shine upon you, and be gracious to you; the Lord lift up His countenance upon you, and give you peace.""*

Aaron the High Priest and his sons were told, *"This is the way you shall bless the children of Israel."* If they would bless the Israelites in this way, God would actually bless them as said in the Scripture. When we take a look at all the Pauline Epistles, we can see that he often said, "The grace of our Lord be with you." This indicated that it was not himself that would give out blessings, but it was God who would do it. Therefore, Paul the Apostle always gave blessing to the saints whenever he ended his epistles.

Paul had the authority to give blessings to God's people. This authority was not given out to all Christian ministers. Instead, it was given only to God's servants. When God's servants make benedictions saying that they truly wish to give out blessings, then God grants them these blessings actually according to the benediction.

God gives heavenly authority not only to His servants, but also to all the born-again saints. God says, *"If you forgive the sins of any, they are forgiven them; if you retain the sins of any, they are retained" (John 20:23).* He grants that kind of authority to all the righteous. Therefore, one should take heed not to confront the born-again saints or His servants, because it is the same as confronting God. For God has granted the authority of blessing and cursing to His Apostles as well as to His servants and the righteous.

Paul the Apostle who wishes to impart the spiritual gift to the saints

Let's read Romans 1:8-12. *"First, I thank my God through Jesus Christ for you all, that your faith is spoken of throughout the whole world. For God is my witness, whom I serve with my spirit in the gospel of His Son, that without ceasing I make mention of you always in my prayers, making request if, by some means, now at last I may find a way in the will of God to come to you. For I long to see you, that I may impart to you some spiritual gift, so that you may be established—that is, that I may be encouraged together with you by the mutual faith both of you and me."*

First of all, for what did the Apostle Paul thank God? He thanked God for the Christians in Rome because they believed in Jesus and through them, the gospel was preached to the other people.

In verses 9 and 10, one could ask the question, "Why did Paul the Apostle want to go to Rome during his mission trip?" The reason for this was because if the gospel of the water and the Spirit were preached in Rome at that time, it would have been spread out to the entire world. Just as the whole world today looks to America, in the ancient times, Rome was the center of the world as there was the saying, "All roads lead to Rome."

We are doing a lot of work of preaching the gospel in America. If we spread this gospel of the water and the Holy Spirit in America, many missionaries will come to rise and walk out into the world to preach this beautiful gospel to others. Therefore, Paul so wished to go to Rome.

The spiritual gift Paul talks about

In verse 11, it is written, *"For I long to see you, that I may impart to you some spiritual gift, so that you may be established."*

What does Paul the Apostle mean by imparting some spiritual gift so that people may be established? The spiritual gift he talks about is the gospel of the water and the Spirit, which we are preaching. In verse 12, it is written, *"that is, that I may be encouraged together with you by the mutual faith both of you and me."* Saying that some spiritual gift would be imparted to people to allow them to be established and to encourage the people with the mutual faiths of both Paul and them, was because by delivering the gospel of the water and the Spirit, Paul wanted to let people rest, get comfort, receive blessings, and to have fellowship within the same kind of faith.

Paul the Apostle's saying that he would want to be encouraged together with them by mutual faiths shows that he longed to preach the gospel of the water and the Holy Spirit once again to the Roman Church. Now, all of our church members understand and believe concretely in the gospel of the water and the Spirit, but there may appear to be some nominal Christians who do not believe in the true gospel with the passage of time. Like this, the Church in Rome might be in need of refreshing the gospel.

Therefore, Paul the Apostle said that he might have been encouraged by the mutual faiths in him. In fact, we receive comfort before God's presence and our hearts can rest in peace thanks to the faith in the gospel of the water and the Spirit. We would not be able to rest in peace without the gospel of the water and the Spirit.

Moreover, it is written, *"I may impart to you some spiritual gift, so that you may be established."* This spiritual gift is the gospel of the water and the Spirit. One can become a child of God and receive blessings only when he/she believes in the gospel of the water and the Spirit.

However, what use is it for people to live virtuously or faithfully by giving up smoking and drinking and without doing any wrongdoings if they don't know the gospel of the water and the Spirit, even though they believe in Jesus somehow? Their doings have nothing to do with God's righteousness. The righteousness of God is much greater than that of human beings. It is easy to draw in people to a church, but it is more important to preach the gospel of the water and the Spirit to these new believers so that they can be forgiven for all their sins and become God's children by being clothed in the spiritual blessings of Heaven.

Paul the Apostle wanted the saints in Rome to be encouraged through his own faith. So he said, *"that is, that I may be encouraged together with you by the mutual faith both of you and me."* Therefore, Paul the Apostle had to preach the true gospel to all the congregation of the church to let them have faith, so they could be established by his own faith in the gospel of the water and the Spirit. He had to deliver the believers of the church in Rome the gospel of the water and the Holy Spirit and teach them what it really was.

This is what made Paul the Apostle different from the other evangelists in today's world. In the Epistle to the Roman Church, Paul the Apostle said that he wanted to let people be established by imparting some spiritual gift, and to encourage them by the mutual faiths of both the people and him. This is what all the preachers of the existing churches of today should learn from Paul the Apostle. Paul the Apostle used to preach the gospel of the water and the Spirit with which one could discern true brethrens from the false ones.

These days, churches let a group of new participants receive the doctrinal teachings for a period of 6 months, and within a year, they finally get baptized. That's it. They get baptized regardless of whether they know about the gospel of the water and the Spirit that Jesus has fulfilled or not. In other words, even though people have become members of a church, they have not been able to become God's children who have obtained His righteousness. The only thing the ministers of today's churches ask their new believers to do is to memorize the Ten Commandments and the Apostle's Creed. If the new believers pass the memorizing test, then they are asked, "Are you going to stop drinking? Quit smoking? Are you going to offer your tithe every month? Will you lead a good life?"

The reason the churches of Europe, Asia, and all over the world became distant from God's righteousness is because they chase after human righteousness. Nowadays, even in Korea, or the so-called 'Jerusalem of Asia,' the population of Christians is declining. Now, the time has arrived in which no one wants to come to church unless there is a special event held inside the church, such as a praising festival or a pop concert. Even if people come, the ordinary sermons that are given to the youth contain themes such as, 'Don't smoke, live a virtuous life, keep the Holy Sundays and do a lot of volunteer work,' have nothing to do with God's righteousness.

Because a human is swift to sin and too fragile to quit sinning, he/she has to rely on the Lord. Therefore, when people come into the church of God, we should deliver them the gospel of the water and the Spirit so that they can obtain God's righteousness. To them, we should really pass on God's righteousness that says that you and I have been made sinless even though we are still insufficient.

Be sure to keep this in mind. One can only live according to God's will after he/she has become sinless by believing in God's righteousness. One can preach the gospel once his/her own problems of sin have been settled. Our work of spreading the gospel to others should not precede the settlement of our own problems of sin. One can never preach the true gospel to others unless his/her own problems of sin have been solved.

It is said that Paul the Apostle did truly impart some spiritual gift to others. The gift Paul talked about is not the gift of strange tongues or healing talked about in the Pentecostal Movement in the present Christianity. Most Christians regard some strange phenomena such as seeing visions, prophesying, talking of other tongues, or healing diseases as the gifts.

However, these things are not the spiritual gifts from Heaven. Seeing visions while making prayers is definitely not a spiritual gift. A person wildly screaming or a person in a cave going crazy whenever he/she hears strange sounds while not being able to sleep for three nights, are not of God's gift. One who claims that he is able to speak other tongues and falls unconsciously to the floor after shouting out strange words 'la-la-la-la' with a twisted tongue is not a sight of one receiving the Holy Spirit. Instead, it's similar to mentally unstable patients in a mental institution going wild. However, there are so called 'charismatic revivalists' who insist that they can teach Christians how to speak other tongues or how to receive the Holy Spirit. They are doing something very wrong and the faiths they possess are definitely not right.

The living water of the Holy Spirit flows out from our

hearts when we faithfully do God's spiritual work and follow the Lord. The water of the Holy Spirit will overflow in our hearts when we lessen the carnal deeds and follow the spiritual deeds instead.

Christians should obtain the spiritual gift of the remission of sin by believing in the gospel of the water and the Spirit. Someone says that numerous Christians are right now heading toward hell through the chairs of today's churches. This indicates that today's churches encourage human righteousness instead of preaching God's righteousness.

Brethren, even if one has piled up a lot of human righteousness after attending church, this doesn't mean that he/she can receive the spiritual gift by such deeds. We should take in God's righteousness into our hearts by the faith in the gospel of the water and the Spirit so that we can obtain the spiritual gift.

Let's read verses 13 to 17. *"Now I do not want you to be unaware, brethren, that I often planned to come to you (but was hindered until now), that I might have some fruit among you also, just as among the other Gentiles. I am a debtor both to Greeks and to barbarians, both to wise and to unwise. So, as much as is in me, I am ready to preach the gospel to you who are in Rome also. For I am not ashamed of the gospel of Christ, for it is the power of God to salvation for everyone who believes, for the Jew first and also for the Greek. For in it the righteousness of God is revealed from faith to faith; as it is written, 'The just shall live by faith.'"*

Paul the Apostle wished to go to Rome. However, he couldn't do so because he had been hindered. Therefore, he had to pray asking for the door of his missionary work to be opened. Likewise, we should give the same kind of prayers while preaching the gospel worldwide through literature ministries. Only when we pray will God's heart be moved and only when God opens up the door and the path for us will we be able to deliver the gospel of the water and the Spirit worldwide.

Paul who owed a debt to all the people

To whom did Paul the Apostle say that he had owed a debt and what kind of debt did he mean in verses 14 and 15? He said that he had become a debtor both to the Greeks and to the barbarians, and that he owed them the preaching of the gospel of the water and the Spirit. He added that he was a debtor both to the wise and the unwise. Therefore, he wished to preach the gospel to these people in Rome as best as he could.

Therefore, the purpose of Paul the Apostle writing to the church was to deliver the true gospel. He found that even in the hearts of the people inside the church in Rome, the gospel of the water and the Spirit did not stand firm by faith, and thus he referred to the gospel as the spiritual gift. Therefore, he preached the gospel of the water and the Spirit even to those who were already inside the church, as well as all the people of the world. He said that he was a debtor to the wise, the unwise, the Greeks, and all barbarians.

What kind of a debt did Paul owe? He owed the debt of having to preach the gospel of the water and the Holy Spirit to all the people in the world. He insisted on delivering all of the debt he owed to the people in the world. Like this, even the people now who have the gospel of the water and the Spirit owe the propagation of the gospel. The debt they have to pay is the work of spreading the gospel. This is the reason why we have to spread the gospel of the water and the Spirit to the whole world at this time.

People mistakenly think that only the blood of the Cross is all of salvation. However, the heavenly gospel the Bible bears witness to is the gospel of the water and the Spirit, which Paul the Apostle also testified to. Therefore, in Romans chapter 6, Paul said that he was baptized into Christ Jesus and also into His death. Because there were nominal Christians in the Church in Rome who believed only in the blood of the Cross, Paul wanted to deliver them the hidden secret of the baptism Jesus had received. Just like this, we should preach the gospel of the water and the Spirit to those who have not been able to hear it, though they have long been inside the church.

When Christians are asked whether they possess sin or not, they think of this question itself as being useless and disregarding their personalities. However, this question is in fact of great importance and enormous value. If humans are destined to go to hell due to their sins, who is there to ask them this kind of question and provide them with a solution? Only a person who is sinless in his/her heart after having been born again by the gospel of the water and the Spirit can ask that kind of question and also give the correct answer to people. Only the born again saints can make sinners to be born again by delivering the sound gospel, that is, the gospel of the water and the Holy Spirit, which sinners have never heard before.

Brethren, even if one believes in Jesus, but has not been born again of the water and the Holy Spirit, then one can neither enter nor see God's Kingdom. Therefore, be thankful when you meet people who allow sinners to receive the remission of sin by delivering you the gospel of the water and the Spirit. You will then receive a great blessing.

The gospel Paul was not ashamed about

In verse 16, what was the gospel Paul the Apostle was not ashamed about like? It was the gospel of the water and the Spirit. Because this gospel is God's power to salvation for everyone who believes, Paul called it as *"my gospel" (Romans 2:16, 16:25),* and he regarded it to be proud and great instead of being ashamed of it. The reason he was not ashamed of the gospel of the water and the Spirit was because this gospel makes people completely sinless and destroys the barrier of sin that divides all mankind from God.

Would the washing away of sin be possible if people believed only in the gospel of the blood of the Cross? It is seemingly possible to wash away the sins committed until now with this kind of faith but it is impossible to cleanse our future sin. Therefore, people with this kind of faith try to wash away their sins by saying prayers of repentance everyday. They confess that their hearts are filled only with sins and that they are inevitable sinners. These Christian sinners who possess sin cannot talk about the gospel sincerely to others, because 'the gospel' they have is no more 'the good news' to them.

The gospel is *'euaggelion'* in Greek, in other words, the gospel that has the ability of blowing away all the sins in this world. The only true gospel is like dynamite. It is this true gospel that eliminates all of the sins in this world. Therefore, a person like Paul, who believed in the gospel of the water and the Spirit that has the ability to eliminate sin, was not ashamed of it. Nowadays, even Christians seem to be ashamed of preaching the gospel. However, those who possess God's righteousness are people that stand out more with dignity and glory when they are preaching the gospel.

Paul the Apostle did not even have the slightest bit of

shame while preaching the gospel. It was because the gospel he was preaching was the gospel of the water and the Spirit. It was because this beautiful gospel was God's power to salvation for everyone who believes.

This gospel is the powerful gospel that allows anyone who believes in it to get his/her sins remitted, no matter who has delivered it to him/her. The sins of the world get completely washed away if the listener takes in the gospel with his/her heart. However, the gospel of only the blood of the Cross tells the incomplete salvation to people, that is to say, it tells people that it only eliminates their original sin and thus their additional transgressions have to be washed away by saying daily repentance prayers. It leaves an aftertaste of sin to its listeners.

Did Jesus only take away a partial amount of sin because His power was not good enough? Since Jesus knew humans so well, He did not leave behind any kind of sin. He took with Him all of the sins with the water, blood and the Holy Spirit. I believe that this beautiful gospel gives complete salvation from sin to everyone who hears and believes the gospel of Jesus' baptism and His bloodshed on the Cross.

Therefore, the gospel has the same power to everyone including the Jews and the Greeks. The gospel of the water and the Spirit allows the same salvation from sin to everyone who believes in Jesus when the gospel is preached to them. On the other hand, when one delivers something other than the gospel of the water and the Spirit, he/she will receive the wrath of God. So Paul said, *"But even if we, or an angel from heaven, preach any other gospel to you than what we have preached to you, let him be accursed" (Galatians 1:8)*. Paul the Apostle clearly said that there is only the gospel of the water and the Spirit that is true out of all the other gospels.

Regardless of whether one is a Gentile or a Jew, or whether one believes in Islam, Confucianism, Buddhism, Taoism, the sun god or anything else, every single person gets the chance to hear the gospel. Moreover, this gospel of the water and the Holy Spirit provides them the chance of getting saved from all their sins. So, we should deliver that Jesus Christ is God, that He created the Universe, that He came to this world in the likeness of human flesh to save us, that He took over all our sins by getting baptized by John, and that He received the judgment for our sins by dying on the Cross.

Therefore, Paul the Apostle was not ashamed of the gospel of the water and the Spirit. Even though the gospel only of the Cross must be a shameful gospel, the gospel of the water and the Spirit cannot be shameful at all; but a sound and powerful gospel that overflows with pride and dignity. Anyone who believes in this gospel receives the fullness of the Holy Spirit by the faith in the fact that he/she has become a child of God. Again I say to you that the beautiful gospel of the water and the Holy Spirit can never be a shameful gospel. However, the gospel that believes only in the blood of the Cross is shameful.

Christians, were you ashamed whenever you had to preach the gospel of only the blood of the Cross? You felt ashamed when you delivered and believed in the gospel of only the blood that does not contain Jesus' baptism. Because you were ashamed to preach that kind of useless gospel, you always had to cry out for the Lord or give fanatic prayers in other tongues to fill up your feelings before you went out to the streets to shout out "Believe in Jesus. Believe in Jesus!"

This is something one can just do with overflowing feelings but something one would never be able to do with a sober mind. That is why those who believe only in the blood of the Cross shout tumultuously and cause disturbances whenever they are out in the streets for evangelism. Having the megaphone close to their mouths, they only shout out the words, "Jesus, to Heaven, disbelief, to hell." However, a believer in the gospel of the water and the Spirit delivers the gospel in a very gentlemanlike fashion; while having opened up his bible, he drinks tea and converses with another.

What is said about the gospel of God's righteousness?

In verse 17, what is said to be revealed in the gospel of Christ? It is said that *"the righteousness of God"* is revealed in the gospel of God. God's righteousness is fully revealed in the true gospel. Therefore, it is said that God's righteousness is revealed in it from faith to faith and that the just shall live only by faith. The gospel that delivers only the blood of the Cross does not contain God's righteousness.

Brethren, if it is said that one has to give prayers of repentance everyday for his/her daily sins even though he/she has already gotten his/her original sin forgiven, and that one can gradually become sanctified to eventually become a perfectly righteous person, then does this kind of faith contain God's righteousness? This is not something in which God's righteousness is revealed. Something that reveals God's righteousness talks about perfect things. The gospel of the water and the Holy Spirit talks about the perfect gospel from the beginning till the end.

You people offer daily repentance prayers because you are committing sins everyday as if you have to make new coverings out of the leaves of a fig tree to cover your shameful sides everyday, or maybe every week or month. A person repeatedly becoming a sinner by saying daily repentance prayers is like covering up his/her own shameful body with the leaves of a fig tree. This is the state of religious lives of those who believe in the gospel of only the blood of the Cross. They are the foolish ones who don't wish to wear the leather coverings that God has given them freely, but instead enjoy wearing the coverings of the leaves of a fig tree.

Jesus' blood on the Cross was the result of Jesus' baptism, and it was not the bloodshed on the Cross by which Jesus was able to take over our sins. He took over our sins at the time He got baptized, then came to the Cross bearing all the sins of the world, and died to atone the sins of the world. Therefore, the Cross was the result of the baptism He had received. Since Jesus had taken over our sins through His baptism, the bloodshed at the Cross was His final deed to atone all our sins. Jesus received all of the curses of sin at the Cross because He had gotten baptized.

Then how can we obtain God's righteousness? We can acquire it by knowing and believing in the gospel of the water and the Spirit. You would ask me, "Are you then a believer in the gospel of the water and the Spirit?" Then I can answer immediately and clearly 'Yes' to this question. The secret to obtaining God's righteousness is to believe in the gospel of the water and the Spirit.

The reason for this is because the gospel of the water and the Spirit is the truth and because it reveals God's love and His righteousness. It is also because the gospel of the water and the Spirit contains the remission of sin God has given to mankind freely, the way to becoming His children, the blessing of eternal life by which one can receive the Holy Spirit, and the physical and spiritual blessings on earth.

Paul the Apostle said that God's righteousness was fully revealed in the gospel of the water and the Spirit that he was preaching. Therefore, putting up human righteousness without knowing God's righteousness is like sinning before God. Moreover, a gospel that believes in only the blood of the Cross, but does not contain God's righteousness, is false.

God's righteousness refers to the sound gospel of the water and the Spirit He has given. The Old and New Testament as a pair save us from our sins. The Old Testament prepares for the New Testament and the New Testament fulfills the words of promise contained in the Old Testament. God saved us from the sins of the world by giving us the true gospel in which His righteousness is fully revealed. Thus He saved mankind from all sin.

Right now, the whole world should return to the gospel of the water and the Spirit. The only gospel that saves people from sin is the original gospel of the water and the Spirit. Brethren, the whole world must return to the gospel of the water and the blood. They have to return to this gospel of the water and the Spirit, which contains God's righteousness.

The reason for this is because the gospel of the water and the Spirit is the only truth that can save us from sin. Only the gospel containing God's righteousness can save us, make us sinless and turn us into God's children. Moreover, the Holy Spirit inside our hearts protect God's people and this Holy Sprit prays for us, blesses us, always stays with us and gives us eternal lives as a gift.

It is very tantalizing to see that there are so many people who don't even pay attention to this gospel. I hope for everyone to believe in this gospel of the water and the Holy Spirit by having clear understanding of Jesus' baptism. The baptism Jesus received from John is not something that Jesus accepted because He was modest. The reason He got baptized was in order to bearing all the sins of this world. John, who was the greatest man among those born of women, laid his hands on Jesus' head when he baptized Jesus. This forms a parallel to the imposition of the High Priest's hands on the head of sin offerings without blemish in the Old Testament (Leviticus 16:21). Jesus' death on the Cross was a result of having taken over the sins onto His body, and it parallels with the sin offering shedding blood and dying after going through the imposition of hands.

Because this gospel of the water and the Holy Spirit has been mentioned in both the Old and New Testaments, anyone who believes in the other gospel while leaving out any part of the original one has a wrong faith. The most important and the very first thing Jesus did when He came to this world was to get baptized by John. It is very wrong for you to believe that His baptism is only a symbol and to think that Jesus got baptized out of His modesty.

What kind of a person is a heretic? In Titus 3:10, it is written, *"Reject a divisive man after the first and second admonition, knowing that such a person is warped and sinning, being self-condemned."* A divisive man is a person who is self-condemned. A self-condemned person means one who admits and confesses that he/she possesses sin. Therefore, a Christian who says, "I'm a sinner" is a divisive man, that is, a heretic. It is written, *"Reject a divisive man after the first and second admonition."*

Because this kind of a Christian is warped and rotten, a sinless saint should not go near such a heretic. He is one who is self-condemned because his own faith and religious life has rotted away. A person who commits unforgivable sins before God is one who does not want to be sinless by believing in the gospel of the water and the Spirit, but instead continues to sin of rejecting His absolute salvation before God while saying that he/she is still a sinner. One who self-condemns while thinking that even though he/she believes in Jesus, he/she has sin and therefore calls himself/herself a sinner, is a heretic heading to hell.

Some Christians attach a sticker on the back of their cars that says, 'It's my fault.' This seems like such a kind and warm saying when viewed by human eyes, but in truth, it means that since it's all one's own fault, such matters as going to hell, becoming a divisive man, and getting cursed is all up to one's own fault. 'It's my fault' is a paradoxical saying that one is going to live virtuously. However, saying that a supporter of such a slogan, who thinks he/she can live virtuously, is directly challenging God's words that defines humans as seeds of iniquity. Those who chase that kind of human thought will eventually receive all kinds of curses.

Are there by any chance people among you who are self-condemned? Then you should once again listen carefully to my sermon on Romans chapter 3 that states that the remission of sin does not refer to the Doctrine of Justification. Romans talks about this in great detail. Paul the Apostle knew in advance what people would say someday and therefore said beforehand that becoming sinless is to become truly without sin and is not just calling a sinner righteous. He also clearly testified that only the gospel of the water and the Spirit is the truth. Therefore, it is natural that those who believe only in the blood of the Cross will become ignorant and dumb while reading Romans.

The Epistle of Paul the Apostle to the Romans is such a great Scripture because it testifies the gospel of the water and the Spirit. One should become righteous after believing in Jesus even if he/she was originally a sinner before coming to believe. One should truly become a righteous person who possesses no sin in one's heart. This is how one gets to possess the right kind of faith.

I hope that even if right at the moment, people's faiths are not complete, their faiths will eventually reach perfection while they lend an ear to the words of the water and the Spirit through the born again church. Please, learn more about the gospel of the water and the Spirit through these sermons and confirm the words of truth.

I believe that God will endow us with the riches of heavenly blessings. ⊠

The Righteousness of God That is Revealed in the Gospel

< Romans 1:16-17 >
"For I am not ashamed of the gospel of Christ, for it is the power of God to salvation for everyone who believes, for the Jew first and also for the Greek. For in it the righteousness of God is revealed from faith to faith; as it is written, 'The just shall live by faith.'"

We must receive the righteousness of God

Paul the Apostle was not ashamed of the gospel of Christ. He stately testified the gospel. However, one of the reasons many people weep though they believe in Jesus is because of their sins. It is also due to their ignorance in acknowledging the righteousness of God. We can be saved by believing in God's righteousness and by giving up our own righteousness.

Why was Paul the Apostle not ashamed of the gospel? First of all, it was because the righteousness of God was revealed in it.

The gospel, *'euaggelion'* in Greek, means 'good news'. When Jesus Christ was born in Bethlehem, God's angel appeared and told the shepherds who were keeping watch over their flock at night, *"Glory to God in the highest, and on earth peace, good will toward men!" (Luke 2:14)* It was good news—'peace, good will toward men.' The gospel of the Lord saved us from all sins and washed away the sins of the world. Jesus washed away all our sins. He, Himself, washed away all the sins of those who squirmed like maggots in dunghills and who sinned in the mud.

Firstly, Paul the Apostle said that the righteousness of God was revealed in the gospel. God's righteousness was revealed in the gospel that blotted out all our sins. The righteousness of God allowed us to become the saints and the righteous. It also permitted us to obtain eternal lives and be sinless.

What is the righteousness of human beings? We people like to show ourselves off before God when we have something to brag about. Piling one's own pride by doing good deeds portrays human righteousness. However, Jesus' righteous act that saved us from all our sins allowed God's righteousness to be revealed in the gospel. This is the righteousness of God.

These days, most Christians preach the gospel without knowing the gospel of the righteousness of God. They say, "Believe in Jesus and you will be saved and become rich." However, these are not the teachings of the gospel of God's righteousness. The gospel seems to be more popular than anything, but most people are ignorant and do not understand the gospel. It is similar to the fact that the Bible is a bestseller, but people still don't know its contents actually. The most precious and beneficial thing in this world is the gospel, which God has given us.

"For in it the righteousness of God is revealed from faith to faith." The gospel of God is like an oasis in the desert. Jesus came to those sinners who had committed many sins and washed all of their sins away. However, people have rejected the gift of His righteousness, which has washed away the sins of the world, while trying to establish their own righteousness.

People who put up their own efforts (service, dedication, zeal, offering, prayer of repentance, fasting prayer, keeping the Lord's day, translating God's word into practice and so on), and refuse God's gift, are those who reject His righteousness. One can receive the righteousness of God only when one's own righteousness is given up.

They sewed fig-leaves together, and made themselves clothing

In Genesis 3:21, it is written, *"Also for Adam and his wife the Lord God made tunics of skin, and clothed them."*

The first man, Adam, sinned against God by falling into the trickery of Satan. What Adam and Eve did right after they sinned was to sew fig leaves together and make themselves clothing. The garments made of sewed fig leaves forms a striking contrast to the tunics made of skins. It was the difference between 'the righteousness of man' and 'the righteousness of God.' Genesis 3:7 said, *"They sewed fig leaves together and made themselves coverings."* Have you ever plaited radish leaves? We Koreans cut off radish leaves from radishes and plait them together with rice-straws to dry them. We cook bean paste stew with them in the winter. It is very delicious!

Adam and Eve plaited fig leaves together and made garments after they had sinned. This sort of acts—good deeds, self-trial and self-sacrifice—constitute human righteousness. It is self-righteousness, not the righteousness of God. The fact that they made their own garments with fig leaves shows the sin of pride by trying to hide their sins with their good deeds before God. Plaiting one's righteousness—one's devotions, self-offerings, self-trials, services, and prayers of repentance into a garment, and covering the sins in one's mind with it is 'idolatry,' which accrues one's pride before God.

Can we hide our sins in our hearts before God by sewing fig leaves together to make garments? Can we hide our sins by our good deeds? Never. The leaves would begin to fall in a day, and on the third day, all the leaves would fall finally. Garments made of vegetables don't last long. People who sew fig leaves together and make garments, namely, those who try to be righteous by serving God well with their own deeds, cannot enter into the Kingdom of Heaven. We cannot receive the forgiveness of sins by the righteousness of our own deeds.

When Adam and Eve tried to hide their sins by making garments with fig-leaves, God called Adam, "Where are you, Adam?" While hiding himself among the trees of the garden, he said, "I was afraid, because I was naked; and I hid myself." A person who has sin tries to hide among the trees. Trees frequently imply men in the Bible. He/she who has sin in the heart tries to hide himself/herself among people. He/she likes to take a seat in the middle, not sitting too far back or in the front of the church where many people gather together. Why? Because he/she wants to hide himself/herself among people.

However, he/she cannot hide his/her sins before God. He/she must be forgiven of his/her sins by giving up his/her own righteousness and by believing in the righteousness of the Lord. Those who have vague faiths and who don't believe in the truth also want to enter into the Kingdom of Heaven, hiding themselves among the same kind of people, but they will end up in hell with those who try to hide their sins with their good deeds. Sinners before God have to be revealed as sinners and give themselves up to God.

God told Adam, who made garments with fig leaves,

"Why did you take the fruit? Who made you eat?" "Oh, God, The woman whom You gave to be with me, she gave me of the tree, and I ate." "Eve, why did you do so?" "The serpent beguiled me, and I did eat." So the Lord God said to the serpent, "Because you did such a thing, you are cursed above all cattle, and above every beast of the field: on your belly shall you go, and dust shall you eat all the days of your life." That is why serpents slither on their bellies. Again God told Adam and Eve, "You also committed sin. You who were beguiled to sin and the ringleaders who made you sin are the same sinners." Nowadays, false prophets also preach their pseudo-gospels, saying, "Receive the fire!" People who are deceived by them will be treated in the same manner as the false prophets and go to hell.

The Lord made tunics of skin for Adam and his wife

The Lord thought, "I will not leave Adam and Eve, who sinned by being beguiled by Satan, as they are. I had originally made up my mind to create men in My image and make them into My sons, so I will save them to accomplish My plan." This plan was in God. Therefore, God passed over their sins to an animal, killed the animal, skinned it and made tunics from its skin and clothed Adam and Eve with the tunics. He made it the symbol of our salvation. In fact, the plant garments made of fig leaves could not last even a day, and it had to be repaired over and over again. God clothed Adam and Eve with eternal life, saying, "You, Adam and Eve, come on, I newly made tunics of skin from an animal, be clothed in it. It's the skin of an animal that died for you." The Lord clothed Adam and Eve with tunics of skin blessed with God's righteousness in order to give Adam and Eve new lives. The Lord God made tunics from skin for Adam and his wife and clothed them, just like God clothed believers with the salvation of His righteousness.

However, the salvation of humankind that was apart from the salvation of God was the plant garment made of fig leaves. God clothed us in tunics of skin, which is the righteousness of God. The Lord clothed the remission of sins with the righteousness of God by giving us His flesh and blood. He took away all our sins with His baptism and crucifixion in order to receive all judgment in our place. God lets us have the forgiveness of sins when we believe in the righteousness of God through the gospel of the baptism and blood of Jesus. It is the gospel that saves sinners from their sins.

There are many people who try to establish their own righteousness, rejecting the righteousness of God in the world. They must discard their own righteousness. In Romans 10:1-4 it is written, *"Brethren, my heart's desire and prayer to God for Israel is that they may be saved. For I bear them witness that they have a zeal for God, but not according to knowledge. For they being ignorant of God's righteousness, and seeking to establish their own righteousness, have not submitted to the righteousness of God. For Christ is the end of the law for righteousness to everyone who believes."*

The Israelites insisted on their legalism in order to establish their own righteousness, while ignoring the righteousness of God. God gave men the law to make them aware of sin. People have the knowledge of sin through the Ten Commandments and have the forgiveness of sin by believing in the righteousness of His salvation, which saves them from their sins through the sacrificial system of the tabernacle. Therefore, the sin offering of the tabernacle implies that Jesus is an exact representation of God in the New Testament. However, the

Israelites didn't know this righteousness of God.

Why was Jesus baptized?

Why was Jesus baptized? John the Baptist baptized Jesus in order to wash away all the sins of this world. Jesus told John the Baptist just before He was baptized, *"Permit it to be so now, for thus it is fitting for us to fulfill all righteousness." (Matthew 3:15)* This is the reason Jesus was baptized. He was baptized so that He could wash away all the sins of mankind. He took away the sins of this world by being baptized. *"Behold the Lamb of God, who takes away the sin of the world!" (John 1:29)* He took away all sins and was crucified to atone the sins. However, the Israelites didn't believe that Jesus became the perfect Savior of sinners.

Israelites have not submitted themselves to the righteousness of God, but Jesus is the end of the law for righteousness to everyone who believes. The end of the law means that Jesus washed away all sins of the world. Christ was judged as the curse of the law for all believers to be sanctified. He ended the curse of the law. Jesus redeemed all people from their sins. Jesus was baptized to wash away the sins of all mankind. He took away all the sins of the world by delivering His flesh up to John to be baptized and by passing all the sins of the world to His flesh. He thereby saved all people from their sins. He ended the judgment of the curse of the law by taking away the sins of this world through His baptism and crucifixion. He perfectly saved us from the judgment and the curse of the law.

It was the end of the law and the beginning of the righteousness of God's salvation. Jesus adequately took away the sins of the world by being baptized by John the Baptist and went to the Cross. How is it possible that one has sin in one's heart, even if one truly believes in the righteousness of Jesus' salvation? *"For therein is the righteousness of God revealed from faith to faith."* The baptism and the blood of Jesus have been the righteousness of God. To believe in the righteousness of God is to believe in Jesus' baptism and blood.

The righteousness of God was legitimately fulfilled by Jesus' baptism. I want you to believe in it. You will then be saved from all your sins. The righteousness was given for sinners to become sinless through Jesus' baptism. Moreover, the righteousness of God's judgment was Jesus' crucifixion. "Christ is the end of the law." The judgment of God will come to those who have not yet been judged as long as the law exists. The law of God reveals sin and proves that the wages of sin is death, a curse and hell itself. Therefore, Jesus' baptism and blood on the Cross ended the curse of the law. Jesus took away all our sins and has ended the law to fulfill all righteousness.

The foolish took their lamps but took no oil with them

Let's look at Matthew 25:1-13. Here is the parable of ten virgins who waited for their bridegroom, the Advent of our Lord. Let's see what the righteousness of God is through the scripture.

"Then the kingdom of heaven shall be likened to ten virgins who took their lamps and went out to meet the bridegroom. Now five of them were wise, and five were foolish. Those who were foolish took their lamps and took no oil with them, but the wise took oil in their vessels with their lamps. But while the bridegroom was delayed, they all slumbered and slept.

And at midnight a cry was heard: 'Behold, the bridegroom is coming; go out to meet him!' Then all those virgins arose and trimmed their lamps. And the foolish said to the wise, 'Give us some of your oil, for our lamps are going out.' But the wise answered, saying, 'No, lest there should not be enough for us and you; but go rather to those who sell, and buy for yourselves.' And while they went to buy, the bridegroom came, and those who were ready went in with him to the wedding; and the door was shut. Afterward the other virgins came also, saying, 'Lord, Lord, open to us!' But he answered and said, 'Assuredly, I say to you, I do not know you.' Watch therefore, for you know neither the day nor the hour in which the Son of Man is coming" (Matthew 25:1-13).

It is written that the Kingdom of Heaven is similar to the ten virgins who took their lamps and went forth to meet the bridegroom. Who enters into the Kingdom of Heaven? Who did enter into the Kingdom of Heaven among the ten virgins? Why were some virgins not able to enter the Kingdom of Heaven, although they believed in Jesus? The Lord tells us about this through the above passages. Five of the ten virgins were foolish and the other five were wise. The foolish took their lamps yet took no oil with them. Lamps stand for 'churches'. The fact that they took their lamps but took no oil with them represents those who go to church without the Holy Spirit (the oil implies the Holy Spirit in the Bible).

What did the foolish do? They took their lamps, but no oil. A man who has not been born again, even though he believes in Jesus, may devotedly attend church. Everybody says, "My church is truly orthodox." Every Christian in this world says so. They're very proud of the founding fathers and some characters in their denominations. Those who were foolish took their lamps and took no oil with them, but the wise took oil in their vessels with their lamps.

What is a human being? A human being is a vessel before God. He/she is dust. A man is made of dust. So humankind is a vessel, which can contain God. The wise took their lamps with oil in their vessels.

The foolish virgins who have only lamps without oil burn their emotions

The Bible tells us that there are foolish virgins among people who believe in Jesus. They take their lamps, but no oil. This means that they have not been born again. Does a wick without oil last long? What we must know here is that a lamp without oil is quickly burned out, no matter how good its wick might be. Believers who have not been born again yet have hot passions of love toward the Lord at first. This lasts for just about 4 or 5 years. Later, the passionate love for the Lord gets extinguished. They must realize that they don't have the remission of sin.

Those who have not been born again, or are without oil (the Holy Spirit), say things such as: "I used to have good faith a long time ago. I was good at first, but now I'm not. You will become like me soon." They are false prophets and false saints who lead religious lives without being born again. They must have the faith of salvation because their faiths are not based on oil (the Holy Spirit). Their faiths are only based on their emotions. They must obtain salvation by believing in the water and the blood of Jesus Christ and receive the oil of God as a gift. The wick stands for the human heart.

Virgins wait for the bridegroom in the above passages. Here, we must well understand the cultural background of

Israelites. They have marriage ceremonies at night and it begins when the bridegroom comes. So, the bride must wait for her bridegroom. This is what the marriage ceremony of the Israelites was like.

"While the bridegroom delayed, they all slumbered and slept." There was a cry, "Behold, the bridegroom comes!" Then, the brides arose and made much ado to fix their countenances. When the ten virgins were waiting for the bridegroom, the bridegroom came with a cry, "Behold, the bridegroom comes." *"Then all those virgins arose, and trimmed their lamps. And the foolish said unto the wise, 'Give us some of your oil, for our lamps are going out.'"* The foolish were always stupid. They should have prepared the oil before the bridegroom came. No matter how weak the wick of the lamp was, Lamp with oil would not extinguish.

The foolish virgins who had lamps without oil burned only the wicks. This means that only their hearts burned. "I have to be born again, lead a life of a born again person, and have to be filled with the Holy Spirit." They burn out their hearts earnestly like this. At the time of our childhood, kerosene lamps used to light up the rooms at night. If we let the lamp burn a strip of paper, it would burn out in the twinkling of an eye. The fire would be over a foot tall and very bright, but it would extinguish immediately.

Foolish virgins who go to hell are those who burn their own hearts (emotions) without oil and whose fires of faith extinguish when they actually have to meet the Lord. They don't have the Holy Spirit in them. They think they believe rightly, even though they don't have the Holy Spirit. "♫Come, Thou burning Spirit, Come♫" They are in a great bustle. Then, women indulge in dancing (they call it the Holy Spirit-dance), fluttering their breasts, saying, "Come on, please come on."

They are foolish and crazy. We must be foolish if we still have sin before the Savior. We would be like foolish virgins if we had sin in our hearts, even though we believe in Jesus. Never be a foolish virgin.

How can the Lord marry a bride who possesses sin?

The Lord is holy God. The bridegroom is God and the Son of God who has no sin. God is our bridegroom. However, how can you try to meet God while possessing sin? Do you want to meet God with sin in your heart? This would be a very stupid and foolish thing to do.

Jesus, our bridegroom, came to the world and made brides to be sanctified. He turned His brides into righteous people by washing away all their sins through His baptism. He chose them as His brides in Him. When the time was full, five of them said, "Please come on." However, five of them were still standing in the dark. How can they have marriage ceremonies when their faces are dark? The bridegroom came and said, "How have you been?" The faces of the latter five brides were darkened because of their sins. They were in deep grief because their sins were attached here and there inside their hearts.

How can the Lord marry a bride who weeps because of her sins? "Thank you, Lord, for sanctifying me like this." This kind of person would be happy with his/her spiritual bridegroom, even though he/she is weak, because the bridegroom loves him/her and washed away all his/her weaknesses and sins. The bridegroom usually leads his bride to apply make-up, sending clothes and all the best perfumes and cosmetics. Then, the bride is dressed up with all those things so that she is ready to meet the bridegroom.

Our Lord was sent to the world as the bridegroom to guide us so we could meet Him as His brides. He gave us His flesh for the remission of sin at the Jordan River. *"And the Word became flesh and dwelt among us, and we beheld His glory, the glory as of the only begotten of the Father, full of grace and truth" (John 1:14).* The Lord Himself took away all our sins so that we would have the fullness of grace, truth and the forgiveness of sin by believing in the Lord. The bridegroom took away all His brides' sins at the Jordan River. The Lord saved His brides from their sins by being judged in their place on the Cross.

Can we buy the Holy Spirit with money and trials?

However, the foolish virgins asked the wise to share oil with them, for their lamps were burnt out, when the bridegroom was near. Can we share the Holy Spirit? Can we buy the Holy Spirit with money? Can we buy the forgiveness of sin with good deeds, trial or money? The wise told them to buy the Holy Spirit from revival service preachers. The foolish thought that they already bought it from them. They thought they could buy the oil with money. They zealously led religious lives, thinking that large offerings and services, attending orthodox churches and praying repeatedly would give them something.

But no matter what, nobody can buy the remission of sin, which the Lord has given, with anything from the earth. The foolish try to burn their emotions until they come to stand before the Lord. One of the five foolish virgins began a religious life saying, "I will follow You, I will also go up a mountain for prayers and prayers of repentance. Let's go to serve Him, let's go abroad to preach the gospel."

The bridegroom came at last with a great fanfare. The foolish went to buy oil when the bridegroom had come, but the virgins who had the forgiveness of sin and had prepared oil (the Holy Spirit) went into the marriage feast. The bridegroom met the brides after He prepared everything. Then He locked the door. Jesus didn't just randomly choose five virgins. The number 'five' means 'grace' in the Bible. The five virgins stand for those who have the remission of sin by grace and believe in His grace and righteous deeds. They recognize the things the bridegroom has done for them and believe in the righteousness of the Lord, which makes them righteous. However, the other virgins eventually came and said, "Lord, Lord, open to us." But He answered, "Assuredly, I say to you, I do not know you."

We can receive the gift of the Holy Spirit only when our sins are blotted out

Those who don't prepare oil cannot meet the Lord. The Lord will take only those who believed in God's righteousness and waited for the Kingdom of Heaven and those who actually had the remission of sin in their hearts, to the Kingdom of Heaven. The Lord told the words of promise. *"Repent, and let every one of you be baptized in the name of Jesus Christ for the remission of sins."* Then, what happens after the remission of our sins? The Bible says, *"You shall receive the gift of the Holy Spirit" (Acts 2:38).* If you receive the gospel of the righteousness of God, the sins in your heart will actually be blotted out and the Holy Spirit will come to you. We cannot physically feel the Holy Spirit of God. Nevertheless, the Holy

Spirit exists. We can say that we have no sin because we have the Holy Spirit and the word of God in our hearts. It truly exists. One who receives the righteousness of the Lord becomes a righteous man, although he is weak. However, one who doesn't have the righteousness of the Lord remains a sinner.

For therein is the righteousness of God revealed

The Lord came by water and blood. He saved us from our sins with His baptism. He took away all our sins when He was baptized and received the vicarious punishment for all our sins by shedding His blood. What do the Apostles John, Peter and Paul say about this? They altogether talk about Jesus' flesh and blood. They talk about Jesus' baptism and His blood on the Cross. Matthew 3:13-17 exactly describes Jesus' baptism. Jesus was baptized to make sinners sinless and to wash away all the sins of the world at the Jordan River.

Let's take a look at 1 Peter 3:21. Peter testified that the antitype of salvation was His baptism. *"There is also an antitype which now saves us—baptism (not the removal of the filth of the flesh, but the answer of a good conscience toward God), through the resurrection of Jesus Christ, who has gone into heaven and is at the right hand of God, angels and authorities and powers having been made subject to Him"* *(1 Peter 3:21-22).*

It is written, *"There is also an antitype which now saves us—baptism through the resurrection of Jesus Christ."* Jesus' baptism, which took away all our sins by His flesh, has been the proof of our salvation. The fact that He shed blood on the Cross is proof to the fact that we had been judged for our sins. Do you see what I am saying? Therefore, the Bible states that

Jesus is the One who came by water, blood and the Holy Spirit (1 John 5:6-9). Jesus was sent to the world in human flesh and took away all our sins in the same way Aaron the High Priest laid his hands on the offerings to pass over the sins of his people.

Water is the antitype that saves us; baptism. It is written that it is not the removal of the filthy flesh. This doesn't mean that we don't sin after we obtain the remission of sin. We receive the forgiveness of sin by believing in the baptism of Jesus. Then, don't we sin with the flesh? Yes, we do. Many people misunderstand the remission of sin and say such things as, "If you have no sin in your heart, you won't sin again." This is a misunderstanding. The Bible says, *"There is not a just man on earth who does good and does not sin" (Ecclesiastes 7:20).* The flesh is still weak. It is weak until it dies. It commits sins until it dies. *"Not the removal of the filth of the flesh, but the answer of a good conscience toward God."* Our consciences change into the good consciences toward God through our faiths in the baptism and the blood of Jesus. Our consciences can call God our Lord and Savior by our faiths in the fact that the Lord took away all our sins by His baptism.

The spiritual nourishment for our hearts is the baptism and the blood of Jesus

Nourishment for the heart is the baptism and the blood of Jesus. Nourishment for the heart and the antitype that washed away our sins is the baptism of Jesus. Thus, Peter the Apostle said that baptism is the antitype, which saved us.

Let's look at 1 Peter 1:22-23. *"Since you have purified your souls in obeying the truth through the Spirit in sincere love of the brethren, love one another fervently with a pure heart, having been born again, not of corruptible seed but incorruptible, through the word of God which lives and abides forever."* Amen.

We have been born again and received the remission of all sins by believing in Jesus' baptism and His blood. We are born again by believing in the written word of the Lord. We have been born again *'through the word of God, which lives and abides forever.'* Hallelujah! Being born again happens through the word that lives and abides forever. The word of God is the canon, which refer to a measuring rod. It's the benchmark for salvation. The measuring rod for the salvation of God never changes.

John the Baptist said in John 1:29, *"Behold! The Lamb of God who takes away the sin of the world!"* The Lamb of God who was baptized at the Jordan River is the real bread of life, which saved us by His flesh and blood.

We are sanctified and saved by believing in the word of God. The Bible says, *"So then faith comes by hearing, and hearing by the word of God,"* and *"For in it the righteousness of God is revealed from faith to faith; as it is written, 'The just shall live by faith'"* *(Romans 10:17, 1:17)*. We can become just by believing in the gospel.

Have you been sanctified? —Amen.— Don't you have any sins? It's the gospel, the good news, *'euaggelion'* in Greek. What is the righteousness of God? It's the fact that the Lord blotted out all our sins by giving His flesh and blood to us. The righteousness of God allowed us to be sanctified. The righteousness of God is that Jesus, who was sinless, took away the sins of the world and was crucified for the sinners. It is the water, the baptism of Jesus that cleansed all the sins of the world. The righteousness of God has been given through the fact that Jesus took away the sins of the world by His baptism and the Crucifixion. The righteousness of God consists of His baptism and death, and the Cross is the antitype of our judgment. This is God's righteousness that was revealed in the gospel. ⊠

The Just Shall Live by Faith

< Romans 1:17 >
"For in it the righteousness of God is revealed from faith to faith; as it is written, 'The just shall live by faith.'"

We must live by faith

What do the just live by? By faith. The just live by faith. In fact, the word 'faith' is very common, but it is the very core of the Bible. The just live only by faith. What do the just live by? They live by the faith in God. I hope we will become enlightened from this section because we have the flesh and the Holy Spirit dwelling within us. We tend to interpret many of the Scriptures with our own thoughts, not knowing the real meanings hidden in the Bible, though we may literally understand the Bible. We simultaneously have the flesh and the Spirit. Therefore, the Bible says that we, the just, shall live by faith because we have the remission of sins.

But the problem is that the flesh cannot do good

But the problem is that we have the flesh also. So, in many cases, we judge according to the flesh. Sometimes, we judge and discern something with fixed thoughts of the flesh, and thus we do not believe fully in His word when it comes to faith. However, the Bible simply says that the just shall live only by faith. Then what does this mean? You may think, 'Where are the just who don't live by faith? Why do you put an emphasis on this verse? Isn't it just one of the verses in the Scriptures?'

Today, I want to tell you about this verse. We must live by faith. We don't realize our ignorance until when we try to explain something, though we think we know well about it in our thoughts. What is the opponent that a sinner fights against? The person who is not born again fights with his/her own thoughts and his/her flesh. Who does the born again person fight with? The flesh and spirit within the person fight each other. You may wonder why I am repeating what we already know, but I would like to explain this repeatedly because it is worth saying.

Even in a born again saint, his/her flesh and spirit continually fight with each other because he/she also has the flesh. There is an instinctive part in the flesh and it prefers to live lavishly, trying to handle all the problems, rather than to live by faith. There is also an instinctive part in the flesh of a righteous person that wants to live lavishly, trying to reach perfection without making any mistake, which is far from living according to the faith God tells them to live by.

So, the flesh of the righteous also wants to reach perfection even in the spiritual works, trying to deal with every spiritual problem perfectly and hoping to reach fleshly perfection at the same time. But can one lead a life of faith by the flesh? Just as Paul said, *"For the good that I will to do, I do not do; but the evil I will not to do, that I practice" (Romans 7:19),* the flesh never does good. We have an instinct in the flesh that wishes to live stately in front of God, even though the flesh cannot help but to act evil.

We cannot lead the life of faith with the flesh

So strictly speaking, trying to live a devout life with the flesh is far from having the correct faith. We have contradictory thoughts and instincts toward God from a biblical point of view. To be perfect in the flesh and to lead a life of faith without any problems with the flesh is impossible. The human flesh is like dust. The Bible says, *"We remembers that we are dust" (Psalm 103:14)*. It is even like a vapor that appears for a little time and then vanishes away because it is incomplete.

Do both the flesh of a born again person and a person who is not born again have the ability not to sin? Can a born again person avoid sinning? We don't need to live by faith if the flesh can survive without sinning. Then would we be able to live by the strength of the flesh? We surely know that it is not possible. The problem is whether we know and recognize that, despite whether or not we have been born again, the flesh is so weak that it continues to sin.

How much do we know about our fleshes? How much do we know about ourselves? You may think you know yourself as well as 100%, but your self-identity is far from your true character because you don't really believe that you are sinful. About what percentage do you think you know about yourself? Even 50% would be too much. People usually understand themselves as little as 10 or 20% at most. In reality, they know about 10 or 20% of themselves, though they think they know themselves 100%. When they think they have done tremendously evil things, they become embarrassed and quit following the Lord. Then, they question whether or not they can keep their faiths to the end, and come to the conclusion that it is impossible.

Filthy water and trash come out in swarms from the

conduit of carnal mind. It seems to be impossible for them to lead devout lives by faith. "Oh! I think it is no longer possible to follow the Lord. I thought my flesh would get better after my sins were blotted out once and for all, but my flesh is still weak and I fall short of perfection, even though it's been a long time since I was born again. The flesh is useless and ugly." We don't know about ourselves at all and we especially don't want to admit the faults of our flesh either. So the result is that we cannot lead faithful lives when we see that many carnal thoughts come out of the flesh. We can never lead lives of faith by flesh. What is the flesh of a human being? Will the flesh of a human being become incrementally sanctified and live a perfect life in front of God if it is well-trained by its own trials? It is absolutely impossible, and the flesh cannot help sinning until its last breath.

Then how do the just live?

"If you sin unintentionally, and do not observe all these commandments which the LORD has spoken to Moses—all that the LORD has commanded you by the hand of Moses, from the day the LORD gave commandment and onward throughout your generations then it will be, if it is unintentionally committed, without the knowledge of the congregation, that the whole congregation shall offer one young bull as a burnt offering, as a sweet aroma to the LORD, with its grain offering and its drink offering, according to the ordinance, and one kid of the goats as a sin offering. So the priest shall make atonement for the whole congregation of the children of Israel, and it shall be forgiven them, for it was unintentional; they shall bring their offering, an offering made by fire to the LORD,

and their sin offering before the LORD, for their unintended sin. It shall be forgiven the whole congregation of the children of Israel and the stranger who dwells among them, because all the people did it unintentionally. And if a person sins unintentionally, then he shall bring a female goat in its first year as a sin offering. So the priest shall make atonement for the person who sins unintentionally, when he sins unintentionally before the LORD, to make atonement for him; and it shall be forgiven him. You shall have one law for him who sins unintentionally, for him who is native-born among the children of Israel and for the stranger who dwells among them" (Numbers 15:22-29).

"If you sin unintentionally, and do not observe all these commandments which the Lord has spoken to Moses." There are many expressions like "sin unintentionally" in the Bible. The flesh sins unintentionally and does what should not be done. I asked you if it was possible for the flesh to become perfect, but it cannot become perfect, even after we have remission of sin. The flesh seems to be perfectly righteous at first, right after we have redemption. But in fact, it does not aid us in disclosing ourselves, but instead hides us. The flesh slops trash and sins all the time. The flesh always commits sins that God hates. Doesn't the flesh sin a countless number of times? Does the flesh always live, as God wants? The flesh always does what God doesn't want. The flesh always sins uncontrollably.

The law of God consists of the Ten Commandments and it has 613 kinds of detailed articles. "You shall have no other gods before me. You shall not make for yourself a carved image. You shall not take the name of the Lord your God in vain. Remember the Sabbath day, to keep it holy. Honor your father and your mother. You shall not murder. You shall not commit adultery. You shall not steal. You shall not bear false witness against your neighbor. You shall not covet your neighbor's house." The first four commandments are the commandments that are to be kept among the relations with God. The rest of the commandments, from the fifth commandment to the tenth, are commandments that should be kept among human beings. But does the flesh please to obey the law?

There are white lines on the road for pedestrians to safely cross the road. But the flesh never wants to keep traffic laws. People cross the road within the lines for fear that other people are watching them. In fact, they don't want to obey the law. They cross the road while denying traffic signs when nobody is around.

The flesh automatically sins. If they are well educated, they should keep to the traffic signs, whether other people watch them or not. However, they would merely be acknowledged through the flesh. We hate to cross the road according to traffic signs and try not to obey them as much as possible.

Then, what's the purpose of God giving us the law? The law gives us the knowledge of sin (Romans 3:20). By the law, we come to know that we are sinners who always disobey the Ten Commandments. We always sin. The law always requires us to do good and not do evil. Nevertheless, our flesh always sins because it is too weak to keep the law. The Bible says that the just shall live by faith. However, how do the just, who have this flesh, live by faith? They also can't live by the law in their flesh so how do they live? The just live by the faith in God.

The spirit wants to follow the will of God, but the flesh always commits sins, disobeying all the articles of the Ten

Commandments. The flesh sins in turns, committing this sin today and that sin tomorrow. There are sins that the flesh prefers to commit; more than other sins. The flesh of a human being sins all his/her life. Is this right or not?

Let us observe the fifth commandment. "Honor your father and your mother." It's utterly reasonable, and people try to keep it even though they cannot keep it all the time. So let us skip discussing it. The next one is "You shall not murder." All of us kill others in our minds, while only a few people actually kill according to the flesh. However, let's skip this as well because killing is such a grave sin. The next ones are "You shall not commit adultery" and "You shall not steal." These sins are easily committed in our daily lives. Some people have an innate talent of stealing and committing adultery. They have made it a habit to commit the sins. Don't they covet, too? (The Bible says to covet is also a sin.) They are also good at taking other's possessions away from their initial places (stealing). The flesh does these kinds of evil deeds whenever it wants to do.

Let us assume that we commit just one or two kinds of sins among ten kinds of sins. Does that make us righteous before God? —No, it does not.— We are not just and righteous by the flesh before God because even the slightest bit of sin is a sin. The flesh repeatedly sins, sinning this today and that tomorrow, until we die. The flesh cannot help but to sin before God until we die. So, have you ever been clean and sanctified in front of God even for a day? Let's look at the flesh, separating it from the spirit. Did you never sin before God, being perfect by the flesh? One sins even when one sleeps. He enjoys looking at vulgar images even while dreaming, thinking of beautiful women through the imagination. We all commit sin.

The flesh does what God tells us not to do and doesn't do what He tells us to do. The flesh is always the same even after our sins are blotted out. How can we become perfect? What is the way to sanctification if our flesh cannot be complete? However, isn't it possible through Jesus Christ?

We are the ones who have committed those sins. Have we sinned before Jesus? —Yes, we have sinned.— Do we sin now or not? —Yes, we do.— Do we continue sinning? —Yes, we do.— We will sin until our dying day as long as we have flesh. We are the sinful beings who cannot but sin until our last breath. Then how can we be delivered from all our sins? First, if you are not born again yet, you must admit that you are sinners in front of the Lord to blot out your sins. After having been delivered, we need not confess that we are sinners, but we have to admit that we have sinned. We should admit our sins after reflecting on ourselves through the law when have sinned, even if we sometimes do good things with the flesh under the pretext of being good. We must admit a sin to be a sin.

We are sanctified by faith

Then how do we handle the problem of sin after admitting it? Are we sanctified by believing that Jesus took away all our sins by being baptized by John the Baptist and was judged on the Cross to redeem us? —Yes.— We are sanctified by believing that all the sins committed by the flesh were passed onto Jesus when He was baptized. Then what does the passage, *"The just shall live by faith"* mean?

To have faith is to believe in the Spirit, not the flesh. Only believing in God, His word, His law, and His redemption can sanctify us, and we can be perfect after we become righteous by having faith in Him. Is this true or not? It's true. The flesh is still weak and far from perfection, even if we become righteous by receiving the remission of sins. The Bible says, *"For with the heart one believes unto righteousness, and with the mouth confession is made unto salvation" (Romans 10:10)*. But the flesh is always weak and imperfect, just as that of the Apostle Paul's. Therefore, we can neither become righteous nor reach righteousness gradually with the flesh. The flesh cannot live a righteous life.

The only way in which the just can live is to believe in God, namely, to accept the remission of sins and blessings, which God has given us. We can be sanctified and remain righteous, while eternally depending on His righteousness, which we received from God, and live eternal lives by our faiths in Him. Our lives depend on the faith in God. So the Bible says that the just shall live by faith. We are sanctified by faith and maintain God's righteousness by having faith and living by it. Even though the flesh is not righteous, it is foolish to try to be sanctified incrementally because it is impossible. We can live only when we receive God's aid by believing Him to be our God, our Lord, and our Shepherd.

So the Apostle Paul says, *"The just shall live by faith,'* quoting it from Habakkuk of the Old Testament. He also says, *"For in it (the gospel) is the righteousness of God revealed."* What is the righteousness of God? Is it the same as the righteousness of human beings? Does reducing sins little by little sanctify us? Are we perfect because we don't sin anymore after believing in Jesus or by having faith?

Only in the gospel, the righteousness of God is revealed and it only sanctifies us perfectly through the remission of sins because we can never be righteous with the flesh. *"For in it is the righteousness of God revealed from faith to faith."* This means that we become righteous only by faith. The just live by having faith in God after becoming righteous. The just become righteous, maintaining God's righteousness and receiving all His blessings through faith.

We must live by faith

To live by faith is like that. A human being's will crumbles more easily than a sandcastle, no matter how strong it may be. He/she would say, "I will do this and that, Lord." However, the flesh cannot do it. We live by faith in the Lord and the word of the redemption from sin and the law, after receiving the remission of sins. Does the flesh change to be good-natured, tall and smart if we lead lives of faith for a long time? Never. So, to live by faith is to absolutely believe in God. We become righteous by having absolute faith in the gospel and live by receiving all of God's blessings through our faiths in Him.

The just shall live by faith. That is, we live by our faith in God. Do you believe this? —Yes.— Do you happen to have too many expectations from your flesh? Do you think, 'I expect only about 20%, my flesh is still good in this part, though my flesh is not right in other parts'? However, the Bible says that the just shall live by faith. God says that one cannot live by the flesh; not even 0.1%. Do you have a mind to keep the faith until the Lord comes again by not sinning, and by having an expectation of the flesh even a little bit?

We are righteous by the faith in Jesus, in spite of how many sins we may have committed. We are sinners in the flesh no matter how good we may be, if we don't believe in Jesus. We become sanctified when we believe in Jesus 100%, but we become sinners when we don't believe in Him 100%. Is God pleased no matter how fewer sins we may commit? Does it please God if we are righteous through the flesh?

The righteousness of God made us righteous

Let's see Roman 3:1-8. *"What advantage then has the Jew, or what is the profit of circumcision? Much in every way! Chiefly because to them were committed the oracles of God. For what if some did not believe? Will their unbelief make the faithfulness of God without effect? Certainly not! Indeed, let God be true but every man a liar. As it is written: 'That You may be justified in Your words, and may overcome when You are judged.' But if our unrighteousness demonstrates the righteousness of God, what shall we say? Is God unjust who inflicts wrath? (I speak as a man.) Certainly not! For then how will God judge the world? For if the truth of God has increased through my lie to His glory, why am I also still judged as a sinner? And why not say, 'Let us do evil that good may come? as we are slanderously reported and as some affirm that we say. Their condemnation is just"* (Romans 3:1-8).

The Apostle Paul said, *"But if our unrighteousness demonstrate the righteousness of God, what shall we say? Is God unrighteous who inflicts wrath?"* Is God unrighteous and wrong if He saves a human being whose flesh sins until he/she dies with His grace? What the Apostle Paul asked in return to those who had brought him into ridicule means, "The more our weakness become manifested, the greater the righteousness of God that saves us form all our sins will be." The Apostle Paul speaks to those who wonder how a human being who sins throughout his/her life can become sanctified. He says that human weakness is to reveal the righteousness of God. Human beings, whose flesh cannot help but to sin until their dying breaths, demonstrate the greatness of God's righteousness through their weakness.

God's righteousness means nothing if one can be righteous with his/her own efforts along with His righteousness; if one can be saved 97% by God's help and by 3% of his/her own efforts. Paul says that God alone perfectly saved those who continue sinning until death through Jesus. So, our unrighteousness reveals the riches of God's righteousness. The flesh cannot help sinning everyday until it dies; it is not able to be perfect for even a day. The fact that Jesus perfectly saved these imperfect sinners from their sins reveals the righteousness of God much more. So, the Apostle Paul says, *"And why not say, 'Let us do evil that good may come'?—as we are slanderously reported and as some affirm that we say. Their condemnation is just" (Romans 3:8).*

Can we become righteous by the flesh? Can our flesh become perfect after receiving the forgiveness of sins? The flesh cannot. Can you and I, leaving all the other people of the world out of the question, become righteous by the flesh? —No.— But has the Lord perfectly saved us or not? —Yes.— The Lord has perfectly saved us from all our sins. Are we with sin if we believe in Jesus with our hearts? —No.— We have no sin however unrighteous we may be.

The Lord said, *"Again you have heard that it was said to those of old, 'You shall not swear falsely, but shall perform your oaths to the Lord.' But I say to you, do not swear at all: neither by heaven, for it is God's throne; nor by the earth, for it is His footstool; nor by Jerusalem, for it is the city of the great King. Nor shall you swear by your head, because you cannot make one hair white or black. But let your 'Yes' be 'Yes,' and your 'No,' 'No.' For whatever is more than these is from the evil one" (Matthew 5:33-37).* Swearing itself is a sin because you cannot keep what you swear. So neither swear nor take a pledge to do something later. Just believe in His words, and then you will live. You can become righteous if you believe in His righteousness and the Lord will help you if you believe in Him.

There are so many illusions. We have the criterion of the flesh and judge according to it because we have flesh. Therefore, there is a judge within us who is not associated with the faith in God's word. There are two judges within us. One is oneself and the other is Jesus. So both of them try to reign within us. We tend to make the laws of the flesh and judge with it because we have flesh. The flesh tells us, "You are good even if you continue to sin. I will approve you to be righteous even if your flesh is not 100% righteous." The judge of the flesh always gives you good marks.

However, the judge of God's righteousness requires us to be 100% sinless. He is holy. We can become righteous only by receiving the remission of sins by faith. Therefore, believers in His gospel have already reached God's righteousness. We have already become righteous. Those who believe in God really live. They are blessed with God's help. The just shall live by faith. This means that unbelievers and those who live by the flesh cannot live. I'm telling you just a small part of the big picture. I am repeatedly telling you and explaining the meaning in detail, just as we boil bones over and over again until the soup turns white.

We need faith

It is important to know the Bible, but how much we believe in it is more important. Some people only believe in God's Creation in the Scriptures. Some people believe both that God created the heavens and the earth and that Jesus only washed away original sin. They believe that their daily sins should be washed away everyday. They make their own judgments according to the law of the flesh. How much do we believe? The just shall live by faith. To become righteous and to live can be possible only by faith. From the beginning to the end, we need faith in God.

So how much do you believe? Do you happen to measure yourself as you please, captured in carnal thoughts, thinking, 'I am quite alright, my flesh is good' or 'I'm too weak to believe in God'? Do you happen to score yourself, giving yourself 80% today and 95% the next day, but only 5% on certain days, thinking, 'It would have been better if I had not been born.' Do you think like that? —Yes.— So do I.

I am seriously like that sometimes. Even when I am relieving myself, I think, "It would have been better if I had not believed in the Lord and known Him. It seems to get harder to lead a devout life by faith. It has been terrible up until now. I am in a dilemma to see the future and to recollect the past. I am praiseworthy to have led a life of faith somehow until now. But I will not be able to walk with You well from now on, Lord. How sensitive to sin I became since I've known You. Many thoughts and criterions have come out of me since I've known You. I have barely followed you, Lord, not exactly knowing You. But now, I have no self-confidence to follow You anymore. Why? Because I know God is holy and perfect. Ah! Lord, I can't follow you anymore. I have no confidence."

Therefore, God tells us to live by faith because He knows us well. He says, "You must maintain being righteous and remain blessed by faith. All your sins were passed onto Jesus Christ through His baptism. You always sin when I reflect your flesh on the law. So admit that you cannot help sinning. Did your Savior take away all your sins or not? —Yes, He did.— Were all your sins passed onto your Savior or not? —Yes.— Then do you have sin or not? —No.— Did the Lord save you or not? —Yes.— Then cloudy and dark days will turn into sunny day like the words in the hymn: "There's Sunshine in My Soul Today."

We can't become sinners again

It may be hopeless when we think of the future, but it's sunny and bright when we look at the Lord with faith. Therefore, God says that the just shall live by faith. Do you believe this? —Yes.— We are saved by faith and also live by it. Who do we believe in? We live by believing in God. Only the just can live by faith. Do you believe that? —Yes.— Can you maintain God's righteousness by training the flesh well? —No.— Does the righteousness of God become invalid when the flesh does evil? Do we become sinners again? —No.—

The Apostle Paul said in Galatians 2:18, *"For if I build again those things which I destroyed, I make myself a transgressor."* A person who believes that all his/her sins were transferred to Jesus Christ through baptism and that He was judged on the Cross for him/her can never become a sinner again. A person who does not deny Jesus becomes sanctified at once and sinless because all his/her sins were passed onto Him and he/she can never be a sinner again. Have you got it?

—Yes.—

God, who saved us, is always our Lord and our Father. God always helps us and is with us to the end of the world. That is the reason He says, "Live by faith. I will help you if you believe in Me. Angels will serve you, who are born again." Angels are the servants between God and us. They tell the Lord everything about us. God made us His children. We were sinners by nature. We can never become righteous by the deeds of the flesh, but we have become righteous by faith.

We give thanks to the Lord. The Lord has became our Shepherd and Father by faith. ✉

The Just Live by Faith

< Romans 1:17-18 >

"For in it the righteousness of God is revealed from faith to faith; as it is written, 'The just shall live by faith.' For the wrath of God is revealed from heaven against all ungodliness and unrighteousness of men, who suppress the truth in unrighteousness."

We must live by faith

It is written, *"The just shall live by faith."* Do we live by faith or not? The only way by which the just live is through faith. Faith allows the just to live. We can live and carry on with all things when we believe in God. Only the just live by faith. The word 'only' means that nobody except the just can live by faith. Then, what about sinners? Sinners cannot live by faith. Do you live by faith now? We must live by faith.

It takes a long time to learn true faith. What we must realize is that we live when we believe in God and die when we don't believe in God. We must realize that it is the fate of the just to live by faith.

Birds have wings, but if they don't use them, they will be caught and killed by beasts that roam the earth. Therefore, the just are destined to live by faith. God has fated the just to live by faith. If they fail to live by faith, their spirits will die.

The life of a Christian and the true path begins with faith. How are the just able to readjust into society after being born again of water and the Spirit? We must know that the only way is for us to live by faith.

Do you understand? It's life to the just. Without faith, we die and have no power to cope with hardships. If a person, who neither lives by faith nor uses faith, undergoes hardships, then he/she will die in the end. When one has faith in God and confesses, "Lord, I believe in You," then one can live, even if he/she is incompetent and weak. He/she can live because of the faith in God. God helps the person and works as much as he/she believes in Him.

When we feel our limitations, we come to learn faith

I want you to think about whether you have lived by faith or not. A person does not live by faith right after he/she is born again. He/she lives by situation at first, so he/she doesn't learn how to live by faith. Why? Because one can live on this earth making money with one's own arms and legs, it is unnecessary to use the faith in God. But we come to feel our limitations when we wonder if we can live only with our physical strengths and efforts. We feel that we can't live. Then how do we have to live? We must use faith. We can never truly live unless we use faith and believe in God.

We must live by faith even through small affairs, saying, "Lord! I believe in You, Please help me." When we believe in God through trivial matters, saying, "Lord! I believe in you, I believe that you help me, I believe in You," we prove that we can live by faith, even when it's a small affair.

We can experience getting stronger and have expectations for things to get done only when we believe. However, when we don't believe in God, we don't realize that God allowed it be done, so we lose because we don't experience by faith. We can't solve the problem, though it can easily be solved by faith. To live by faith is good in all ways, so we must learn how to live by faith.

People in the Old Testament lived by faith and it is also proper for people in the New Testament to be saved by faith. How do we have confidence in our salvation? Have we become righteous by believing in what Jesus Christ did? Yes, we have. God helps us when we live by believing in Him. At first, just believe in God and ask whatever you seek, and then God helps us. God gives us other things, just as He gave us salvation. Faith is available in all parts of our lives. It's life. Life to the righteous is faith. Faith is life. It's the same as the blood of the flesh. When a person who is born again doesn't have faith, his/her spirit dies just as a human dies when his/her flesh doesn't have blood. We should believe in God and confess, "God, I believe in You. I believe that You help me and solve the problem."

It is faith that seeks the Kingdom of God first, before we seek what we need and believe that God will certainly answer our prayers. We must live by faith. The just cannot but live by faith. What we have in the flesh will be exhausted someday while living on the earth. And we will encounter with danger or inevitable situation someday. At that time, the most important thing we need is the faith in God; the faith that God saved us, helps us, and that He is good.

Moreover, we also need the faith that God gives what we pray for and seek, if it is proper to God. Faith leads us to live in His grace when what we have in the flesh is exhausted. The faith in God becomes a motivational power for us to accomplish what we hope for before God.

We must use faith from small affairs

How do we have to live? We have to pray like this. "God, I believe in You. I lack this and that, so help me, Lord." I'm not talking about our original weakness. Let us live by faith, saying, "I need this and that in my daily life. Please help me, Lord. I believe You will do it for me." A person who lives by faith must seek God, starting from small affairs. For example, "Lord, I don't have toothpaste. Please give me toothpaste. I believe in You." Therefore, we come to experience that God answers when we believe in Him and seek Him.

By what do sinners live? Sinners live by their own strengths, but the just live by faith. We can use faith in our lives when we know that the just live by faith. We do not live by what we have, but by faith. Do you see it? "The just shall live by faith." What the just need most is faith, but we come to use faith only when we are at the end of our resources.

We come to use faith when all our strength and resources have been used up. However, we must know that to live by faith is the truth and it is God's commandment, based on His promise, which we certainly need in our lives. Live by faith. Believe in God and seek. Then we can receive and obtain what we need. We must learn how to live by faith from our small affairs, and then we can gradually have stronger faiths.

David killed Goliath with five smooth stones by faith. He killed Goliath with the faith that God was with him, thinking, 'God, I believe in You. To kill him is Your will.' And he yelled at Goliath, *"You come to me with a sword, with a spear, and with a javelin. But I come to you in the name of the Lord of hosts"* (1 Samuel 17:45). By faith Abraham, when he was called, obeyed by going out to a place which he was to receive for an inheritance; and he went out, not knowing where he was going.

The just shall live by faith. There are many similar expressions like 'live by faith' in the four Gospels. However, how many people know that to live by faith is the life of the just, the life of Christians? I'm not saying that we should give up all our physical strengths and properties we've depended on. I just advise you to abandon your dependant mind on something on earth to live by faith. Then, believe what? God. God works when we believe in Him and seek what we need. Believe that He answers our prayers and believe the leader of the church. Join with church and serve the Lord. Do you believe? We have to live by faith because we are the just individually.

We must give up what we depend on with our hearts. We must believe in God, seek and obtain through faith, no matter how trivial the task may be. We must live by faith and experience it. Then, we can reign with the Lord and not be ridiculed by the people in the world. God says that He *"prepares a table before me in the presence of my enemies" (Psalm 23:5)*. To have great recompense is to be blessed before God. It is not to live according to the development of the situation, but by faith.

Have you ever lived by faith? Countless people have never lived by faith, but there are people who have experienced God's works when they prayed. We must continuously experience this, not just once. Again and again. It's the way the just should live. We must not rely on the earthly things of the world, but believe in God. It's the life of the just. We must live like that. Only by faith can we live and get all the blessings from God.

What we most need before God is faith

Having faith seems to be very hard, but in fact, it's easy. Nothing is needed except the belief in God. We only have to believe in God. People think that it is difficult to believe in God, but it actually isn't that hard. I call my father "Father" and believe he is my father because he is a real father to me. His being my father doesn't depend on my own belief. The faith in God starts from this point. I believe in God. Why? Because God always stands by the just, loves them and becomes their Father and Savior. Secondly, if we believe in Him, we ask Him what we need, just as a child asks his/her father what he/she needs. Lastly, God the Father hears and answers what we seek. Believing in God is based on and starts from such a simple confidence.

We have to live by faith because God is the Alpha and the Omega, the first and the last. All our lives are related to faith. We have been saved by faith and have been taken care of by Him through faith. It is faith that allows us to say, "Lord, I believe in You. Keep me and please take care of me." What shall we do when we are weak and scared due to Satan's threats? We have to believe in God, saying, "Lord, I believe in you." We may think incorrectly and as a result, may be caught and defeated by Satan. In that case, because we pray and believe in God, saying, "Lord, please keep me. I believe You surely keep me," and because God is our Father, He keeps us. God takes care of us somehow, even if we offer improper prayers, because He knows us well. The most important thing is to believe. It's very simple. Just use your God given faith, and then He will lead you from faith to faith. It is useless if we don't believe, even if God exists. We come to live by faith if we believe in God.

From faith to faith

Romans 1:17 states, *"For in it is the righteousness of God revealed from faith to faith."* When we use our faith again and again, we become people of faith. I want you to understand this. God doesn't exist to us if we don't believe in God, even if He really does exist. You reach faith by faith when you believe consistently that God is alive and saved us.

When you become a person of faith, all things of God become yours by faith. What the Bible says in Romans 1:17 is that the beginning and the conclusion of faith is faith *"For in it is the righteousness of God revealed from faith to faith."* Therefore, we can be saved and can be people of faith also if we believe God saved us. We cannot be children of faith if we don't believe. God answers when we earnestly seek what we need in our lives while believing in Him.

What the Apostle Paul talks about in Romans 1:17 is a very significant, though the passage is short. Do you now understand how the just live? *"The just shall live by faith."* Faith is certainly essential to the just, not to sinners.

The first thing needed for sinners is the belief that Jesus is their Savior. However, we, the born again Christians, can have faith in our lives. Do we need just one or two things when we live? No. There are many things to be done whether they are serious or trivial. The just shall live by faith in all affairs. Do you understand this? We must live by faith. We are saved by faith and taken care from risk by faith. When we pray by faith, God answers. We have to live by faith and pray even if we are weak. In all things, from marrying to preaching the gospel, we need faith. When we preach the gospel to someone, faith makes us pray like this. "God, I believe You saved that soul." We do everything by faith.

We cannot preach the gospel without faith. We can preach the gospel only by faith. People become saved when we preach the gospel by faith. Have you ever lived by faith? People live without faith, not knowing that they must live by faith, so they hit rock bottom when they meet with hardships. They seek only when they use up their power, so in the end, they always lack something. They don't have confidence in faith and unwillingly live, as they say, "I unwillingly live because I cannot die."

But the just live their lives of faith spontaneously and positively; they believe, seek and get answers. Useless thoughts and unbelief become present if we don't have faith. Then, we cannot walk with the church. How can we walk with the Lord without faith? Is there anything to believe in the flesh? Nothing. How can we believe? We cannot have faith if we don't believe in God. We can follow the church when we live by faith and to live by faith is due to faith. Do you see it? Do you believe in God? Then seek what you need. Believe in God, and then all will go well. The only problem is to not realize that we must live by faith.

I give thanks to God who has led us to live the remainders of our lives by faith. ✉

Those Who Suppress the Truth in Unrighteousness

< Romans 1:18-25 >

"For the wrath of God is revealed from heaven against all ungodliness and unrighteousness of men, who suppress the truth in unrighteousness, because what may be known of God is manifest in them, for God has shown it to them. For since the creation of the world His invisible attributes are clearly seen, being understood by the things that are made, even His eternal power and Godhead, so that they are without excuse, because, although they knew God, they did not glorify Him as God, nor were thankful, but became futile in their thoughts, and their foolish hearts were darkened. Professing to be wise, they became fools and changed the glory of the incorruptible God into an image made like corruptible man—and bird and four-footed animals and creeping things. Therefore God also gave them up to uncleanness, in the lusts of their hearts, to dishonor their bodies among themselves, who exchanged the truth of God for the lie. And worshiped and served the creature rather than the Creator, who is blessed forever Amen."

To whom is the wrath of God revealed?

We can see that Paul the Apostle preached the same gospel as the gospel we preach. To whom is the wrath of God revealed? The judgment of God is revealed to sinners who suppress the truth in unrighteousness, namely, to those who have sins and block the truth with their own thoughts.

Paul the Apostle clearly says that the wrath of God is revealed, first of all, to those who block the truth in unrighteousness. Those will be judged by God. What wrath will the wrath of God be like? The wrath of God will drop their flesh and spirits to hell.

We must not think that only the flesh will be judged because men also have spirits. Therefore, God will judge both the flesh and the spirit. There are ones who block the truth of God with their earthly thoughts. There are ones who are against the righteous, possessing sins. The wrath of God and His judgment are revealed to those with the sin of hardened hearts, who are not afraid of God.

Paul the Apostle says in Romans 1:17, *"The just shall live by faith."* He also says that the judgment and wrath of God are revealed to those who block the truth with their sins.

Unbelievers are under the wrath of God

God pervasively gave the truth of salvation to the world. The truth and love of God are pervaded on the earth. Therefore, there is no excuse for ignoring the truth and the love of God. God will judge all those who don't believe in the gospel of the truth and who are against it.

Let's think about the people who have not received the love of the true gospel. We see what God made; namely water, grass, trees, the sky, birds, etc. How can these things exist without the creation of God? The Bible says, *"For every house is built by someone, but He who built all things is God (Hebrews 3:4).* Isn't it their fault for not believing in God and the word of the truth?

Therefore, it is reasonable for people who don't believe in the grace of the forgiveness of sin to be judged by God. They insist in the theory of evolution. They persist that the universe has naturally evolved itself. They also say that at first, there was an explosion called the Big Bang about 15 billion years ago, and that then, a certain living being came about. They say, this original reality of life changed and it evolved into fishes, beasts and eventually into humans. If this theory were right, mankind would have to eventually change into another life form after one or two thousand years.

"For since the creation of the world His invisible attributes are clearly seen, being understood by the things that are made, even His eternal power and Godhead, so that they are without excuse" (Romans 1:20). People deny and reject God, although they can apparently see that God is alive when they look at the wonders and mysteries of nature. Unbelievers are under the God's wrath. Many people didn't glorify God or were thankful, so they became futile in their thoughts. Their foolish hearts were darkened; professing themselves to be wise, they became fools, and changed the glory of the incorruptible God into images of corruptible men, birds, four-footed beasts, and creeping things. The judgment of God is apparently waiting for those men. All the people who have not been born again are under the judgment of God, whether they believe in Jesus or not.

God gives unbelievers up to uncleanness

"Therefore God also gave them up to uncleanness, in the lusts of their hearts, to dishonor their bodies among themselves,

who exchanged the truth of God for the lie, and worshiped and served the creature rather than the Creator, who is blessed forever. Amen. For this reason God gave them up to vile passions. For even their women exchanged the natural use for what is against nature. Likewise also the men, leaving the natural use of the woman, burned in their lust of one another, men with men committing what is shameful, and receiving in themselves the penalty of their error which was due" (Romans 1:24-27).

What is this passage trying to say? God leaves the men who worship and serve creatures to sin as they please. He also gives them up to Satan. God permits Satan to do as he wishes. Therefore, we must believe in God and be saved anyway. *"For even their women exchanged the natural use for what is against nature. Likewise also the men, leaving the natural use of the woman, burned in their lust of one another."* This is like denying God and it is what caused AIDS.

God gave the natural use. A man should live with a woman. However, the fact that men have relation with men and women with women shows that they deny the natural use that God has given. The Book of Romans was written about 1900 years ago. Paul the Apostle predicted that those who leave the natural use of their sexes would pay the penalty for their sexual disorder. God's word is achieved in reality these days. We know that AIDS is prevailing especially among the homosexuals.

It is completely adequate for them to pay the penalty for their sexual sins. The wrath of God is revealed against the men who change the natural uses of their sexuality. They deserve to receive the penalty of AIDS. This disease is surely caused by the disbelief in God. God gives over unbelievers to a reprobate mind. In other words, it surely is the curse of God.

They are opposed to the righteousness of God

Men who don't like to retain God in their minds are like the following. *"Being filled with all unrighteousness, sexual immorality, wickedness, covetousness, maliciousness; full of envy, murder, strife, deceit, evil-mindedness; they are whisperers, backbiters, haters of God, violent, proud boasters, inventors of evil things, disobedient to parents, undiscerning untrustworthy, unloving, unforgiving, unmerciful; who, knowing the righteous judgment of God, that those who practice such things are deserving of death, not only do the same but also approve of those who practice them" (Romans 1:29-32).*

What do 'those who practice such things' do to those who practice the same evil? They 'approve' of them. What do men who are against God do to the righteous, who obey the word of God? They persecute the righteous, saying, "You are heretics." The righteous are persecuted for righteousness' sake after they believe in Jesus. They are blessed.

People sympathize with those who wander by the flesh. However, strange to say, we see that they object and prevent others from believing in Jesus and becoming righteous by the forgiveness of sin. This is like living as a servant of sin because they neither believe in God nor obey the word of the truth.

Therefore, unbelievers and Satan say that we should neither be perfectly sanctified nor have the perfect forgiveness of sin, although they permit us to believe in Jesus Christ. Unbelievers and disobeyers think and say that they must believe in Jesus in order to go to Heaven even though they have sins in their hearts. That is why they feel comfortable when they believe in Jesus as sinners. The ones, who don't know and believe in God, although they are Christians, don't receive God in their knowledge and oppose Him. They oppose the righteousness of God. They also worship Satan and all the sins. Those, who are not born again, although they believe in Jesus, are like that. There are so many nominal Christians who have not been born again. Those who believe in Jesus with sins in their hearts don't obey the word of the truth of God and oppose born again Christians who have obtain the remission of sin and got sanctified by believing in the truth of Jesus Christ.

Those who are not born again oppose the born again

Paul the Apostle says in the Bible that the wrath of God is revealed to men who suppress the truth in unrighteousness. He also says that the judgment of God is revealed from heaven against all ungodliness, and unrighteousness. Everything is done according to the truth. The truth is that the Lord has blotted out all our sins. The judgment of God is revealed to those who are against the truth and block it. We learn through the word of God that all the believers who are not born again are going to be judged by Him. God will judge those who are not born again, even though they believe in Jesus.

Believers who have not been born again like to slander the born again, with hearts full of maliciousness. Those will go to hell. God expels them to hell. They are full of malice and whisper to each other. Sinners who whisper together against the righteous, who have the forgiveness of sin, are to be judged. Do you see what I mean? We should sympathize with them. They oppose God with their sins, not knowing that they are against Him, whispering, "It's strange for them not to have sins. It sounds strange."

The judgment of God is revealed to those who are against

God with their evils. Those people take pleasure in those who do so. They admit whisperers and slanderers to be right. Christians who are not born again whisper to each other and slander the righteous. They backbite and hate the righteous, pride themselves, and plot evil things together. Do you know how they devise evil things? They commit evil acts by uniting with one another. They oppose the righteous with good slogans such as "Let's believe in Jesus well. Let's have the right kind of faith. Let's be the light of the world." They commit such sins uniting themselves, because it's not fun to sin alone.

Therefore, God says in Psalm 2:4, *"He who sits in the heavens shall laugh; The Lord shall hold them in derision,"* because the kings of the earth are against God. 'Oh! It's funny. Nothing will ever happen to Me no matter what your challenge against Me is. You guys bribe me to be judged.' God is waiting for the time of judgment because it is too laughable.

Those who judge the righteous will be judged by God

Those who are against the truth of God and who have not been born again commit sins. Those who are born again also have malice and imperfections in the flesh. However, it's basically different, in fact. We believe in God and the truth. We have received the remission of sin through God. However, they don't believe in God at all. These people are against 'the righteousness and the truth of God.' *"Therefore you are inexcusable, O man, whoever you are who judge, for in whatever you judge another you condemn yourself; for you who judge practice the same things" (Romans 2:1).*

Paul the Apostle talks to the Jews and Christians who have not been born again and only stuck to the law. They judge others, saying, "Don't murder, don't commit adultery, don't steal, and only serve God", while they themselves don't keep the law. Only God justly judges, and only His children, who have been born again, can judge according to the word of God.

These kinds of people are to be judged because they judge the righteous arbitrarily. God will judge all of those who have not been born again, that is to say, the Jews and the legalist-Christians. The wrath of God is revealed to those who lead religious lives by keeping the law, while not being born again, and who believe that they will go to hell if they don't obey God and that they will go to heaven if they do as God has said. A person of faith is one who becomes righteous after he/she believes in Jesus Christ. We must be discriminate. Those who can believe in God and lead pious lives without being born again judge the righteous according to their own criterion.

However, God will surely judge them. They don't know they are judging themselves according to their own criterion. Oh, you men who judge the righteous without having the forgiveness of sin, with wrong faiths, not receiving the grace of the truth of God, do you think that you can escape the judgment of God? These people are going to be judged by God.

The judgment of God is righteous

"But we are sure that the judgment of God is according to truth, against them which commit such things" (Romans 2:2). We are sure that the judgment of God is according to truth, against those who judge other people while not being born again, even though they believe in Jesus. We must know that God sends these people to hell and that He judges them according to His truth.

God sends sinners to hell because His truth is right, and because the judgment of God is accurate. Whether one goes to hell or not doesn't depend on the Doctrine of Predestination that preaches, 'God loves some, but hates others unconditionally.' God chose all men in Jesus Christ before the foundation of the world (Ephesians 1:4).

Whoever believes that Jesus Christ blotted out all his/her sins receive the remission of sin. God predestined this. Therefore, all of those who have not been born again, even though they believe in Jesus, will go to hell. They will go to hell according to the judgment of God and this is the truth.

The judgment of God, which sends sinners to hell, is right. Why? Because they rejected the great love of God and neither received the salvation of God nor believed in Him. It's proper for Him, according to the truth, to send those who are not born again to hell.

Some would say, "Why didn't God preach the gospel to me?" Didn't He? God preached the gospel to you so many times. Try to obtain salvation by widely opening your eyes. There are a few churches that preach the true gospel in this world. However, you can meet the truth if you really search for it. In my case, I really tried to find it! After preaching a sermon, when I was not born again yet, I prayed, "Oh, Lord. I'm a sinner before God, even though I have preached Your word to people like this. What I told people were things I was saying to myself. I'm a sinner. Please meet me. Please save me."

I don't know how much I have tried to find the truth. God wants to meet whoever seeks Him. God wants to redeem even those people who didn't seek Him. *"I will call them My people, who were not My people, And her beloved, who was not beloved" (Romans 9:25).* God says that He is our Savior who came to this world to save us. People who have sought God earnestly will surely meet Him. Some others haven't sought God, but come to get an opportunity to meet the Lord when the gospel preachers come to them and preached the gospel. Some would be interested in the gospel, but others would not. Men who will go to hell will end up there because they rejected the good news.

It is proper for those who deserve to go to hell to end up in hell according to the truth of God. Those who deserve to go to the Kingdom of Heaven reach it by believing in Jesus according to the right discrimination, even though they don't have any outstanding exploits. It happens through the right judgment of God.

God doesn't send one person to hell and the other to the Kingdom of Heaven at random on account of His favoritism for some people. But instead, He judges according to the right judgment in truth. Therefore, we must preach the gospel. *"And do you think this, O man, you who judge those practicing such things, and doing the same, that you will escape the judgment of God? Or do you despise the riches of His goodness, forbearance, and longsuffering, not knowing that the goodness of God leads you to repentance?"* (Romans 2:3-4)

Jesus already blotted out all the sins of the world through His love

Paul the Apostle says to sinners, the Jews and the legalist-Christians, who neither receive the love of Jesus nor are born again, that they will be judged. They are destined to go to hell. But what is the gospel? In Romans 2:4, God says, *"Or do you despise the riches of His goodness, forbearance, and longsuffering, not knowing that the goodness of God leads you to repentance?"* The love of God has accurately appeared to all people and has justly prevailed.

Nobody is excluded from the grace of the salvation of God. Jesus blotted out all the sins of the world. Jesus perfectly sanctified us. Does He only blot out the original sin and forgive us for our daily sins whenever we pray for forgiveness of them? No. The Lord already blotted out all the sins of the world once and for all. Nonetheless, those who are against God ignore His goodness and love. "How did Jesus save us? How can I say, 'I have no sin', even though I constantly sin? It's nonsense. How could God blot out all my sins while I continuously sin, even though He is the Savior and Lord God?"

People think according to the flesh like this, yet God has already washed away all the sins of the world with His love. The Lord came to the world and perfectly blotted out all our sins. The Lord knows the imperfections and infirmities of men (The flesh cannot but sin again and again). Therefore, He blotted out all the sins of the world once and for all with His baptism and by shedding His blood on the Cross. The Lord knows the infirmities of the flesh very well. "I saved you because I knew you would sin again and again until you die."

The Lord washed away the sins of the world. The Lord has accepted all of us by redeeming us. The Lord paid the wages of sin for sinners and sanctified them with His power and righteousness (Jesus was baptized by John the Baptist at the Jordan River). The Lord allowed us to be blessed, become His children and enabled us to go to the Kingdom of Heaven by paying the wages of our sins with His life (blood). The Lord turned sinners into His righteous children.

Unbelievers must repent and turn their hearts to the Lord

"Or do you despise the riches of His goodness, forbearance, and longsuffering, not knowing that the goodness of God leads you to repentance?" God sentences those who despise and deny the goodness, riches, forbearance and long-suffering of God to go to hell. It is certain that Jesus Christ washed away all the sins of the world, and that the gospel pervades all over the world. However, people still go to hell because they don't believe in it. Jesus saved us by washing away all our sins to prevent us from going to hell, even if we wanted to go to hell by despising the forbearance and riches of His goodness. Even if we desired to go to hell, He saved us.

Therefore we must believe in the water and the blood of Jesus Christ to be saved. Believe, and be saved. Those who despise the love and salvation of God will go to hell. Hell is a place that God has prepared for those who despise the grace of His salvation and the riches of His goodness. Unbelievers have already bought their tickets to hell. People who are destined to go to hell must repent and turn their hearts to the Lord. You also must say good-bye to the Kingdom of Heaven unless you have faith in the true gospel.

People go to hell because they reject the love of God

"But in accordance with your hardness and your impenitent heart you are treasuring up for yourself wrath in the day of wrath and revelation of the righteous judgment of God" *(Romans 2:5)*. Those who have impenitent hearts and people who don't repent will go to hell. Some people go to hell

because they have rejected the great love of God. Sinners who reject the truth with stubborn hearts and pursue their own thoughts will go to hell, due to the wages of their sin. Those who refuse to receive God's love and persist in doing repentance prayers to reach gradual sanctification will eventually go to hell. To have stored God's wrath until the day of revelation and His righteous judgment is due to denying the Lord's love.

In His plan of redemption, God decided to save sinners and make them righteous, even before Satan corrupted us into sin. God sent His Son to save and sanctify us. However, sinners have not accepted this. They have stored His wrath full to the brim by refusing God's love and will be judged on the day of wrath and revelation of His righteous judgment. The righteous judgment of God is to send those who have sins in their hearts to hell.

Why? Because God washed away all the sins of the world and made everyone in the world be saved by faith. Unbelievers will surely go to hell. They are stubborn and volunteer to go to hell, so they will ultimately regret their foolishness. Sinners will go to hell if they don't accept God's great love.

People think that God is unreasonable because He sends some people to hell and others to the Kingdom of Heaven at random according to His own authority. However, this is not true. God invented hell for those who are stubborn to deny His love and truth so that there would be an adequate place for them to go.

The Bible says that hell is a lake that burns with fire and brimstone. There are wriggling dirty maggots for those who prefer to have sin. They may cry, "No, No. I hate this place." But God would say, "I had washed away all your sins, but you said that it didn't matter if you possessed sin. Therefore, I give you maggots as a gift, as your friends, because you didn't like to have the forgiveness of sin." "No, I hate it, Lord."

"You've asked for it, even though you hate it. I'm the Lord of righteousness. I gave you what you wanted. I give hell to all those who like to have sin in their heart." It is the right judgment of God. Human beings sin while they live in this world, yet they should not ignore the gospel of the salvation of God that has washed away all the sins of the world.

People go to hell because they are hard-hearted. We should not be stubborn before God. We should believe that He already washed away all the sins of the world. You must believe, even if it is not visible.

God tells us that He already loved us

God tells us that He already loved us. "I already washed away all of your sins." You must believe this fact. When God says that He created the heavens and the earth, we must believe it because the word of God is true. Faith begins with the belief in God's word. People believe something only when they understand it with their small heads and don't believe when they can't understand. Unbelievers who don't believe that God saved all sinners from their sins will go to hell. They are the ones who make up their minds to go to hell.

There was a prominent Christian who once declared publicly, "I confess before God that I'm a sinner until I die." He died and surely went to hell. He said to God, "I declare that I'm a sinner before God and can never be righteous before Him." He persisted in being a sinner until the time of his death. He rejected God's love and the truth up to his last breath. Then the Lord said, "You are so faithful to your own faith! It's proper for you to go to hell according to your faith. I send you to hell because sinners can never enter into the Kingdom of Heaven."

If I had believed,

The man who said, "I declare that I'm a sinner until I die," went to hell. Even God can't help these people. Not only have they declared that they are sinners, though they may end up in hell the day after tomorrow, but they also taught believers who trusted in them, "We are sinners until we die and will still be sinners when we stand before God." Therefore, many believers also follow the same religious route. God said that sinners would go to hell. However, innumerable Christians follow this teaching in today's Christianity. God said that those sinners would eternally regret, grinding their teeth in the hot flames of hell, saying, "If I had believed; if I had only believed it."

"If I had believed in the fact that Jesus washed away all my sins and abandoned my own thoughts, I would have entered into the Kingdom of Heaven!" "If I had believed; if I had only believed." There are going to be many people uttering things like this in hell. They will say, "If, If, If I had believed, If I had received the truth, I would have been His son. Why had I been so stubborn...."

We the righteous will ask God at that time, "Lord, please show us what the sinners are doing now. They had persecuted us, the righteous." "No, it's not good for you, My children, because you heart will suffer after seeing your acquaintances among them. Do you really want to see people you know suffering?" "Please show us just one time!" The Lord may show it to us someday because He is so generous. So let's assume that we see it. There would be a lot of outcries heard such as: "If I had believed, if I had believed." We would then wonder, "What is this noise? Are they singing?" "Listen carefully whether they are singing or regretting." Men and women in that flame singing in chorus and regretting, "If I had believed."

Stubborn people will go to hell unless they are stubborn in the right way. We really need persistence in holding fast to the truth. Man should not be indecisive. We should be persistent when we have to be persistent. We all have to be persistent in the right way and we have to break our persistence when it is needed.

God will render to every man according to his deeds

God *"will render to each one according to his deeds: eternal life to those who by patient continuance in doing good seek for glory, honor, and immortality"* (Romans 2:6-7). God renders to every person according to his/her deeds and judges him/her so. 'Render' means to 'reward in accordance with a deed.' What kind of a person uses patience to continue doing good whiling seeking glory, honor, and immortality? He/she is the one who believes in Jesus' perfect salvation.

There are many people in the world, but God gives eternal lives only to those who endure for righteousness and believe in His truth, no matter what other people say. God gives the glory of the eternal Kingdom to those who want to become the righteous and wish to lead eternally happy lives. They continue in doing good and seek glory, honor, and immortality; wanting to be the sons of God. They would endure and continue in doing good to follow and pursue after the righteousness of God.

God gives those people eternal lives. God allows them to live eternally and makes them His children. The sons of God are gods in His Kingdom.

"But to those who are self-seeking and do not obey the truth, but obey unrighteousness—indignation and wrath" (Romans 2:8). "But to those" refers to the group of people who are opposite to the blessed. The indignation and wrath of God are given to those who disobey His righteousness, are contentious and don't obey the truth. God sends them to hell. Those who are not born again and don't obey the truth are contentious and against the truth as a group.

Those who are not born again are contentious and like to form factions. Throughout Korean history, our ancestors made factions and contended each other in political problems. The ruling group would be decided according to the fact who became king. When one of Lee families became king, men of the Lee family were placed on high social positions while others were expelled or persecuted. But when the throne changed to the Kim family, everything was completely changed. People formed factions for their own advantages, not for achieving just causes.

The present Christianity is similar to this. They form denominations and sects. What for? To disobey the truth as a group. They say unanimously that they have sin, though Jesus washed away the sins of the world. They pretend to be righteous and saved, but don't obey the truth. They condemn the righteous as heretics, saying that they are right to have sin. The Lord says that sinners who are contentious to the righteous are wrong and that they must all go to hell.

Those who obey the truth and God obey the word of the Lord. We, the righteous believe the judgment of God is according to the truth.

Can Christian denominations send us to the Kingdom of Heaven?

Denominational bodies cannot send us to the Kingdom of Heaven. My wife provoked her mother-in-law to fury when she said to her, "A religious body can't send you to the Kingdom of Heaven." Frankly speaking, I don't know why my mother got angry at the assertion still now. Do you think a religious body can send you to the Kingdom of Heaven? We individually get saved and enter into the Kingdom of Heaven by believing in the word of God. Can the religious bodies of the Presbyterian Church send you to the Kingdom of Heaven? Can a denominational body of the Baptist Church send you? Can the Holiness Church? Can the Seventh-Day Adventist Church? No. We can enter into the Kingdom of Heaven only when we believe in the forgiveness of sin that Jesus prepared for us.

We have to abide in the church of God

Paul the Apostle apparently separated sinners who would go to hell from the righteous who would enter into the Kingdom of Heaven among all Christians. The gospel is equal to everybody, to Jews and to Greeks alike. Here, the Greeks stand for Gentiles and the Jews stand for Israelites. God does not look at the outward appearance of people. God looks for a man who believes in the word of God with his heart. Do you believe that Jesus is God? Do you believe that Jesus is our Savior? We can go to the Kingdom of Heaven only when we believe that Jesus took away all the sins of the world with His baptism. We have to believe this and not betray it. The Holy Spirit within us keeps us from betraying our faiths and helps defeat our enemies when danger is upon us. We have to be careful.

In the Bible, there is a parable of the four kinds of fields, but some fields imply those who can't be saved. The seeds sown on those fields die as soon as they spring up. Such case is the same as being a dead seed. It has the same result, which is death. Then, can we keep our faiths by ourselves? No. We can keep our faiths only when the Lord gives us the strength to endure any trouble and the remedy for every spiritual sickness while we abide in the true vine.

The church of God is the vine. The Lord gives us blessings, remedies, consolations, and the faith to endure persecution while we abide in the church of God. But what will happen to us if we don't abide in the vine? We would die quickly. The hearts of the righteous can't endure against Satan's attacks and eventually get sick if they don't willingly unite with the church, though they may have many abilities and powers. Do you see it? They gradually fall and become more and more useless. The Bible says, *"You are the salt of the earth; but if the salt loses its flavor, how shall it be seasoned? It is then good for nothing but to be thrown out and trampled underfoot by men" (Matthew 5:13).*

Even the righteous are good for nothing if they live apart from the church. They can shine their lights and are blessed when they abide in the church. But they come to be ruined when they live apart from the church and can't overcome the world when they go astray into the world apart from the church. How long can you uphold your own beliefs? How long can you stand apart from the church of God? Even the servants of God can't prevail. However, if we abide in the vine, our household shall be saved, and many people can have the remission of sin through us. Where did Lot go after pursuing a carnal desire? He went to Sodom. He lived well there. What was the result? He became ruined. The Bible says that all the descendants of Lot were ruined. The Moabites and the Ammonites came from Lot's daughters.

Why were the descendants who were against God born from a righteous person, Lot? It was because he departed from the church. The reason why I am not disappointed in any hard times is that God set up His church. God blesses the church where the righteous gather together and becomes the Shepherd and Lord of the church for every single saint. It's His promise and assurance.

"For as many as have sinned without law will also perish without law, and as many as have sinned in the law will be judged by the law (for not the hearers of the law are just in the sight of God, but the doers of the law will be justified; for when Gentiles, who do not have the law, by nature do the things in the law, these, although not having the law, are a law to themselves, who show the work of the law written in their hearts, their conscience also bearing witness, and between themselves their thoughts accusing or else excusing them.)" (Romans 2:12-15)

A person who doesn't go to church doesn't know the law these days. Then his/her conscience becomes the law because he/she doesn't know the law. He/she does the evil, though he/she knows it's right or wrong in his/her conscience. Then, it is a sin and he/she must seek the Lord to be saved from sin. God meets whoever really wants to seek Him.

We must seek His mercy before God and believe in Him. We must believe in Him while abandoning our pride. We must live by faith. We must not leave the church of God; we must seek, believe, and abide in the church. God does not expel us when we abide in the church, even though we are infirm and weak.

The sin of Jews

Now the Apostle Paul starts to preach the gospel in full scale to the Jews after separating them from those who are going to the Kingdom of Heaven.

"Indeed you are called a Jew, and rest on the law, and make your boast in God, and know His will, and approve the things that are excellent, being instructed out of the law, and are confident that you yourself are a guide to the blind, a light to those who are in darkness, an instructor of the foolish, a teacher of babes, having the form of knowledge and truth in the law. You, therefore, who teach another, do you not teach yourself? You who preach that a man should not steal, do you steal? You who say, 'Do not commit adultery,' do you commit adultery? You who abhor idols, do you rob temples?" (Romans 2:17-22)

We must know the following. God originally spoke to the Jews, so they had the word of God and the sacrificial system. He promised the Messiah through the Jews and showed His plan through His Jewish servants. So, Moses and all the prophets were Jews. However, the Jews thought they understood what would please God and what His law was, diligently reciting and memorizing the word of God. Nevertheless, Paul the Apostle said, *"Indeed you are called a Jew, and rest on the law, and make your boast in God."* Jews were not saved, though they boasted of God and ministered sacrifices earnestly. Those who don't believe fully in Jesus as their Savior are the same as unbelievers. It means that they neither believed God's promise that He would save them as in the sacrificial system, nor believed in Jesus, the Savior.

Jews will go to hell because they don't believe in Jesus, the Savior. It was useless for them to lay their hands on the head of sheep again and again. They didn't truly believe that 'Laying on of hands' meant 'to pass sins' in the time of Malachi, at the end of the Old Testament. They had believed it well to the time of David, but their faiths had begun to falter from the time of Solomon. During the age of the divided Kingdom, they worshiped other gods like Baal and Asherah while they ministered formalistic sacrifices at the Temple. Ministering formalistic sacrifices is the same as not believing in God. God is satisfied when we believe and abide in His word.

In the sacrificial system of the tabernacle, the sins of a person were passed onto the head of a sacrificial animal when he laid his hands on it. But they didn't believe in it, teaching other people, though they knew what was wrong and right. It was the sin of the Jews. Not to believe in the truth of God's word, knowing His word to the letter, and preaching the word to other people was the sin of the Jews.

It is the same as not believing in God. It's a fatal sin. *"Indeed you are called a Jew, and rest on the law, and make your boast in God, and know His will, and approve the things that are excellent, being instructed out of the law, and are confident that you yourself are a guide to the blind, a light to those who are in darkness, an instructor of the foolish, a teacher of babes, having the form of knowledge and truth in the law."* Paul pointed out the sin of disbelief among Jews.

It is to defile God to believe in Jesus with sins in the heart

We can apply the same blunder of the Jews to most Christians today. Jews are the same as those who don't believe that Jesus have sanctified them by blotting out all their sins. *"You who make your boast in the law, do you dishonor God through breaking the law? For 'the name of God is blasphemed among the Gentiles because of you,' as it is written" (Romans 2:23-24).* It is to defile the name of God if we believe in Jesus in the wrong way. It's to defile the name of God, if we don't exactly believe what Jesus did and if we are not born again.

It is to defile God to believe in Jesus without being born again. *"For circumcision is indeed profitable if you keep the law; but if you are a breaker of the law, your circumcision has become uncircumcision. Therefore, if an uncircumcised man keeps the righteous requirements of the law, will not his uncircumcision be counted as circumcision? And will not the physically uncircumcised, if he fulfills the law, judge you who, even with your written code and circumcision, are a transgressor of the law? For he is not a Jew who is one outwardly, nor is circumcision that which is outward in the flesh; but he is a Jew who is one inwardly; and circumcision is that of the heart, in the Spirit, not in the letter; whose praise is not from men but from God" (Romans 2:25-29).* We must all receive the word of Jesus with our hearts.

Which one came first, circumcision or the law?

Which one came first, circumcision or the law? Which one did God give to Israel first? Circumcision. God told

Abraham to be circumcised. Abraham had no legitimate son, even though he was 99 years old. However, God had promised Abraham a son when he was 75 years old. God told Abraham, "Come outside, I will give you as many descendants as the stars in the sky." Abraham believed in the word of God and waited for 25 years. The promise was finally fulfilled after 25 years. Therefore, his son was given to him when he was 100 years old. He waited 25 years, even though he was a little disappointed and made many mistakes while he was waiting. God also promised to give him and his sons the land of promise, Canaan that implies the Kingdom of Heaven spiritually.

After promising the Kingdom of Heaven, God told Abraham and every male among the men of his house to be circumcised. God said that circumcision should be a sign of the covenant between God and them. Therefore, Abraham circumcised the flesh of his foreskin. All the male of his household performed this rite. Circumcision is the same as the faith by which we believe and receive the gospel of the truth.

Israel denied to be circumcised in the heart

However, Israel boasted of being the descendants of Abraham and being circumcised, asked the Gentiles arrogantly, "Have you been circumcised?" We must be circumcised in the heart. We are saved when we receive the word that Jesus blotted out the sins of the world and believe it with our hearts.

No other country has been invaded more than Israel. They were in deep grief as a homeless people for nearly two thousand years. God trod on Israel. Why? Because they didn't believe.

They defiled the name of God because they didn't believe,

even though God loved Israel and wanted them to believe that God washed away all their sins. He wanted to defeat their enemies as the Shepherd of Israel and wanted to bless, love, and give glory to them.

God promised to give glory to all people and make them His children if they believe in Him with their hearts and have the remission of sin. Through the example of Israel, God warns all the people of the world that He will send them to hell, if they don't receive His promise.

God has promised that whoever believes the gospel of His truth can receive all the blessings that Jesus promised, even though he/she is insufficient in deeds. The only way to avoid the judgment of God is to believe in the gospel. Believe in it, and you will then be saved and be able to avoid hell.

I wish for the grace of the Lord to be on all souls. ✉

CHAPTER

2

Introduction to Romans Chapter 2

In this world, there are only two groups of people that believe in God: the Jews and Christians. Among these two groups of people, the former believe in Jesus while the latter do not. God regards the faiths of those who do not believe in Jesus as useless. However, the most serious problem Christians face is that they believe in Jesus somehow but have not yet been remitted of their sins. The Apostle Paul talks about this theme in Romans chapter 2 not only to the Jews and Greeks but also to today's Christians.

The Jews judge others easily

The Apostle Paul reproaches both the Jews and Christians who have the same kinds of faiths. In Romans 2:1, Paul, saying *"O man, whoever you are who judge,"* reproaches those who are intoxicated with the sense of superiority in being Jewish or Christian. Even those who have not been born again after believing in God know what is wrong by the law of consciousness in their hearts. That is why they tell others not to steal. However, they commit adultery themselves and do not keep the Lord's words, yet guide others with God's commandments while professing themselves to be believers of God. These are the people, among Jews and Christians, who have not been born again.

Those who believe in God tell others not to worship idols or commit murder, boasting that they keep the law of God.

Therefore, they dishonor God by breaking His laws.

People who do not know God's righteousness, but believe in Jesus, also say that Jesus is their Savior. But their faiths are not based on God's righteousness, so they oppose the true righteousness of God that has already blotted out all their sins. They themselves do not know that they are opposing the true believers in God. We can see that many people call themselves Christians but reject the gospel that contains God's righteousness, without knowing Jesus' love, or the spiritual circumcision. They claim to follow God's will, but in truth they have not accepted Jesus and have crucified Him to the Cross on a charge of blasphemy that Jesus identified Himself as the Son of God.

The Apostle Paul said that an outward Jew is not a Jew, but an inward Jew is a genuine Jew. They claim that they are God's people and that they are a part of God's nation. But how can the Jews believe in God when they have rejected Jesus as their Savior?

The Apostle Paul says, *"Circumcision is that of the heart, in the Spirit, not in the letter" (Romans 2:29)*. Those who believe in the spiritual circumcision are the true believers in God. They are righteous by faith.

From whom should the believers of God receive recognition and praise? They should receive it from God. Paul said, *"Whose praise is not from men but from God" (Romans 2:29)*. If we believe in God's righteousness, we win His praise and receive a reward from Him. If you believe in Jesus outwardly yet hold sin in your heart, you do not believe in God's righteousness actually; you are only mocking Him. Therefore, you will receive the judgment of an unbeliever.

Who are those who ignore God's truth? They are the people who follow human words more seriously than God's word. They organize themselves into various religious sects in Christianity and oppose God. They reject and stand against the righteousness of God's salvation with their united power. Can you guess what kinds of punishments will come down on these people?

The punishment to those who oppose God

Verses 8 and 9 state, *"But to those who are self-seeking and do not obey the truth, but obey unrighteousness—indignation and wrath, tribulation and anguish, on every soul of man who does evil, of the Jew first and also of the Greek."*

Tribulation and anguish will come down upon each of the souls of mankind who do evil. Here, the expression "anguish" is the punishment to be received in hell. To those who commit evil, there are tribulations and hell's anguish.

What kind of a curse do those who reject God receive? God brings down fearful judgment upon those who reject His love. How do you expect those who have opposed God's love, which comes from spiritual circumcision, to live peacefully in body and mind? Some people will live ruined lives now and after death because they deserve God's wrath. They have opposed God's righteousness and cannot hold true satisfaction in their hearts. They do not know the love that comes from spiritual circumcision; even when they go to church confessing that they believe in Jesus, they still suffer from not having their sins remitted.

You cannot know this secret just because you believe in Jesus. Only those who believe in God's righteousness know it. Be advised you wrong believers in God that you should understand and believe in the gospel of the water and the Spirit, which is God's righteousness. Then you will be able to free yourselves from the suffering curse.

If a man says that he has sin in his heart even when he believes in Jesus, it means that he believes in the wrong way and has to believe in the true gospel that bestows God's righteousness. No matter in what denomination people believe in Jesus, if they claim to believe in Him somehow, yet hold sin in their hearts, they are committing the sin of ignoring God's righteousness. What is the right result of believing in God? If you believe in Jesus as your Savior in truth, you will surely be sinless. However, if you have sin in your heart even after believing in Jesus, it means that you have not fully understood God's righteousness.

The Lord who saved all the sinners from their sins has already come in flesh, saved the sinners, and become the Savior of all believers. Then, can a person who truly believes in the water and the Holy Spirit have sin? The person should not have sin if he/she truly believes in God's righteousness from the moment he/she first believes in Jesus. But it is because he/she ignores God's righteousness while believing in Jesus somehow that his/her heart comes to have sin.

Therefore, you have to give up your stubbornness right now. "I have believed in Jesus wrongly! Then in what way should I know Jesus and believe? I have come to understand that the Cross is important in believing Jesus, but His baptism is also very essential. Now I come to understand that Jesus was crucified on the Cross and received vicarious judgment because He took over all the sins of the world through the baptism." You have to realize these truths and believe them.

Those who remain stubborn against the Lord will receive God's retribution in accordance. The result is being put into the fires of hell. That is why Matthew 7:22 states, *"Many will say to Me in that day, 'Lord, Lord, have we not prophesied in Your name, cast out demons in Your name, and done many wonders in Your name?'"* When the Lord comes again, those who do not believe in God's righteousness and have sins in their hearts while outwardly pretending to believe in Jesus will be judged before God. They will say to the Lord, "Have I not believed in You well? Have I not cast out demons in Your name and spoken in tongues? Have I not served You, Lord?"

However, the Lord will say, "Depart from Me, you who practice lawlessness (this indicates those who do not believe in God's righteousness)! How can you say that you believe in Me when you do not believe that I have blotted out all of your sins by receiving baptism and dying on the Cross? Liar, you shall enter the eternal burning fire. Your sin is that of a false prophet and have led many people to hell." Those who do not believe in His righteousness and give up their stubbornness will receive God's fearful wrath.

The biggest example of this kind of faith is of the Jews, and they still remain stubborn before God. To this day, they do not believe in God's righteousness through Jesus Christ. Even among the Protestants, there are so many stubborn Christians who say that their daily sins can be forgiven every time they offer prayers of repentance. These people should give up their stubbornness of not believing in God's righteousness in order to avoid His indignation.

Does Jesus forgive those for their self-crimes whenever they repent and pray for His forgiveness everyday? He doesn't. John the Baptist, who was the last High Priest of the Old Testament and the representative of all mankind, baptized Jesus 2000 years ago and He shed blood on the Cross. For thus, He fulfilled the righteousness of God and blotted out all of mankind's sins at once.

Where did Jesus take over our sins? Jesus burdened himself of all the sins of mankind all at once when He was baptized by John at the Jordan River. He also saved the believers eternally from sin by going up the Golgotha to shed blood on the Cross and receive vicarious judgment for all the sins. But all the Christian-sinners are still stubborn and do not believe in God's righteousness. If their hearts have already been cleansed of all sins by the blood on the Cross, then why do they have to ask for forgiveness for their sins until they pass away? They are being stubborn. Jesus' blood on the Cross is important, but Jesus' baptism received from John is also so important that people should believe and have their sins forgiven in one time in order to obtain God's righteousness.

Everyone is stubborn! But before God, you should give up your stubbornness of rejecting His righteousness. Those who believe in God should obey and believe in His words. I am also a very stubborn person, but I gave up my stubbornness before God and became righteous by His grace.

True repentance is giving up one's stubbornness and receiving the remission of sins by accepting the righteousness of God in mind. After being forgiven, we have to change our wrong ways and acknowledge our mistakes, trying to live better lives spiritually in front of God. The latter is the repentance in actual life of a born-again saint.

Those who believe in Jesus, yet do not know God's righteousness will be destroyed. These people should give up their stubborn ways, repent, and believe in the baptism and the Cross of Jesus for the remission of their sins (Acts 3:19). The Lord gave us this commandment in order for us to receive the remission of sins in one time by believing in His righteousness. We have to listen to God and listen to His words so that we can be perfectly righteous people and be forgiven for all our sins at once by believing in the truth that Jesus atoned all our sins through His baptism and crucifixion. When a person believes in God's righteousness, he/she will be forgiven for all sin and receive the Holy Spirit as a gift. All the Apostles and disciples of Jesus believed in God's righteousness and received the remission of sins in one time. You, too, should not be stubborn before the truth. You should be stubborn at the right times. If you do not understand the spiritual circumcision well, you have to learn and believe it. It would not do to remain stubborn. You have to repent and believe.

People reject the truth and mock it without knowing the truth of spiritual circumcision. "That is wrong! How can a person become righteous when he commits sins everyday? You know, God just calls the believers in Jesus righteous even though they are still sinful. It is the Doctrine of Justification. You are not called righteous because you really do not have any sin in your heart." However, you should know it is a very erroneous teaching.

In the Bible, God said that through the gospel of spiritual circumcision that gives us the remission of sins, "I have blotted out all of your sins. You are sinless now. Because I have taken over all of your sins, you are righteous." "Do you believe in My righteousness? If you believe in the words of the spiritual circumcision, then you are one of My people and you are sinless." God talks about His complete deliverance, but nominal Christians slander and mock the born-again Christians who believe in spiritual circumcision. They say, "How can a person become righteous when he/she commits sins ceaselessly? You can call a person 'as sinless' only through the Doctrine of Justification. How can we think of a person as really sinless? A person cannot help but sin every day." They slander like this and remain stubborn because they do not believe in the righteousness of God.

But God gives eternal lives to those who are patient in doing good. Those who seek glory, honor, and immortality by patient continuance in doing good will become God's children, but those who do not do so will receive punishment. Everyone wants to become a child of God and live eternal life. Jesus gives eternal lives to those who earnestly want to live forever and have sinless lives.

"What I truly want Lord is to believe in the remission of sin through the spiritual circumcision so that I may live a life without anything shameful in my conscience. I want to become Your child. I want to believe in Your righteousness and make You happy. I want to become sinless. Please save me from all my sins." To those who seek God's righteous salvation and wishes to be forgiven for all their sins, God listens to all of their wishes and forgives all of their sins by giving them the gospel of God's righteousness. To those who want to live eternally, God gives eternal life.

What is the spiritual circumcision?

It means the remission of sins accomplished through Jesus' baptism and His blood on the Cross. The blood of the Lamb is the vicarious judgment and Jesus' baptism from John means that the sins of the world were passed onto Jesus. Even today, Christianity cannot ignore the Old Testament because then, it cannot believe in the New Testament. In the Scriptures, we can find that the spiritual circumcision and the blood of the lamb at the Passover ritual are closely related.

In 1 John 5:6, it says that Jesus came *"not only by water, but by water and blood."* Jesus did not come only by water or by blood, but by both. You have to believe in the spiritual circumcision contained in the words of the water, the blood, and the Spirit in order to be delivered from all your sins.

Reading Exodus chapter 12, I had some questions about the spiritual circumcision. What does Exodus chapter 12 mean? I looked carefully into the entire chapter and all the related passages in the Bible again and again. And I came to realize that the Israelites were able to participate in the Passover Feast because they had received circumcision and in the New Testament, it said that Jesus did not simply shed blood on the Cross, but shed blood because He was baptized by John.

God told the Israelites two ordinances for the lawful Passover Feast: to receive circumcision previously and then to eat the meat of the Passover lamb. This was the spiritual circumcision of the Old Testament! In the New Testament, it said that our sins were passed onto Jesus by John's baptism and that He shed blood on the Cross. I found out that accepting these facts resulted in the truth of receiving the spiritual circumcision. Jesus Christ was baptized by John at the Jordan; that is how He burdened the world's sins and why He had to die on the Cross to receive judgment in our place.

You can experience the salvation from all the sins and iniquities by accepting this truth in your heart. For a person to receive salvation from all sin, he/she needs to believe in God's righteousness, which can give us the spiritual circumcision. People need to realize this truth. You readers have to perceive the truth that the spiritual circumcision in the Old Testament and the baptism of Jesus in the New Testament form a pair when concerning the remission of sins. Jesus did not receive judgment because He had sinned, but He died on the Cross for mankind because He had been baptized and borne the sins of the world with His body. This is the faith of those who have received the spiritual circumcision.

Those who believe in God's righteousness through the spiritual circumcision have no sin because they truly believe in Jesus. I pity those who believe in Jesus somehow, yet have not received the spiritual circumcision from God. They have to believe in the truth that Jesus took over all the sins of the world when John baptized Him.

Unfortunately, most Christians believe only in the Cross and not Jesus' baptism. Thus, they do not have the faith of believing in God's righteousness. We have to know that we must believe what God has told us in the Scriptures.

We have to tear down no matter what doctrines and teachings of theologians, and only believe in God's words that will lead us to His righteousness. This is because words without His righteousness are not truly God's words. The gospel without the spiritual circumcision is not complete. That is why in the Bible, God spoke so frequently about the circumcision in the Old Testament and the baptism of Jesus in the New Testament. In other words, it talks about the circumcision and the blood of the Passover lamb in the Old Testament in parallel with Jesus' baptism and His blood in the New Testament. We have to believe in this truth to receive the spiritual circumcision. However, if we do not believe in this truth, we will be set aside from God's Kingdom.

Is God's righteousness fulfilled only by His blood on the Cross? This is not so. God's righteousness was completed both by Jesus' baptism and His blood on the Cross. So, we received the spiritual circumcision in our hearts not only by His bloodshed on the Cross, but by the baptism He received from John. The spiritual circumcision can be possible for us since Jesus actually blotted out all our sins through His baptism and His atoning death on the Cross.

Circumcision means to cut out

Isaiah prophesied that the Messiah, Jesus Christ would receive the vicarious judgment for our sins by being wounded and bruised. Therefore, there is something we should know before we go on. Why did Christ have to be crucified on the Cross?

In the Old Testament, a sinner had to lay his/her hands on a sacrificial lamb to pass on the sins and then had to kill the lamb. Then, the priest took some of the blood of the sin offering with his finger, put it on the horns of the altar of the burnt offering, and poured the rest of its blood at the base of the altar (Leviticus 4:27-30). A sinner of the Old Testament Age could be remitted of his/her sins this way. Then wouldn't Jesus, who came as the Lamb of God (John 1:29) to save us from our sins, had to have had hands laid on His head as in the Old Testament in order to take all of mankind's sins?

Then, when and how did the Lord take the sins of the world? Is that not shown in Matthew 3:13-17, where John baptized Jesus at the Jordan? This is as in Leviticus of the Old Testament where it continuously says the sinner *"shall lay his hand on the head of the sin offering" (Leviticus 1:4, 3:8, 4:29)* to pass on the sins. The High Priest in the Old Testament had to lay his hands on the head of the lamb and pass on his and all the Israelites' sins (Leviticus 16:21). Then, he took some of its blood and put it on the horns of the altar of burnt offering and poured its remaining blood at the base of the altar. They received the remission of sins this way.

In a way like this, our remission of sins was made possible by Jesus' baptism from John and His blood on the Cross. This was God's righteousness and the spiritual circumcision that God wanted to give us within the Bible. Therefore, we who believe in God's righteousness had our sins cut off by Jesus' baptism from John and His blood on the Cross. When we perceive the meaning of Jesus' baptism in the New Testament in relation to the circumcision in the Old Testament, we come to believe in God's righteousness and we truly come to receive the spiritual circumcision in our hearts.

The true spiritual circumcision in the New Testament

Let us see Matthew 3:13-15. *"Then Jesus came from Galilee to John at the Jordan to be baptized by him. And John tried to prevent Him, saying, 'I need to be baptized by You, and are You coming to me?' But Jesus answered and said to him, 'Permit it to be so now, for thus it is fitting for us to fulfill all righteousness.' Then he allowed Him."*

John the Baptist baptized Jesus at the Jordan. He laid his hands upon Jesus' head and baptized him. (To baptize, *'baptizo'* in Greek, means to immerse or to submerge under water.)

In order for Jesus to die on the Cross for our sins, He first had to take our sins through the baptism. So, He was baptized by John first, and then submerged under water. Why was He baptized? It was because when He was baptized, all of God's righteousness could be fulfilled. It was just and fitting that He took mankind's sins through baptism and that He became our God and Savior. It was very suitable for Jesus to die on the Cross bearing all our sins on His body through His baptism.

The first thing Jesus ever did in His public life was to receive baptism. Baptism, *'baptisma'* in Greek, implies "to wash, to bury, to transfer and to pass over." In the Old Testament, the 10th day of the seventh month was the Day of Atonement of the Israelites, and Aaron laid his hands upon the sacrificial goats to pass on all of the sins of the Israelites. Of the two goats, one was offered to God and the other was made as an offering for atonement in front of the Israelites (Leviticus 16). In the New Testament, Jesus received all of our sins by being baptized by John.

On the next day of His baptism, John pointed his finger at Him and said, *"Behold! The Lamb of God who takes away the sin of the world!" (John 1:29)*

You have to admit that the spiritual circumcision is not possible only by the faith in His blood.

Let us see starting from 1 John 5:4. *"For whatever is born of God overcomes the world. And this is the victory that has overcome the world—our faith. Who is he who overcomes the world, but he who believes that Jesus is the Son of God? This is He who came by water and blood—Jesus Christ; not only by water, but by water and blood. And it is the Spirit who bears witness, because the Spirit is truth. For there are three that bear witness in heaven: the Father, the Word, and the Holy Spirit; and these three are one. And there are three that bear witness on earth: the Spirit, the water, and the blood; and these three agree as one. If we receive the witness of men, the witness of God is greater; for this is the witness of God which He has testified of His Son. He who believes in the Son of God has the witness in himself; he who does not believe God has made Him a liar, because he has not believed the testimony that God has given of His Son. And this is the testimony: that God has given us eternal life, and this life is in His Son. He who has the Son has life; he who does not have the Son of God does not have life" (1 John 5:4-12).*

What is the proof of the spiritual circumcision? It is the faith of believing both in Jesus' baptism and His blood as our salvation. The victory that has overcome the world is the water and the blood. *"This is He who came by water and blood— Jesus Christ; not only by water, but also by blood. And it is the Spirit who bears witness because the Spirit is truth. And there are three that bear witness on the earth: the Spirit, the water, and the blood."* These witnesses, that show God is our God and our Savior, testifies that God came to earth in human flesh, took all of our sins unto His body through His baptism, shed blood on the Cross on our behalf, and thus delivered us from all our sins.

In the New Testament, the gospel of the spiritual circumcision consists of the water and the blood. In the New Testament, the water is the baptism Jesus received from John and the blood means His death on the Cross. Jesus' baptism is the counterpart to the circumcision in the Old Testament. Jesus' baptism from John is proof that our sins have been passed onto Him by it. Those who believe in the truth will be able to stand in front of God and say, "God, you are my Savior. I believe in Your righteousness, therefore, I have no sin. I am your flawless child and You are my God." What is the basis in the Scriptures that let's you confidently shout in this way? It is the faith in Jesus' baptism and His blood on the Cross, which constitute

God's righteousness. Accepting God's righteousness as my righteousness cannot be possible only by Christ's blood. Both His baptism and blood create it.

Let us look at the passage about the indispensability of Jesus' baptism in our salvation. 1 Peter 3:21 is the proof of this truth. *"There is also an antitype which now saves us—baptism (not the removal of the filth of the flesh, but the answer of a good conscience toward God), through the resurrection of Jesus Christ."*

The Apostle Peter is now talking about the doubtless evidence of our salvation. Jesus' baptism is the circumcision in the Old Testament. Do you understand? As the Israelites cut off their foreskins for circumcision in the Old Testament, in the New Testament, Jesus was baptized by John and took all the sins of the world, enabling us to receive the spiritual circumcision. The baptism and the blood on the Cross created God's righteousness. The spiritual circumcision and the baptism mean the same thing. You have to understand that Jesus' baptism implies the spiritual circumcision to all of us.

"There is also an antitype which now saves us—baptism." How do we receive God's righteousness? By believing that Jesus was baptized and died on the Cross for our sins. Matthew 3:15 states, *"For thus it is fitting for us to fulfill all righteousness."* Because all of mankind's sins have passed onto Jesus' head, sinners' sins are blotted out absolutely. Every sinner becomes righteous by believing in Jesus' baptism and His blood. Jesus Christ shed the blood of judgment on the Cross after bearing all the sins of the world; all of mankind's sins were atoned this way. Believing that Jesus took over the world's sins by being baptized and that He received vicarious judgment on behalf of us is to have faith in the truth that will

bring God's righteousness to believers. Believe in this truth.

John 1:29 states, *"Behold! The Lamb of God who takes away the sin of the world."* Jesus is God's Son and as our Creator, He fulfilled His promise of circumcision by taking all sinners' sins. This is the true faith that brings in our hearts the spiritual circumcision, which is God's righteousness. Jesus is our true righteousness. We must thank Jesus. We must thank Him for His baptism and blood that enables us to receive the spiritual circumcision.

1 Peter 3:21 continues, *"Not the removal of the filth of the flesh, but the answer of a good conscience toward God."* A person's filth of the flesh is not removed just because he/she believes in Jesus as his/her real Savior. You can receive the remission of sins by believing that all your sins have been passed onto Jesus by His baptism and His blood shed on the Cross. Receiving the remission of sins by confessing Jesus as your Savior occurs in your heart. It takes place in the believer's heart. If you believe in the Savior with your heart, you will be remitted of your sins, while your flesh is still filthy and commits iniquities everyday; but there is no sin. You receive God's righteousness by believing that when Jesus was baptized, all of the sins were passed on to Jesus and that there are no more sins in your heart.

You have to believe in the truth to make it yours

In John 1:12, it says, *"But as many as received Him, to them He gave the right to become children of God, to those who believe in His name."*

What words have you received and accepted? You have to accept the things that were done by God's Son. What was

God's work? God's Son came to earth in the likeness of sinful flesh, and when He was thirty, He got baptized to take all of mankind's sins and gave us the spiritual circumcision so that our sins would be blotted out. Then He died on the Cross as the Lamb of God and made atonement for us. The Lord became the eternal sin offering for all sinners and saved us eternally. This is true faith. We become righteous by believing in this truth.

Can we receive the spiritual circumcision only by Christ's blood? No, we cannot. Jesus' baptism cut out the sins from us and the judgment He received on the Cross by shedding blood for the sinners was the vicarious judgment for you and me. We are saved from sin and are exempt from judgment because we believe in the gospel of God's righteousness, that is, the gospel of Jesus' baptism and blood on the Cross. Receiving Jesus as the Savior can blot out all the sins in a sinner's heart. Receive the spiritual circumcision in your hearts. Then, the righteousness of God will become yours.

True spiritual circumcision should take place in the heart

In Romans chapter 2, the Apostle Paul says, *"Circumcision is that of the heart."* How do you circumcise yourself in your heart? This is possible by believing that Jesus Christ came to earth in human flesh, that He was baptized to take all "the sins of the world," that He died shedding blood on the Cross, and that He resurrected again to be our eternal Savior. The Apostle Paul said that circumcision should be done in the heart, and you can be circumcised in your heart by believing in Jesus' baptism. If you want to receive the spiritual circumcision in your heart, believe in Jesus' baptism. Then, you will truly become one of God's children. Righteous is the person who believes that Jesus' baptism and blood delivered him/her from all his/her sins. Amen.

Until He was 29 years old, Jesus lived a private life supporting His family, but when He became 30, He started living His public life. During His public life, He blotted out all of mankind's sins and delivered all the sinners from their sins. The first thing He did was to receive baptism in order to deliver the sinners from their sins and make them righteous. *"Then Jesus came from Galilee to John at the Jordan to be baptized by him" (Matthew 3:13).* Why did Jesus try to be baptized? We have to know that He did this in order to take all the sinner's sins. We must not misunderstand the true meaning of His baptism. Baptism is to wash away sins by transferring them. That is why Jesus, in order to take sinners' sins, asked John to baptize Him.

Who is this John who baptized Jesus? John is the representative of all mankind. This is explained well in Matthew 11:11-14. *"Assuredly, I say to you, among those born of women there has not risen one greater than John the Baptist; but he who is least in the kingdom of heaven is greater than he. And from the days of John the Baptist until now the kingdom of heaven suffers violence, and the violent take it by force. For all the prophets and the law prophesied until John. And if you are willing to receive it, he is Elijah who is to come."*

Starting from the days of John the Baptist, the age of God's Covenant ended. This is because Jesus, the Person who was to fulfill His promises, had come. Then, who were the persons that were to fulfill the promises in the Old Testament? They were Jesus and John the Baptist. John the Baptist passed the sins onto Jesus. John the Baptist was the last prophet in the

Old Testament who was sent to pass all the sins onto God's Lamb, who came in the New Testament. John did this task by laying his hands on Jesus' head according to the lawful way established in the sacrificial system. All the sins of the world were cut off and transferred onto Jesus when He was baptized. "For thus," God gave the spiritual circumcision in all the hearts of mankind.

Hold fast Jesus' baptism and His blood as your atonement. Jesus has already taken all of the sins of the world and has also born all of the judgment. The gospel of God's righteousness is the truth that Jesus was baptized and shed blood to atone all our sins. Now, we can receive the remission of sins just by accepting God's righteousness in our hearts. If you receive it, you will be able to enter *"the genealogy of Jesus Christ, the Son of David, the Son of Abraham."* There are people who already know of God's righteousness and those who do not and are still outside of Jesus Christ. The sun is going to set. Believe in Jesus' baptism and enter Him. The faith of believing in the baptism will become your oil prepared for the wedding feast. I hope you know the secret so that you can prepare the oil for the lamp to meet our second coming Lord Jesus just by believing in Jesus' baptism and His blood on the Cross.

Jesus received baptism so that He would blot out everyone's sins. Jesus is the Son of God and God Himself. He is our Creator. He came to the earth with His Father's will in order to adopt us as God's children. Who do all the prophecies in the Old Testament talk about? They prophesy about Jesus. They were prophecies about how He would come to earth and take over our sins and eliminate them. As the prophecies in the Old Testament said, Jesus came to earth about 2000 years ago and took over all of our sins by being baptized. He had borne all of mankind's sins, starting from Adam and Eve, down to the last person.

Receive the spiritual circumcision in your hearts. *"Circumcision is that of the heart" (Romans 2:29).* When you believe in Jesus' baptism, you will automatically receive the circumcision of the heart. Circumcision of the heart means the elimination of the sins in our hearts when we acknowledge that all the sins were passed onto Jesus by His baptism. Have you received the circumcision of the heart? By believing in the circumcision in the heart, "all the sins will be cleansed by faith."

Do you really accept the truth of the spiritual circumcision in your heart?

It has been about 2000 years since Jesus came to earth, was baptized and died on the Cross. We should only accept this fact and receive it in our hearts today. *"Circumcision is that of the heart."* We can receive circumcision in our minds and hearts by faith in the truth. We all have received deliverance by believing in God's righteousness. Even if God's judgment on earth comes, we will not be afraid. Those who believe in God's righteousness do not receive God's judgment. God's judgment falls upon those who have not accepted God's righteousness in their hearts.

Why do Christians today believe in Jesus, yet go astray? Why do they live in agony? It is because they believe only in Jesus' blood for their salvation. Now you should admit that you have inflicted God with your stubbornness and return to the truth that Jesus took all of our sins by being baptized at the Jordan. Then, the spiritual circumcision will take place in your heart.

If you believe both in Jesus' baptism and His blood, the spiritual circumcision will take place in your heart and you will not receive God's judgment, but become one of His children. God will become your God and you will become one of His people. If there are those among you who believe in Jesus but are dependent only on Jesus' blood, I would like to ask you a question. Is our spiritual circumcision and God's righteousness only by the blood of the Cross? Our salvation is completed not by the blood only, but by Jesus' baptism, His blood and the Spirit.

God's righteousness attained by being united with Christ

Let us study Romans 6:3-8. *"Or do you not know that as many of us as were baptized into Christ Jesus were baptized into His death? Therefore we were buried with Him through baptism into death, that just as Christ was raised from the dead by the glory of the Father, even so we also should walk in newness of life. For if we have been united together in the likeness of His death, certainly we also shall be in the likeness of His resurrection, Knowing this, that our old man was crucified with Him, that the body of sin might be done away with, that we should no longer be slaves of sin. For he who has died has been freed from sin. Now if we died with Christ, we believe that we shall also live with Him."*

Verse 5 states, *"For if we have been united together in the likeness of His death, certainly we also shall be in the likeness of His resurrection."* The Bible says that the wages of sin is death, that is, whoever has sin will perish and go to hell. Did not all of you have sin before believing in the truth of Jesus Christ completely? —Yes.— Even if you have the slightest amount of sin, you will go to hell and receive the judgment of *"the lake of fire burning with brimstone" (Revelation 21:8).* If we were to pay the wages of our own sins, which is death, we would never be able to be saved from sin at all. So, God sent Jesus Christ to this earth and passed all the sins to Him and judged Him instead of us.

God saved us all because He loved us so much. God the Father sent His only begotten Son to the world, passed all the sins of the world onto His Son through the baptism, and crucified Him with nails so that He would shed blood to atone all the sins. Believing in this is being united with Jesus. The wages for sin is death. We all had sins in our hearts and were supposed to go to hell because of those sins. But instead of us, who were destined to go to hell, Jesus took care of the sins in the Jordan by being baptized and punished vicariously on the Cross. Thus, His death became our deaths because His baptism took away all our sins. This is the faith of uniting with Christ.

Many people still believe in Jesus in the "religious" way. They go to church and shed tears while confessing their sins, asking for forgiveness. Stop doing that right now and believe in God's righteousness, and you will gain the peace from God in your heart. Jesus was baptized and died on the Cross in order to save us, and I hope you believe in this gospel.

God taught us through Moses about the remission of sins. Moses accepted God's command that he go to Egypt to deliver the Israelites, His people. So, he went to Egypt with his wife and child on a donkey. That night, God's messenger appeared and tried to kill Moses. Then, his wife Zipporah, hastily took a sharp stone and cut off the foreskin of her son and cast it at Moses' feet, and said, *"Surely you are a husband of blood to me!" (Exodus 4:25)*

The truth in this passage is like this. Even Moses' son would not have been considered as one of God's people if he had not yet received circumcision; therefore, God was going to kill him. God said that the Israelites would not be considered His people if they had not been circumcised. The circumcision in the Old Testament was a sign of being one of God's people. God had to make Moses realize this. So, Moses' wife quickly cut off her son's foreskin and threw it saying, *"Surely you are a husband of blood to me!"* God tried to kill Moses because of his son's uncircumcision.

Even if a person were Abraham's descendant, he would be cut off from the Israelites if he hadn't been circumcised. Only the circumcised could eat the meat of the Passover lamb and strike the lintel and the two doorposts with the blood of the lamb. Like this, only the spiritually circumcised can participate in the Holy Communion. Those without this faith can never enter God's righteousness and therefore, will not be able to participate in God's glory.

The Apostle Paul was a Jew. He was circumcised when he was eight days old and brought up at the feet of Gamaliel. He was proficient in the Old Testament. So, Paul understood well as to why Jesus Christ had been baptized at the Jordan River and why He had to die on the Cross. Therefore he could preach the gospel of the water and the Spirit in much assurance. That is why he said, *"Circumcision is that of the heart" (Romans 2:29).*

Of course, the Apostle Paul talked more frequently about Jesus' death on the Cross. Why? Because even if Jesus performed our spiritual circumcision of taking our sins; if He had not been sacrificed on the Cross, in other words, if He had not received judgment, we could not have been saved. That is why Paul spoke about the Cross more frequently. You have to keep in mind that the Cross is the conclusion and completion of our spiritual circumcision. However, most Christians today do not have the slightest idea of the causality between Jesus' baptism and His death on the Cross, and thus are doomed to hell. If the power of faith in the spiritual circumcision had been passed on well through generations, today's Christianity would not have been this way.

Some people are very grateful when they first meet Jesus, but they become disappointed at their immutable infirmities and become worse sinners as time passes by. Ten years may pass after first believing in Jesus, but they may have become worse sinners. Can they be sinners even after believing in Jesus? They sing the hymn just in words.

"♪Weeping will not save me! ♫ Though my face were bathed in tears, ♫ That could not allay my fears, ♫ Could not wash the sin of years! ♫ Weeping will not save me! … ♪Faith in Christ will save me! ♫ Let me trust thy weeping Son, ♪Trust the work that He has done; ♪To His arms, Lord help me run: ♪Faith in Christ will save me. ♫"

They sing, "Weeping will not save me. Faith in Christ will save me." But, that's in word only. They pray shedding tears every time they sin. "God, please forgive me. If you forgive me this time, I will be good from now on." When a Christian sins, he/she confesses, cries and asks for forgiveness, and then feels better. But a person who repeats this for years becomes more sinful in his/her heart than when he/she first believed in Jesus ten years before. That person regretfully asks the question, "Why did I believe in Jesus so early? I should have believed in

Him when I turned 80, or just before my last breath. I believed too early." It is because he/she was supposed to live according to God's will, but didn't.

To every person's sin, there must be a judgment. That is why Jesus was baptized and judged on the Cross, shedding His precious blood so that He could save us from our sins. He arose again from the dead in three days. God the Father raised Jesus to life again. A person who believes in the spiritual circumcision can and has to live the life of spreading the gospel. Spiritual circumcision is the evidence that we have to become God's children and it is God's righteousness. Jesus' baptism is the evidence that our sins have been passed onto Him, and His precious blood on the Cross is the evidence that He has paid all the wages of our sins by receiving the vicarious judgment.

Do you believe in Jesus, yet remain sinful in your heart? That is the faith of a heretic. Titus 3:10 states, *"Reject a divisive man after the first and second admonition, knowing that such a person is warped and sinning, being self-condemned."* Those who have heretical faiths are self-condemning sinners. They insist that they are being sinners even when they are threatened with death. They are too stubborn to change their misunderstanding. God tells these sinners, "You are a heretic. You are a sinner; you are not My child and you will enter the eternal fires of hell."

Those who believe in Jesus, yet have not accepted God's righteousness, or the spiritual circumcision of Jesus' baptism and blood, are heretical Christians and the great sinners who cannot but confess their sinfulness before God. Sinners who do not believe in Jesus' righteousness cannot enter His Kingdom.

Those who have become righteous after believing in Jesus have the evidence of receiving the spiritual circumcision in their hearts. The following are the evidences: Jesus is God who came in a flesh of a man, and He was baptized and shed blood on the Cross. Jesus came to the earth and was baptized by John the Baptist in order to take the sins of the world; He received judgment on the Cross to make perfect the faiths of those who believe in the spiritual circumcision. He resurrected from the dead in three days and became our living Savior. This is the very correct salvation of God's righteousness that is not only by the blood, but by the water, the blood and the Holy Spirit. These are the conclusive evidences of the spiritual circumcision that bears witness to His perfect salvation of us.

My dear Christians, accept in your hearts that our salvation was not made possible only by Jesus' blood, but by the water, the blood, and the Holy Spirit. God has cut off the sins of the world and completely eliminated the condemnation from us. Not only did He cut off my sins, but also the sins of the world, starting from Adam's to the sins of the last person on earth. He took them all with His baptism and blood. Receiving the spiritual circumcision will save whoever believes in God's righteousness, which was fulfilled by Jesus who came by water and blood.

All the sins of the world have been cut off by Jesus' baptism from John. Now those who believe in the spiritual circumcision cannot have sin in their hearts. Jesus rose again among the dead and raised our souls that had been lost with sin with His righteousness. God is looking for us with the gospel of Jesus' baptism, His blood, and the Spirit, and we now can be saved by the spiritual circumcision. The spiritual circumcision was God's plan in Jesus even before Creation, for those who believe. Now, you who believe in God's righteousness have also received the spiritual circumcision. ✉

Those Who Ignore God's Grace

< Romans 2:1-16 >

"Therefore you are inexcusable, O man, whoever you are who judge, for in whatever you judge another you condemn yourself; for you who judge practice the same things. But we know that the judgment of God is according to truth against those who practice such things. And do you think this, O man, you who judge those practicing such things, and doing the same, that you will escape the judgment of God? Or do you despise the riches of His goodness, forbearance, and longsuffering, not knowing that the goodness of God leads you to repentance? But in accordance with your hardness and your impenitent heart you are treasuring up for yourself wrath in the day of wrath and revelation of the righteous judgment of God, who 'will render to each one according to his deeds': eternal life to those who by patient continuance in doing good seek for glory, honor, and immortality; but to those who are self-seeking and do not obey the truth, but obey unrighteousness-indignation and wrath, tribulation and anguish, on every soul of man who does evil, of the Jew first and also of the Greek; but glory, honor, and peace to everyone who works what is good, to the Jew first and also to the Greek. For there is no partiality with God. For as many as have sinned without law will also perish without law, and as many as have sinned in the law will be judged by the law (for not the hearers of the law are just in the sight of God, but the does of the law will be justified; for when Gentiles, who do not have the law, by nature do the things in the law, these, although not having the law, are a law to themselves, who show the work of the law written in their hearts, their conscience also bearing witness, and between themselves their thoughts accusing or else excusing them) in the day when God will judge the secrets of those by Jesus Christ, according to my gospel."

Legalists always judge other people, while they are not able to keep the law

Let's talk about the law. Paul the Apostle said to the Jews who rested in the law, *"Therefore you are inexcusable, O man, whoever you are who judge, for in whatever you judge another you condemn yourself; for you who judge practice the same things. But we know that the judgment of God is according to truth against those who practice such things. And do you think this, O man, you who judge those practicing such things, and doing the same, that you will escape the judgment of God?"* (Romans 2:1-3) Legalists think that they honor God well. These kinds of people do not believe in God with their hearts, but with their false pride that is based on their own deeds. These people like to judge others and are good at it. However, while they judge others with God's words, they don't realize that they are exactly the same as those being criticized and make the same mistakes.

For example, they don't keep the Sabbath day holy, though they tell others to keep it according to God's Commandments. They tell others to obey and keep the law, but they themselves don't keep it. Paul the Apostle said to these kinds of people, *"And do you think this, O man, you who judge those practicing such things, and doing the same, that you will escape the judgment of God?" (Romans 2:3)*

Legalists cannot be saved before God. The law can never deliver us, so God will judge us if our religious lives are based on the law. Legalistic lives cause the wrath of God. Those who have not been saved have legalistic faiths. They tell others to live in certain ways, according to the law, but they shouldn't say such things these days.

A long time ago, most Christians in our country used to be like that. Legalistic ministers used to rebuke women who had permed hairstyle, saying they would be sent to hell. If we were under the instruction of ministers who taught church members with the deeds of the law in this way, we would certainly believe that those with permed hair would automatically go to hell. This was something that happened only about 15-20 years ago. If a woman used lipstick, it meant that she would be sent to purgatory under the instruction of such ministers.

These people were legalists. They physically appeared to be holy before God; teaching people not to use lipstick or have permed hair, to always walk gently, and to neither buy or sell any goods. These legalists told believers which things were right or wrong in the views of God's words, while they themselves were hypocrites.

The Jews were just like this

The Jews were just like that. They judged the Gentiles with the law, saying things like, "They don't know God and serve idols. They are damned to hell and are brutal people." However, they themselves loved the material things of this world along with other foreign gods more than God.

"Therefore you are inexcusable, O man, whoever you are who judge, for in whatever you judge another you condemn yourself; for you who judge practice the same things." The Jews judged others according to the law, but they never followed their own teachings. Furthermore, those who don't believe in God's righteousness or have the salvation of Jesus in their hearts, think they live exactly according to God's word, but they are just like the Jews.

Legalists will be judged

People from younger generations here have probably never led religious lives in this manner. However, those of the older generations have probably heard the sermons based on the law. Ministers used to scold those who had permed hairstyle just because it looked lewd. Ministers cannot do such a thing these days. It became the target of criticism to say such words as 'the righteous' or 'be sanctified completely' a long time ago. Nowadays though, many people generally use the expression 'the righteous.' This means that Christianity has changed. False teachers cannot tell random lies because even their congregations have been delivered the true gospel through books and tapes. Therefore, they cannot speak to their hearers without reason.

The most important thing to know is that legalists who ignore the perfect salvation of Jesus Christ and who lead religious lives according to the law will be judged before God.

Verse 4 talks about God's judgment. Let's read it, *"Or do you despise the riches of His goodness, forbearance, and longsuffering, not knowing that the goodness of God leads you to repentance?"* God will judge legalists. Brethrens, the legalistic faith opposes God. Legalists oppose the love of God with criterions that are based on their own deeds. Legalists ignore the gospel of salvation that states that God has forgiven all their sins and iniquities through the riches of His goodness, forbearance, and longsuffering.

Those who lead religious lives according to the law will be judged before God. However, many people lead their religious lives according to the law before God's presence. We must not think, 'We are exempted from His judgment because we have been saved.' Paul the Apostle said that legalists could not be saved, but would instead be perished and judged. We must know what kinds of people lead religious lives according to the law so that we can come up with a plan to deliver the gospel to them.

There are many legalists in the world including the Jews

Paul the Apostle didn't only talk about the fact that Jesus washed away all the sins of the world. He also spoke about how people who lead religious lives within the law, such as the Jews, oppose God and will be judged. They ignore God's love, through which He showed sympathy for us. They ignore the gospel of the remission of sins, which states that God has blotted out all the sins of the world for we were pitiful in His eyes.

Aren't there many legalists around you who lead religious lives such as this? There are many legalists who believe that God feels no mercy for the world and that He didn't washed away all our sins. Nevertheless, there are some who accept

God's love and are called to be 'the righteous' before Him. There are also those legalists who ignore His righteousness and despise God's salvation with their own thoughts, even at this very moment. The latter is an absolute majority, and they look coldly upon the former.

I want you to know that there are many people around you who ignore the riches of God's goodness, forbearance, and longsuffering just like the Jews did. Is it true or false? —Yes, there are many people like this.— A legalist despises others in front of God. What do legalists despise? God's perfect salvation.

So many people who are living in this world despise the fact that Jesus is the Son of God, including the Jews. The Jews are the people of Israel. They say, "How is He the Son of God? He is just one of the prophets." They acknowledge Jesus only up to this point. The Israelites despised the Son of God and slapped Jesus' cheek with their hands, saying, *"He has spoken blasphemy" (Matthew 26:65).* They also despise Him now. The Jews despise God because they don't believe in His Son. It's understandable that the Israelites disregarded Jesus because they did not believe in Him. However, what do legalists among the Gentiles despise? They despise the riches of God's love and righteousness.

Legalists live based on their own deeds

In a legalistic denomination, the legalists teach their followers to turn the left cheek after being slapped on the right cheek. They should never get angry. They are also instructed on how to preach the doctrine, to walk gently, how to smile, and so on. They think they know all about the Scriptures and insist that their original sin was forgiven, but they receive the forgiveness of daily sins by offering repentance prayers every single day.

Something like this is also a faith based on the law. These things also make people despise the riches of God's love and salvation. They say, "You are so proud to say you have no sin, that you are righteous, and that you have received the forgiveness of all sins by believing Jesus washed them away!" They think that God calls them to be righteous, even if they are not actually righteous. All legalists believe these false Christian doctrines. Therefore, we must keep away from such legalists.

After believing in Jesus, is it legalistic to receive the forgiveness of daily sins through repentance prayers? Or isn't it? —Yes, it is.— Does it derive from the law of deeds or doesn't it? —Yes, it does.— It's not of faith. People who declare that they live by the deeds of the word are legalists. There are a countless number of people like this around us.

Paul the Apostle received the complete remission of sins by just believing in Jesus Christ. However, the Israelites, who believed in the Old Testament according to the law, believed in Judaism. Were all those who became one of these people a legalist or not? They were the ones who followed the law; teaching outward deeds, such as how one should walk, what one should do, or what one should not do.

Therefore, Paul the Apostle blamed these people in acrid tones. He did this in a well-mannered way. Today's Christians lead legalistic lives according to the law as well. They believe that, though they are sanctified by faith, their sins are forgiven daily when they offer repentance prayers for their sins. They are legalists and their faiths are of the law.

Many pastors are good at preaching, saying, "We are

saved by faith." However, they say in the end, "But we must confess what we have sinned and repent." These pastors are legalists. They depend on their own deeds for their salvations, while not believing or relying themselves on Jesus Christ.

Were we legalists before we were saved? —Yes, we were.— Before we were born again, we thought doing good deeds could save us. There are many people in this world who think in this way. God tells them to repent. *"Repent therefore and be converted, that your sins may be blotted out, so that times of refreshing may come from the presence of the Lord" (Acts 3:19).* However, these people do not repent. How stubborn they are! So, Paul the Apostle once again talks to the stubborn.

Legalists declare that they are sinners until they die

Let's look at Romans 2:5, *"But in accordance with your hardness and your impenitent heart you are treasuring up for yourself wrath in the day of wrath and revelation of the righteous judgment of God."* God's wrath will be treasured up until the day when God's righteous judgment will finally be revealed on legalists.

However, legalists are so stubborn that they would confess that they are sinners before God even if they had knives pointed to their throats. When faced with danger, they would still confess that they are sinners before God. Some people declare that they are permanent sinners before God until the day they die. How stubborn they are! They say that they are sinners because they can't live according to God's word, even if they believe in Jesus Christ.

What does God say? He says, "Because you cannot live

according to the words, I saved you. I blotted out all your sins and saved you absolutely." They neither possess the faith in Jesus Christ nor try to accept God's righteousness to be delivered from their sins. Instead, they insist that they are sinners until the day they die because they try to be saved by both the deeds of the law and the faith in Jesus Christ. They must know that the time will come when they will be judged for their own faiths and deeds.

"But in accordance with your hardness and your impenitent heart you are treasuring up for yourself wrath in the day of wrath and revelation of the righteous judgment of God" *(Romans 2:5).* Paul the Apostle meant, "How stubborn you are. You are to be judged for your hard and impenitent hearts. You are treasuring up His wrath." Jesus Christ blotted out all our sins, regardless of whether one believes this or not. Thus everyone can be saved from all his/her sins through Jesus Christ. We were saved by our true faiths in the fact that Jesus Christ washed away all our sins. We could not live according to the law while we repented our daily sins to receive His forgiveness, so we returned to Jesus Christ from the Gentile religions. We are destined to sin until the day we die, so we cannot become righteous by the deeds of the law, but by the faith in the Lord.

Do you declare that you are righteous until you die in front of God? Or do you declare that you cannot but remain a sinner until you die? —We declare that we are righteous.— Is this merely possible through brainwashing? Some people may say that this is like brainwashing. Who would possibly fall for this kind of indoctrination? No one.

Let's assume that somebody indoctrinates you every single day. You would resist strongly by saying, "Why is that?

So? So what?" Wouldn't most people react in this way? We come to believe in something only when we heartily confirm that it is true. If a person tries to deceive us into believing in anything that is not biblical with beautiful words, it would never work. Not even the slightest bit. We know that humans are very stubborn, but we become meek and believe in the truth if it is of the word of God.

How stubborn legalists are

How stubborn they are. They declare that they are sinners until the last minutes of their lives. There are many people who believe in Judaism. Are there many people among today's Christians who believe in Judaism actually? Or aren't there? —There are many.— "Lord, a sinner came here. Please forgive my sins." There are many who declare that they are sinners before God because they look at their weaknesses and daily sins with their own thoughts, even if there are over a billion Christians in the world and ten million Christians here in Korea. These people are law-abiders.

Legalists are like the Pharisees

I was also a legalist before I believed in the gospel of the water and the Spirit. I used to think, "How can I become righteous while sinning everyday?" This is not so nowadays. Many people you know behave stubbornly. Where do these kinds of people go, according to the Bible? They will end up in hell for they have gathered up God's wrath because of their hard and impenitent hearts. Legalists must also repent once to convert themselves while living in this world by giving thanks and truly believe that Jesus Christ blotted out all their sins.

However, they are too stubborn to repent. These people deserve pity. They don't repent even though they should. There are so many people who behave just like the Pharisees. They gently greet people in front of church saying, "How are you? How have you been?" while holding the Bible under their arms. They have their eyes halfway closed in an arrogant manner when they meet people on Sundays. They try to look even more divine than Jesus. How good would it be if they were actually divine like this every single day?

Do you know what wives of legalistic pastors say? They say they are happy when their husbands preach a sermon on the pulpit because their husbands speak in gentle words saying things in such "holy and merciful" manners. However, they change as soon as they get home. Once, a wife of a legalistic pastor made herself a home at the back of the pulpit, taking with her the oven, blankets and rice, because her husband was like a hoodlum at home but gentle at the back of the pulpit. The pastor asked her what she was doing there. His wife said that she liked it there because he was gentle and his voice sounded soft behind the pulpit, but at home he would change and harass her.

We must preach the gospel

Frankly speaking, I lost many marks from my wife. This is because my wife says, "The only thing you ever care about is the gospel." I cannot do everything well because I am not a perfect man. The first thing that I must do well is the work of God. Secondly, I must take care of my home. Thirdly, I must run other errands. These are my preferential orders. This is not only because I am a pastor. I do so because I take charge in serving the gospel. I cannot serve the gospel after taking care of all my affairs. So, I lay a strong emphasis on preaching the gospel and take care of all my other affairs after preaching the gospel. I don't think I could preach the gospel while finishing up all my affairs anyway.

Legalists act like angels when they stand on the pulpit. They teach believers to weep over their sins. Every legalist should receive the forgiveness of sins after believing in Jesus because only then can one truly be happy that he/she has become sinless. This is the only way one's soul can be happy. People sin and do immoral things while carrying on with their lives, and thus if one has sin in his/her heart, it would be even worse than hell for him/her. God judges these kinds of people.

I cannot help saying that many people are treasuring up wrath before God. Those who neither repent, convert nor believe in Jesus Christ, while pretending to truly believe, will be judged by God's wrath. They cannot deceive God. We cannot deceive, whether we have true faiths before Him or not. We will get judged if we do not believe. The wrath of God is revealed to those who don't possess faith. They will be burnt in the sizzling fires of hell. There are many people who will be burnt in hell due to their unbelief.

Therefore, we must preach the gospel. We should also continuously spread the word of God. Every time we gather together, we should think of the gospel and not only think about ourselves, but also take time to care about others. The reason we must preach the gospel is to help people be exempted from God's wrath, even though they persecute us and despise God's love.

We must know the following. There are many people around us who will receive this wrath. We must carefully think about whether we must really testify it or not, why we must do our best to preach the gospel and take up offerings for other people. Will God be pleased if we let them be judged by His wrath? We cannot just leave them as they are. Knowing this very well, we must preach the gospel worldwide.

If there is a legalist in your family, the whole family will be judged by His wrath. What is wrath? We say, "If you don't obey, you will get hit," when children don't obey their parents. Parents will then beat their children up if they cannot bear their children anymore. Children admit their wrongdoings and beg for pardons. Parents forgive their children because they are their offspring. In verse 4 it is written, *"Or do you despise the riches of His goodness, forbearance and longsuffering, not knowing that the goodness of God leads you to repentance?"* However, until when does God forbear? God forbears for 70-80 years on this earth, but people strike their children with canes after forbearing two or three times. God forbears until our lives end.

God prepared the fire of hell for legalists

It will be the end when the Lord takes a cane in His hands. God prepared a melting furnace for legalists, which contains boiling molten rocks and sulfur. God resurrects the dead into immortal bodies with His wrath. God makes their bodies immortal so that they eternally feel pain, and He puts them in the melting furnace that never extinguishes. The wrath of God resurrects them into eternal bodies and makes suffer eternally. They never die from burning, even if they are too hot and say,

"Please dip the tip of your finger in the water and cool my tongue by dropping a drop of water into my mouth, for I am tormented in this flame" (Luke 16:24).

We must preach the gospel to them because it is apparent that they will be judged. The reason why we must preach the gospel to the legalists around us, though we may be despised and persecuted, is to save them from wrath and destruction. Do you understand why we do our best, why we are interested in saving others, and why we spend most of the church's finances in the literature ministries? We could be rich if we spent the money for our church only. We could eat and live well.

However, lots of material things are needed to spread the gospel worldwide. Do you know why? Because in this way, other people can be saved. Therefore, we devote ourselves to the preaching of the gospel all over the world. If we did not do so, would others possibly be able to receive the forgiveness of sins?

If we had not preached the gospel to you, could you have been saved, even if God already saved you? No you couldn't. All of us had been legalists before we were born again. We were with sin though we thought we believed in Jesus. We would have perished in this world if we had not heard of this good news.

Can we just let them go to hell and perish? No, we cannot. We cannot let them go to hell because we know the gospel of the Lord and salvation. We know who will go to hell and who will enter the Kingdom of Heaven. Therefore, we worry about them, and pray and preach the good news. The reason why we secure finances and spend so much money for this ministry is because of the following: To save a soul is better than to obtain everything in this world.

The reason why we preach the gospel with forbearance and endurance, in spite of being despised and persecuted by legalists, is to save the souls that are going to be judged by God's wrath.

You may think, 'You had better write readable books on the true gospel and scatter them worldwide like leaflets.' We would have done so if it had been a good way to preach the true gospel. However, since it doesn't work, we frequently try every possible means and keep praying.

We the gospel preachers are not trying to preach the gospel to earn anything. They preach the gospel to save souls because they know all the sinners will surely go to hell. However, many legalists in this world actually pursue their worldly lust while they are proud of their devotion to Christianity. We must understand the reason for teaching the gospel to legalists.

We must also know why the Lord commended us to keep the Sabbath-day holy in the Ten Commandments and why those who didn't keep the Sabbath-day were stoned to death. The Sabbath-day implies the gospel that Jesus washed away all our sins. We must keep in mind that Jesus washed away all our sins. We must also preach it by the faith in the Lord, which includes the fact that the Lord blotted out all the sins of the world.

It seems that I have satisfied my resentment on legalists during this sermon. But we must forgive and be broad-minded to them. They are destined to go to hell if we keep our mouths shut. We the gospel preachers cannot permit legalists to despise us with their money or to make a display of their carnal influence to us.

We must preach the gospel to our families and to other souls

We must preach the gospel to everybody, including many other people. We know that all souls are as precious as our own family members. We should consider other people to be precious because we are all the same before God.

I cannot help speaking of the truth of salvation whenever I preach because souls are being sent to hell. We must save them from going to hell. We must preach the gospel to our families and friends, preach it with literature if it leaves something to be desired, and pray for the things we need. We must preach it in many different methods. We prepare a feast when a soul comes back. We gain souls whenever we have a revival meet for preaching the gospel. Sometimes, people go back to the world even though we barely manage to preach the gospel to them. Then, we become full of grief. But in the end, we preach the gospel without feeling any disappointments.

I want you to know one thing today. Remember the fact that there are many legalists Christians around us and that we must preach the gospel to them. They pretend to keep the law, even if they cannot help sinning everyday, and they think they can receive the forgiveness of their daily sins by offering prayers of repentance daily.

They reject the gospel that says that Jesus already blotted out all our sins. They think that Jesus took away only their original sin, excluding their daily sins, because they don't know the true remission of sins. Those who don't know the salvation of the truth are called legalists. We must save them from their sins by preaching them the gospel of God's righteousness. ⊠

Circumcision is
That of the Heart

< Romans 2:17-29 >

"Indeed you are called a Jew, and rest on the law, and make your boast in God, and know His will, and approve the things that are excellent, being instructed out of the law, and are confident that you yourself are a guide to the blind, a light to those who are in darkness, an instructor of the foolish, a teacher of babes, having the form of knowledge and truth in the law. You, therefore, who teach another, do you not teach yourself? You who preach that a man should not steal, do you steal? You who say, 'Do not commit adultery,' do you commit adultery? You who abhor idols, do you rob temples? You who make your boast in the law, do you dishonor God through breaking the law? For 'the name of God is blasphemed among the Gentiles because of you,' as it is written. For circumcision is indeed profitable if you keep the law; but if you are a breaker of the law, your circumcision has become uncircumcision. Therefore, if an uncircumcised man keeps the righteous requirements of the law, will not his uncircumcision be counted as circumcision? And will not the physically uncircumcised, if he fulfills the law, judge you who, even with your written code and circumcision, are a transgressor of the law? For he is not a Jew who is one outwardly, nor is circumcision that which is outward in the flesh; but he is a Jew who is one inwardly; and circumcision is that of the heart, in the Spirit, not in the letter; whose praise is not from men but

from God."

We must be circumcised in the heart

"Circumcision is that of the heart." We are saved when we believe with the heart. We must be saved in the heart. God says, *"Circumcision is that of the heart, in the Spirit, and not in the letter; whose praise is not from men, but from God" (Romans 2:29).* We must have the remission of sin in our hearts. If we don't have the forgiveness of sin in our hearts, it is invalid. Man has an "inner self and an outer self," and every one must receive the remission of sin inwardly.

The Apostle Paul says to Jews, *"Circumcision is that of the heart."* Then what did the Jews circumcise? They circumcised a part of the flesh. However, the Apostle Paul says, *"Circumcision is that of the heart."* Jews circumcised outwardly, but Paul says that circumcision is that of the heart. God tells us in our hearts when we become His children.

Paul does not talk about the outward circumcision, but the circumcision and the remission of sin in the heart. So when he says, *"For what if some did not believe?" (Romans 3:3)* He means, "If some did not believe in the heart." He does not talk about outwardly believing, but says, "Believe in the heart." We must know what the Apostle Paul means and what the remission of sin is. We must also learn how to obtain the remission of sin in our hearts though God's word.

"For what if some did not believe?" means "For what if Jews did not believe in Jesus Christ as their Savior, even though they are Abraham's descendants by the flesh? " Will their unbelief make the faithfulness of God without effect? Shall the fact that God blotted out all our sins including the sins

of Abraham's descendants become invalid? Never. Paul says that even the Jews, who are the descendants of Abraham by the flesh, can be saved when they believe that Jesus Christ is the Savior, the Son of God, who took away the sins of the world through His baptism and crucifixion. He also says that the salvation and grace of God through Jesus Christ cannot become invalid.

Romans 3:3-4 states, *"For what if some did not believe? Will their unbelief make the faithfulness of God without effect? Certainly not! Indeed, let God be true but every man a liar. As it is written: 'That You may be justified in Your words, and may overcome when You are judged.'"* The Lord promised with His word and sanctified believers by accomplishing His promise by Himself. God wants to show His righteousness and to justify those who have faith in Jesus through His word by accomplishing what He promised when He is judged. Even we, who have the remission of sin in our hearts, also want to be judged by His word and want to overcome with His word when we are judged.

The Apostle Paul tells about the outer and inner self

Paul talks about his "outer and inner self." We also have an outer self and inner self, which are the flesh and the spirit. We are the same as him. Now Paul deals with the issue.

Romans 3:5 states, *"But if our unrighteousness demonstrates the righteousness of God, what shall we say?"* Paul does not mean that his outer self is clean. His flesh is dirty and continues sinning until he dies. This includes all the people in the world. However, if God had saved those people, wouldn't it demonstrate His righteousness? Wouldn't God be righteous if He had saved human beings, though their outer selves are infirm? So Paul says, *"Is God unjust who inflicts wrath? (I speak as a man.) Certainly not! For then how will God judge the world?" (Romans 3:5-6)* Paul explains that we are not saved just because our outer selves are clean.

We have outer and inner selves. However, Paul deals with the realm of the heart saying, "For what if some did not believe? Will their unbelief make the faithfulness of God without effect? Circumcision is that of the heart." It is not true faith if we become a righteous person once and then a sinner the next day by establishing our faith on the basis of our outer self who sins and has infirmities.

Outer man always sins until he dies

The Apostle Paul did not place his hopes on his outer self. Those whose sins are blotted out also have outer and inner selves. How do they feel when they see their outer selves? They cannot help being disappointed. Let us see our outer selves. Sometimes we are good, but sometimes we are simply abominable. But the Bible says that our outer selves were crucified with Jesus Christ. Our outer selves died, and Jesus Christ forgave all the sins of our outer selves.

We who are saved are frequently disappointed with our outer selves when we look at our outer selves. We seem to be hopeful when our outer selves do well, but become disappointed when they don't meet our expectations. We tend to think that our faiths are wrecked when we are disappointed with our external selves. However, this is not right. Our outer selves were already crucified with Christ. Those who have the remission of sins also go on sinning through their physical bodies. But isn't that a sin? Yes it is, but it is a dead sin. It's dead because the sins were taken to the Cross with the Lord. The sin that the outer flesh commits is not a serious problem, however it is a serious matter that our hearts are not right in front of the Lord.

We must believe in God with the heart

More iniquities are revealed to the righteous just after receiving the remission of sin. Therefore, God's salvation would become imperfect if we set our basis of salvation upon our outer men who cannot but sin every moment. Our faiths would deviate from the faith in God, which Abraham had, if we set our faiths on the basis of the deeds of the outer flesh.

The Apostle Paul says, *"Circumcision is that of the heart."* We become sanctified and righteous by believing in the heart, not according to the deeds of the outer men. Sanctification does not depend on whether our outer men do as God says or not. Do you understand this? The problem is that we have both the outer and inner selves and they coincide. Therefore, we sometimes tend to place more weight on the outer man. We become confident if our outer selves do well, but disappointed if they don't. Paul says this is not the right faith.

"Circumcision is that of the heart." What is the real truth? How do we know and believe with the heart? In Matthew 16, Jesus asked Peter, "Who do you say that I am?" Then Peter confessed his faith, saying, "You are the Christ, the Son of the living God." Peter believed like that with the heart. Jesus said, "Blessed are you, Simon Bar-Jonah, for flesh and blood have not revealed this to you, but my Father who is in heaven."

Jesus said Peter's faith was right.

Abraham had no son. God led him with His word and promised that He would give him a son and that he would be a father of many nations. He also said that God would be God to him and his descendants after him. God told Abraham, his family and his descendants to be circumcised as a sign of the covenant between God and Abraham. "The scars of cutting a part of the flesh is the covenant that I am God to you," said God. Abraham believed the covenant with his heart. He believed that God would be God to him and bless his heart. He also believed that God would be God to his descendants after him. He believed in God Himself.

We are made righteous by believing the gospel of the water and the Spirit with the heart

We are made righteous by believing with our hearts that God is our God, our Savior. We are saved by believing with our hearts. We are not saved by anything else. We have become righteous by believing with our hearts that God is our God and He blotted out all our sins with the baptism of Jesus and His death on the Cross. Believing with our hearts saves us. So the Bible says, *"For with the heart one believes unto righteousness, and with the mouth confession is made unto salvation"* *(Romans 10:10).*

What we must make clear at this time is that we are made righteous by believing with our hearts, and not by virtuous deeds of our flesh. We would not become righteous if Jesus attached a condition to our outer selves, saying, "I will blot out all your sins, but under one condition. You can be my child if you avoid sinning. You cannot be my child if you fail to do so."

We are made righteous by believing with our hearts. Could we have been made righteous if God had attached conditions to our outer man? Do you believe that God saved you by taking away your sins through His baptism in the Jordan River, being crucified and judged in your place? How do you believe this? Don't you believe with your heart? Could you have been saved perfectly if God had said, "I will forgive your small infirmities but will not forgive the big ones. I will make your deliverance invalid if you fail to keep this condition"?

We must separate outer man from inner man

Our flesh, the outer man, is always weak and cannot reach the righteousness of God by itself. We are made righteous by believing with the heart in front of God because He promised to save those who believe with their hearts. Seeing our faith that we admit what God did and that Jesus took away and blotted out all our sins with the heart, God makes us His righteous children. It is the covenant of God, and He saved us by fulfilling His promise.

God says that when He sees faith in our hearts, we are His people. We must separate our outer man from our inner man. Nobody in the world would receive the remission of sin if we set our benchmark of salvation on our deeds of the outer flesh. *"Circumcision is that of the heart."* We are saved by believing in Jesus Christ with our hearts. Do you understand this? *"For with the heart one believes unto righteousness, and with the mouth confession is made unto salvation" (Romans 10:10).* The Apostle Paul apparently separates the outer man from the inner man.

Our outer man is worse than dog shit. It's worthless. We don't need to use Abraham as an example. Look at yourself. See your worthless flesh. The flesh resorts to trickery in trying to obtain a high social position and to live in affluence. Doesn't the flesh always do nothing but seek its own interest? The flesh would be judged more than twelve times a day if it were judged on how it thinks and acts. The flesh is against God.

Fortunately, God does not care about our outer man, but He take notice of only our inner man. He saves us when He sees us really believe that Jesus is the Savior with our hearts. He tells us that He saved us from all our sins.

We can never be saved by our own thoughts

Let us look into our own thoughts. We think we can believe merely with our thoughts. We can believe with the thoughts of the flesh, thinking, 'I was saved because God saved me.' However, we cannot be saved by our thoughts. The carnal mind changes all the time and always does evil. Is this true? Thoughts of the carnal mind want to do this and that according to its lusts.

Let's suppose someone put his/her faith on the basis of his/her thoughts. He/she can have confidence in his/her salvation while his/her present thought agree with his/her former thought, that is, 'Jesus took away all our sins in the Jordan River.' However, because thoughts of the flesh are not stable, he/she cannot have confidence in His salvation any more, once a slight bit of doubt invades his/her feeble thought on salvation. The wrongly built faith based on fleshly thought will fall down at a stroke of a doubt.

We cannot truly believe in Him and the truth if we lay the

basis of our faith on our own thoughts. Such a faith is like a house built on the sand, *"And the rain descended, the floods came, and the winds blew and beat on that house; and it fell. And great was its fall" (Matthew 7:27).*

Therefore, the faith of a person who believes with thoughts is far from the faith based on God's word. God said, *"That You may be justified in Your words, and may overcome when You are judged" (Romans 3:4).* Our salvation should be based on His word. The Word became flesh and dwelt among us, and God is the Word. The Word came to the earth in the likeness of men. Jesus saved us and was taken up after His 33 years of lifetime on the earth and led His Apostles to write the word of promise, which is the accomplishment of the Old Testament that He also told to His servants before. God wrote what He said and did in the Bible. God appears in and with the Word, speaks with the Word and saved us with the Word.

We cannot have the perfect remission of sin with our own thoughts, while not believing in God's word, thinking, 'I seem to be saved sometimes, but I cannot believe the salvation of the Lord sometimes.' We cannot be saved with thoughts because our thoughts always change and they are not always true.

Therefore, the Apostle Paul says that circumcision is that of the heart and we believe His righteousness with the heart. When our heart believes in His word, the heart apparently testifies that God promised this in the Old Testament and accomplished His covenant. He saved us like this in the New Testament by His word. We are saved and become God's children by believing in His words with our hearts.

We are saved from our sins by believing the gospel of the water and the Spirit with the heart

We are saved by faith because the heart can admit God, but our thoughts of carnal mind may not admit Him. We become God's children by believing with our hearts, not by the deeds or thoughts of our outer man. It is clear that we become God's children by believing in His word with our hearts. Do you believe with your heart? Are you circumcised in the heart? Do you believe in your heart that Jesus is your Savior? The one who believes in the Son of God has the witness in himself. Do you have the witness of the word that Jesus perfectly saved you, not the witness of personal experience? Do you have the word of God in your heart? Do you have the word that gave you the remission of sins? To have true faith is to be saved by faith.

We receive the remission of sins by believing in God's word with our hearts. However, we are frequently disappointed when we look at the weaknesses of our outer man. And then we are apt to retreat from out faith in God. One who does not fully understand the truth is under an illusion. Most Christians set the benchmark of their faith on their deeds. That's a great mistake. We must not measure our faiths on our own thoughts. We should not set the basis of our faith on out flesh because the flesh is useless. The Old Testament and the New Testament tell us that one is made righteous when he/she believes in God's word with the heart. We are not saved from sins by thoughts or deeds, but only by faith. We cannot be saved by the deeds of the flesh. Whether we sin or do good deeds has nothing to do with God and His glory.

Therefore, true faith means to be saved by believing the truth of salvation of God's word with the heart. Our faiths are wrong when our hearts are wrong and our faiths are right when our hearts are right. Right behavior comes from right faith. Wrong behavior may come out because the heart is weak. But the important thing is that God looks at the heart. God looks at the heart and investigates it. God looks whether the heart is right or not. God looks whether we really believe with the heart or not. Do you understand? Do you know that God looks at our hearts? God looks on whether we believe in Jesus Christ with our hearts when He looks at our hearts. Do you believe with your heart?

God observes whether we believe with the heart or not when He looks upon us. He looks in our hearts. We must check up our hearts in God's presence. Circumcision is that of the heart. Do you believe with the heart? God looks at the heart. He looks at whether we really believe with our hearts or not. He looks at whether we really know the truth and whether we want to pursue it or not. He looks at whether we have faith in our hearts or not and whether we want to follow Him and believe in His word.

There is a religious body that puts a great importance on the exact time of being born again

It is important to have an exact knowledge of what Jesus Christ did and believe it with the heart. There is a religious body that tells the brothers and sisters in our church that they are not saved. I feel pity for the souls in that religious body. I want to let them understand me and teach them the gospel of the water and the Spirit. Are your sins blotted out? —Amen.— Do you believe it with the heart?

But there are some people who say that our faiths are not right. They say that we must not believe the word as it is

written and believe only what is proved with science. They say
that is perfect salvation and perfect faith. They say that a born
again person should know exactly time he/she was born again
(hour, date, month). When brother Hwang to meet with one of
them, the person asked brother Hwang when he was born again,
so brother Hwang answered that he did not know the exact date
and hour, but that he was born again by believing in the gospel
of the water and the Spirit, sometime last year. Then he said
that brother Hwang was not saved.

Of course, we can say the exact hour and date and month
and year if we trace back to when we were born again. We can
even say whether it was A.M or P.M; or the morning, afternoon,
lunchtime or suppertime. However, salvation depends on
believing with the heart. It doesn't matter if you can't
remember the exact time.

Circumcision is that of the heart

The Lord took all our sins onto Him at the Jordan River
and was crucified in our place to be judged for the sins. He was
wounded for our transgressions and bruised for our iniquities.
He took away all the sins of our outer and inner man. Our
spirits rose again from the dead and now we can follow the
Lord as He pleases, even though some people may viciously
tell us that we are not saved.

What does the Bible say about the outer man? More and
more infirmities seem to be revealed after we receive the
remission of sin. All of our infirmities have not been revealed
yet; more insufficiencies will be revealed. However, we are
saved if we believe in our hearts that God is our God and that
Jesus took away all our sins in the Jordan River through His

baptism and was crucified.

We cannot be compared with people who put an importance on the date when they were born again and believe only what is proved by science. Clearly, they are not saved. We believe with our hearts to become righteous. Do you believe that Jesus Christ is our Savior? —Amen.— Faith begins from that point and the Lord leads our hearts from that time. The Lord says that we are His righteous children and our faiths are true. He blesses our hearts and wants us to follow Him with our hearts by faith. God leads us and blesses us when we walk with Him through the faith in our hearts.

"Circumcision is that of the heart." We were saved by believing with our hearts. Many people on the earth say that believing the gospel with their hearts saved them. However, they actually add their deeds to the faith. They regard the deeds of the outer man as essential condition of their faith. They say that having faith in the gospel of the water and the Spirit cannot lead them to salvation because they mix believing with the heart and their own virtuous deeds.

As a result, they are more concerned with how well the outer man does and how often they offered the prayers of repentance. They are far from salvation even though they think they are saved from their sins.

God looks on the heart

We believe to become righteous in our hearts. It is purely separated from the outer flesh and has noting to do with our deeds. Salvation itself has no relation with our deeds. Are you refreshed after learning that all your sins have been blotted out? Do you want to serve the Lord with joy? Do you preach the gospel with joy? Do you want to engage yourself in His beautiful mission? The heart becomes grateful and joyful because God approves our faiths when we believe with our hearts. Therefore, the heart is very important before God. ⊠

CHAPTER

3

Introduction to Romans Chapter 3

Paul said that people's disbelief did not make the faithfulness of God without effect. Continued from chapter 2, the Apostle Paul pointed out in this chapter that the Jews had no advantage over the Gentiles. In this chapter, Paul compared the law and God's law of righteousness before he talked about the law of God's righteousness, which allows sinners to receive His righteousness and leads them to true life. He also emphasized in this chapter that the salvation from sin is not through our deeds, but through the faith in God's righteousness.

The Apostle Paul said that even if the Jews and other people do not believe in God's righteousness, their disbelief does not make His righteousness without effect. God cannot lie and the faithfulness of His righteousness will not disappear. The effect will not be nullified just because the Jews do not believe in His righteousness.

The righteousness of God that Paul preached about cannot be nullified just because people disbelieve. Whoever believes in the salvation God gave to sinners receives the righteousness of God, and this righteousness is perfect beyond human morality or thought.

Paul blamed those who did not believe in God's righteousness for making Him a liar. God said that He completely saved the people from their sins through His righteousness but they did not believe in this, therefore, He was made into a liar. However, God's righteousness is not affected by their disbelief.

How is God's righteousness revealed?

Those who do not believe in God's righteousness will be judged for their sins. We can all confirm God's righteousness with the salvation that He gives. Those who believe in His righteousness receive the forgiveness of sins and obtain eternal lives. Therefore, everyone can be blessed by believing in the faithfulness of God's righteousness.

God's righteousness is not false, but true. Everyone is a liar before God. But God works as He promised and fulfills the promises. Therefore, God's faithfulness wins over human lies. Human beings have to believe in God's righteousness. God does not change what He said, while humans frequently change their attitudes according to their circumstantial judgments. God always keeps true to what He has told mankind.

Romans 3:5 states, *"But if our unrighteousness demonstrates the righteousness of God, what shall we say?"* Mankind's unrighteousness reveals the righteousness of God.

God's righteousness is revealed further by our weaknesses. This is because as recorded, Jesus Himself acted righteously in order to save sinners from all their sins. Therefore, God's righteousness shines even more brightly because of people's infirmities. This truth can be found in the gospel of the water and the Spirit, which is filled with God's righteousness. The reason for this is because all people sin until the day they die and God's love is greater than those sins. God's love saves all the fragile sinners from their sins.

Our Lord overcame all the sins of the world and

completed His salvation through the forgiveness of sins. No person can live a sinless life. Since people were meant to go to hell, God takes care of them with His love, and this is His righteousness.

We people were liars from the day we were born and rejected God's righteousness by not believing in His words. Mankind was due to be doomed before God because none of their deeds were acceptable in the sight of Him. But God saved us from our sins with His love because He pitied us. All people were due to go to hell because they were corrupted by the deception of Satan and all of them sinned. However, God sent His only begotten Son to save the people from the hands of the devil and the power of darkness.

The Apostle Paul said that a human being may try to behave decently everyday, but he/she cannot help but commit sin throughout his/her entire life. However, that person's evilness will further reveal God's righteousness and love. In truth, humans have no righteousness and thus need a messenger like the Apostle Paul. He knew and received God's righteousness, and thus had the indwelling of the Holy Spirit. That was why he could preach His righteousness.

The gospel Paul preached was based on God's righteousness

The gospel Paul preached was based on God's righteousness. Paul had to preach the gospel because God loved sinners and saved them from their sins. God's love of deliverance is in the gospel of the water and the Spirit. Therefore, the forgiveness of sins depends on our belief in God's righteousness. However, the problem is that people generally think that they have to live virtuously to be saved before God. Human beings cannot be good based on their basic instincts; being good outwardly only becomes an obstacle in accepting God's righteousness. People have to break their fixed thoughts of living virtuously in order to accept the gospel of the spiritual circumcision, which God gave.

Nobody on earth can truly be good. Then, how could sinners be saved from all of their sins? They must throw away the thought that they should live good lives to be saved. Many people refuse to give up their thoughts and standards; therefore, they cannot be completely saved from their sins. God's righteousness, which is revealed in the gospel of the spiritual circumcision, made us aware of how our unrighteousness served to only demonstrate God's love and how great His righteousness was. For this reason, those who believe in God's righteousness are proud of His righteousness and not their own. The righteous only boast of God's righteousness and raise His righteousness on high because it comes from God.

The Apostle Paul teaches the role of the law to legalists who believe they will go to Heaven if they do good deeds, but if they do not live virtuous lives after believing in Jesus, they can never reach God's righteousness. The law is like a mirror that reveals human sins. Paul teaches that people have regal faiths and that their faiths are wrong. This is Paul's teaching and his guidance to God's righteousness.

Paul speaks to those who follow false teachers who don't think they can be righteous and sinless after believing in Jesus. He teaches unbelievers to believe in God's righteousness and to be free from condemnation. Paul says that those who do not believe in the salvation of Jesus' water and blood are under the judgment and since they do not believe in God, it is proper for them to be judged. He says that sinners should return to God's righteousness and receive His righteousness in order to be delivered from the dreadful judgment.

Then can we sin more because we believe in God's righteousness?

Verse 7 states, *"For if the truth of God has increased through my lie to His glory, why am I also still judged as a sinner?"* Then if we are called sinless, can we sin freely? Paul demonstrates this point. Since God saved you with His righteousness, then are you allowed to lie more freely? If you believe so, then you should know that you do not know God's righteousness and that you are slandering His righteousness.

Even today, there are many people who slander God's righteousness in their hearts; it is not very different from the old times. Paul wrote this Scripture nearly 2000 years ago and even back then, there were people who were wrapped up in their own ways of thinking.

Still today, most Christians, who have not yet been born again, misunderstand that if one becomes sinless, he/she might commit sins on purpose. Those who have not been born again slander the righteous, who are born again of water and the Spirit, according to the thoughts of their flesh and speak ill of the born-again saints. Nominal Christians have slandered the truly born again Christians with their faithless thoughts. True faith cannot be understood by human flesh. Sin is something you commit all your life. Both the righteous and unrighteous inevitably sin. However, those who reject God's righteousness are with sin while those who believe in it are without sin.

176 Introduction to Romans Chapter 3

Paul said to unbelievers, *"For what if some did not believe? Will their unbelief make the faithfulness of God without effect? Certainly not!"* *(Romans 3:3-4)* Just because humankind does not believe in God's righteousness, their unbelief cannot nullify His righteousness. If a person believes in God's righteousness, he/she is saved. However, if the person does not, he/she cannot receive His righteousness. That's it. God's righteousness will stand steadfast forever. Those who go to hell do not believe in Jesus' baptism and blood and will never be able to cleanse their sins. God's righteousness, which leads believers to be born again, will never be made without effect just because people do not believe in it.

Obtaining God's righteousness is regardless of human effort

Obtaining the righteousness of our Lord has nothing to do with our human efforts. It is simply related to our faiths in the truth that God's righteousness is the remission of our sins. A person who believes in the truth of the water and the Spirit receives God's righteousness by faith, but one who does not believe in God's righteousness receives judgment according to the truth of God's words.

Therefore, God sent Jesus to this world and made Him become a stumbling stone and a rock of offense to those who are disobedient to God's righteousness. There are many people who voluntarily ask for hell because they don't want to believe in God's righteousness, even though Jesus, a stumbling block and a rock of offense, gave them the righteousness of God by becoming their Savior. Even the most evil person was given the way to becoming righteous and obtaining eternal life. Even a person who does many good works cannot be delivered from destruction if he/she doesn't believe in God's righteousness, which makes him/her receive the remission of sins and born again.

Because the wages of sin is death, anyone with sin will go through the judgment. Jesus becomes a stumbling stone and a rock of offense to those who try to establish their own righteousness and enter Heaven without believing in God's righteousness. Therefore, the reason people get ruined, though they somehow believe in Jesus, is because they don't believe in His righteousness.

Some people say that they are sinners who have been saved from their sins, but there is no such thing as a 'saved sinner.' How can one become a sinner again after being saved from sin? One is sinless if one has been saved from sin, and one is with sin if one has not yet obtained salvation from sin. There won't be a single person with sin in the Kingdom of Heaven. God says, *"Therefore the ungodly shall not stand in the judgment, nor sinners in the congregation of the righteous"* *(Psalm 1:5)*.

People pose themselves the big question of how they can become righteous while committing sins everyday. However, there is no need for them to worry about that. Becoming righteous by believing in God's righteousness is possible only because the Lord already took all the sins of the world, along with their future sins, onto Him by receiving baptism at the Jordan River and dying on the Cross, thereby fulfilling all the righteousness of God. Sinners can become righteous just by believing in God's righteousness. Are you still debtors even if all of your debts have been paid off?

Our Lord eliminated all of our sins with His righteousness.

The Lord saved those who have complete faith in the gospel of the water and the Spirit, so there is no condemnation to them, no matter how weak they may be. We can all become righteous by believing in God's righteousness.

Human thoughts lead us to death

Human thoughts lead us to death and they originate from the carnal mind. Spiritual thoughts originate from the faith in God's righteousness. It is possible for the devil to dominate human thoughts. Human beings have no other choice but to sin with their flesh. However, a person who has faith in God's righteousness becomes righteous by the faith in the baptism and blood of Jesus. One cannot become righteous by avoiding the committal of sin. One cannot become completely sinless by going through a physical transformation to reach a holy state. It is foolish for a Christian to think that he/she can enter Heaven by becoming a holy person who never commits sin in front of God.

We can be saved from our sins all at once by believing in God's righteousness. Moreover, every sinner can be completely saved from his/her sin if he/she believes in the grace of the gospel of the water and the Spirit, which leads believers to be born again. It may seem impossible for one to become sinless from a human point of view. However, it is possible by the faith in the word if God. One cannot live without sinning through the human body, but one's heart becomes sinless if one truly believes in God's righteousness. Human bodies need to satisfy their desires and it is impossible for bodies to restrain from sinning since they constantly crave pleasure. God speaks the truth; one can become righteous only by having faith in the gospel of the water and the Spirit, which our Lord has given. We cannot enter the Kingdom of Heaven by doing good deeds with our flesh. We can only enter Heaven by believing in the righteousness of God.

There is a difference between a spiritual mind and a carnal mind

Carnal minds cannot understand the truth that they can only become sinless by faith and that they are able to become the righteous, the born-again Christians. Because they think that even if a person repents for his/her wrongdoings, he/she will sin again the following day.

However, even though it is not possible for a person to become righteous through the human deeds, it is perfectly possible by God's righteousness. This is because one can receive His righteousness by believing in Jesus' baptism and His blood. God's righteousness is capable of eliminating the sins of all the people. It allows us to be righteous and to call God our Father. Therefore, you should know that true faith starts with the faith in God's righteousness. True faith does not start with the carnal mind, but with the faith in the words of truth.

Many people who have not been born again are unable to escape from their own thoughts because they are always locked up inside them. These people can never say that they have become righteous because they think only with carnal minds, even though they say they believe in Jesus. One can say that he/she is sinless before Jesus only when he/she believes in the words of the spiritual circumcision, which contains God's righteousness.

Therefore, if a person wants to receive God's righteousness, he/she should listen to the words of truth from the truly born again people and believe them with their hearts. The Holy Spirit dwells in every saint who believes in God's righteousness. I hope you brethren keep this truth in mind. If you truly wish to obtain the blessing of being born again, God will allow you to meet a born again person who believes in His righteousness.

You say that there is none righteous?

Verses 9 and 10 state, *"What then? Are we better than they? Not at all. For we have previously charged both Jews and Greeks that they are all under sin. There is none righteous, no, not one."* It is written that there is none righteous, no, not one.

What does this mean? Do these words talk about our state before or after we are born again? We were all sinners before we were born again. The words *"there is none righteous"* refers to the state before Jesus fulfilled the ministry of eliminating all the sins of the world. One cannot become righteous without believing in Jesus.

Therefore, the words 'incremental sanctification' came to exist through people who served heretic religions or idols. *"There is none righteous, no, not one."* Do you think that a sinner can possibly become righteous by going through self-training and cultivation? One cannot become righteous on one's own.

"There is none righteous, no, not one." There is no one who will become righteous or has become righteous through

one's own decent living. There is not a single person who has become sinless through his/her own efforts. It is only possible through the faith in the spiritual circumcision that contains God's righteousness.

Verse 11 also states, *"There is none who understands; there is none who seeks after God."* There is no one who understands his/her own evils. In other words, there is none who understands that he/she is one who will be sent to hell. A sinner is not even able to understand that he/she is a sinner. A sinner lives while not even clearly understanding that he/she will go to hell due to his/her own sins. Therefore, such a person has to try to receive salvation from sin by understanding that he/she deserves to go to hell due to sin. However, there is not even one who understands one's sinful nature before God or his/her fate to go to hell.

Are we profitable or unprofitable beings in front of God? The whole of mankind is useless until they are born again. Even though we all have become righteous thanks to Him, weren't we once people who fought against God, refused to believe in the truth and even blamed Him?

Then, how can a sinner glorify God? How can a sinner, who has not even settled his/her own problems of sin, praise God? Praising God in a sinner's state cannot be true adoration. How can a sinner possibly praise God? A sinner can never give glory to God, and He doesn't accept anything from such a person.

Nowadays, praise ministries have been spread throughout the world. However, only those who believe in God's righteousness can praise God. Do you think that God will be pleased by the praise of a sinner? A sinner's praise is like Cain's offering. Why would God accept the meaningless praises and sinful hearts of sinners?

Verse 12 states, *"They have all turned aside; they have together become unprofitable. There is none who does good, no, not one."* Those sinners who have *"turned aside"* do not know the great works God has done for them, and do not believe in Him or the Word of truth. Moreover, sinners not only refuse to uphold God's word or to believe in it, but they always think of carnal biases based on their own thoughts. So, they can never discriminate between what's right and wrong before God.

Correct judgment is only possible by the words of truth that contain God's righteousness. Good decisions and correct judgments can only be made within God's righteousness. You should know that all lawful judgments do not rest inside humans, but inside God's righteousness. Human thoughts have all turned aside and rejected God's righteousness. People say, "I think in this way and believe according to my own thoughts, no matter what the Bible talks about." But, I hope you realize that one who does not discard one's own thoughts such as this is one who rejects God's righteousness with one's egocentric stubbornness. Therefore, thinking this way does not allow one to return to God's righteousness.

The carnal mind leads one's spirit to death

One who has not been born again is one's own judge. These kinds of people don't really care about what is written in God's words, but instead, if something is different from their own thoughts, they say it is wrong and agree only with a part of the words that tally with their own thoughts. The Bible states that humans turned aside to their own thoughts and self-centeredness. If one hopes to be delivered from his/her sins in the most proper way, he/she needs the righteousness and justice of God. Then what is His justice?

God's justice is God's righteousness and you should know that the word of God is the criterion for the righteous justice of God. *"In the beginning was the Word, and the Word was with God, and the Word was God" (John 1:1)*. Who is this Person who is called *"the Word"*? Who is the Person who was with God the Father and the Holy Spirit? He is our Savior, Jesus Christ. Jesus Christ became our Savior and the King of kings. Jesus is God.

It was said in John that there was the Word in the beginning, and the Word was with God. Yes, the Lord Jesus is our Savior. The Word is God and He is the express image of His Person (Hebrews 1:3). The Savior is God. Therefore, because the Word is God Himself, His words of righteousness are different from the thoughts of us humans. You have to realize that sinners dare to understand God's righteousness through their own perceptivity when they are ignorant in His righteousness. One who stands fast by the faith in God's righteousness is a profitable person who will be put into good use by God. One who stands fast and holds the word of God is a person of faith and is profitable in front of God. This kind of person is also blessed.

All people fight against God with their own thoughts and sins. You should know that one's pretending to be holy and good, or pretending to be kind and having mercy on others, are all hypocritical deeds that come from human thoughts that deceive God. Pretending to be good is against God. No one is good but Him. If a Christian does not accept the love He accomplished and His righteousness of salvation without having been born again, it is against God and disobedient to the truth.

Do you think that only those who commit great sins in this world are going to receive the condemnation of God? All those who do not believe in God's righteousness will not be exempted from God's furious rage.

One who does not believe in Jesus in truth is filled with the imperative conception of having to live a good life. Who taught such ideas? It was Satan who did it. However, human beings are not capable of living good lives starting from their births. Therefore, the word of God tells us that we must receive the remission of sins. Does this mean that we should do evil things on purpose so that grace may abound? Certainly not. Since human beings were infected with sin starting from the day they were born, they are destined to go to hell due to the wounds of contaminated sin. Therefore, God told them to receive the remission of sins Jesus had already prepared for them. He is the God of salvation and advises all of us to receive salvation by accepting the word of His righteousness, which is the truth, into our hearts.

What is a human being by nature?

Verses 13-18 state, *"Their throat is an open tomb; with their tongues they have practiced deceit; the poison of asps is under their lips; whose mouth is full of cursing and bitterness. Their feet are swift to shed blood; destruction and misery are in their ways; and the way of peace they have not known. There is no fear of God before their eyes."*

"With their tongues they have practiced deceit." How well all those people deceive! In John, it was written, *"When*

he speaks a lie, he speaks from his own resources" (John 8:44).
"I'm telling the truth, it's the truth. Do you understand me?"
All of the words that a person who has not been born again
strongly asserts to be true are false.

A person who has not yet been born again cannot help but
tell lies whenever he/she talks to people. He/she stresses that
all of what he/she has said is true, but it is the paradoxical
evidence that proves that every time he/she tells a lie, he/she
deceives people by saying that it's the truth. All of the things
that a person who has not yet been born again says are false
because he/she does not believe in God's righteousness.

A swindler can never make fraudulent practices to people
after they all know that whatever he does is fraudulent. He talks
as if it were genuine. He talks to people realistically and
sincerely to make them trust him. "I tell you the very, very, very
truth. If you invest some money in this, you will earn tons of
money in return. Just invest a million dollars and within a year,
you will get about two million dollars more than you have
invested. In the next couple of years, you will earn so much
money. This is the newest type of business and it is absolutely
safe. Come on, you must hurry and make up your mind because
many others are waiting." This is what a swindler tells people.
You should keep in mind that a person who has not received the
forgiveness of sins practices deceit with his/her tongue.

The Bible says that when Satan speaks a lie, he speaks from
his own resources. Everything a person who has not been born
again from sin says is a lie. It is no wonder that a minister who
has not been born again deceives the church members by
saying they will become rich if they offer large amounts of
tithes to the church. Moreover, he may say that once a person

becomes an elder of the church, the person will become rich by 'the irresistible blessings of God.' Why do people try so hard to become an elder? It is because of the lies of the false ministers who claim that God will fill one with material wealth once he/she becomes an elder. There are so many Christians who have been deprived of their properties after trying to be an elder. They have paid excessive devotions for their swindling ministers because they wished to be elders.

Let's pay attention to Romans 3:10 again. The phrase, *"as it is written,"* indicates to us that the following verses are quotations from the Old Testament. Rather than giving additional explanations, Paul quoted the exact phrase from the original Scripture: *"For there is no faithfulness in their mouth; Their inward part is destruction; Their throat is an open tomb; They flatter with their tongue" (Psalm 5:9). "Their feet run to evil, And they make haste to shed innocent blood; Their thoughts are thoughts of iniquity; Wasting and destruction are in their paths" (Isaiah 59:7).* People who go to hell because they do not know God's righteousness are so pitiful.

Verse 19 states, *"Now we know that whatever the law says, it says to those who are under the law, that every mouth may be stopped, and all the world may become guilty before God."*

The law brings about wrath (Romans 4:15). God gives the law to those who have not yet been born again in order to make them perceive themselves as sinners. The law teaches every sinner that he/she is incapable of living according to His law. It was clearly said that God did not give us the law for us to live by it. Then does God make the law void? No, He does not do that. God said that He gave us the law through Moses in order to teach us that we are sinners. He wants us to realize our sinful natures through the law and that it was not given for us to keep it. The role of the law is to point out how insufficient and infirm we are as human beings.

So, verse 20 states, *"Therefore by the deeds of the law no flesh will be justified in His sight, for by the law is the knowledge of sin."* No flesh will be justified in His sight by the deeds of the law. Not only for Paul himself, but also for all the other servants of God, *"by the deeds of the law no flesh will be justified in His sight."* There is none who can keep the law, none who will be able to keep it, and none who has kept it. Therefore, the conclusion is that one cannot become righteous by the deeds of the law.

Can we be transformed into righteous people by keeping the law? When we see these passages, we can easily think that we may become holy, step-by-step, to finally reach sanctification by living good lives through our deeds after we become believers in Jesus. However, this is not true at all. Saying that one can enter the Kingdom of Heaven by being sanctified incrementally is absolutely false.

All those who have not been born again are still under the law of God, the law of sin and death (Romans 8:2). It is because once a person becomes a Christian, he/she thinks that he/she must live by God's words. Christians feel obligated to keep the law with their deeds, but in actuality, they cannot live by the law at all. That's why they come to say prayers of repentance every day. They don't realize that they are falling into the mire of a hopeless religion; namely Christianity. This proves that living this sort of religious life is wrong from the start. Trying to keep God's law after misunderstanding the law leads Christian-religionists to the confrontation of God's righteousness, even though the law is only there to teach people that they are sinners.

The Doctrine of Incremental Sanctification in Christianity is the same religious doctrine as of the heathenish religions of the world. Similar to the doctrine of entering Nirvana in Buddhism, in Christianity, the Doctrine of Incremental Sanctification states that one's flesh and spirit becomes holier and holier after one starts believing in Jesus, and one finally becomes holy enough to enter Heaven.

One who has been born with the infection of sin can only do the work of spreading sin during one's entire lifetime. The reason for this is because one has already been infected with sin. The virus of sin comes out of one's body even if one does not mean to spread sin. There is only one cure for this disease. It is to listen and believe in the word of the gospel of truth that contains God's righteousness. One can be saved from all sin and even receive eternal life if one hears and believes in the words of the true remission of sins, which enables us to receive the spiritual circumcision.

How can there be a person in this world who lives perfectly according to the law even after he/she is born again? There is none. The Bible states, *"By the law is the knowledge of sin" (Romans 3:20).* Isn't this truth clear and simple? Adam and Eve left the word of God by not believing and falling into sin by being deceived by Satan in the Age of Innocence, and they came to pass on all the sins to their descendents after the incident. However, even though all human beings inherited sin from their ancestors, they did not even know that they were truly born as sinners.

Since the time of Abraham, God gave mankind the concrete knowledge on His righteousness to let all people receive the remission of sins by believing in the word of God.

Paul talks about the righteousness of God apart from the law

Verses 21-22 state, *"But now the righteousness of God apart from the law is revealed, being witnessed by the Law and the Prophets, even the righteousness of God, through faith in Jesus Christ, to all and on all who believe. For there is no difference."*

It is said that the righteousness of God is revealed, *"being witnessed by the Law and the Prophets." "The Law and the Prophets" implies* the Old Testament. Now, Paul talked about the gospel of God's righteousness that was revealed through the sacrificial system of the tabernacle. The Scriptures clearly show us God's righteousness by which one can receive the remission of sin through the sin offering, and Paul's faith was also based on the faith in God's righteousness, which is revealed in all the Scriptures.

Paul declares that anyone who has faith in Jesus Christ can indiscriminately obtain God's righteousness. One's being saved or not is absolutely up to one's belief or unbelief. So, he says that the righteousness of God is revealed *"through faith in Jesus Christ, to all and on all who believe. For there is no difference."*

What is true faith? Who is the substance of faith? It is Jesus Christ. Hebrews 12:2 states, *"Looking unto Jesus, the author and finisher of our faith."* We should learn about God's truth from a born again saint and receive salvation in Jesus Christ by believing in this truth and then live by the faith in God's words. Believing in the Lord's righteousness with the heart is to have true faith.

Romans 10:10 states, *"For with the heart one believes*

unto righteousness, and with the mouth confession is made unto salvation." We can become righteous by believing in Jesus' baptism and blood with our hearts and be confirmed in our salvations by confessing our faiths with our mouths. The remission of sins cannot be obtained by our deeds, but just by our faiths in God's righteousness.

Verses 23-25 state, *"For all have sinned and fall short of the glory of God, being justified freely by His grace through the redemption that is in Christ Jesus, whom God set forth as a propitiation by His blood, through faith, to demonstrate His righteousness, because in His forbearance God had passed over the sins that were previously committed."*

The Bible states that all have sinned, and therefore, they fall short of the glory of God. Sinners had no other choice but to go to hell. However, through the redemption that is in Christ Jesus and God's righteousness, people received the remission of sins freely. People became sinless because they believed in God's righteousness. God set forth Jesus as a propitiation by His blood through faith.

When we take a look at verses 25-26, it is written, *"whom God set forth as a propitiation by His blood, through faith, to demonstrate His righteousness, because in His forbearance God had passed over the sins that were previously committed, to demonstrate at the present time His righteousness, that He might be just and the justifier of the one who has faith in Jesus."*

Here, the phrase, *"to demonstrate His righteousness"* refers to God's righteousness, which was accomplished by the righteous act of Jesus Christ. The reason Jesus shed blood on the Cross was because prior to His death, He had fulfilled all the righteousness of God by being baptized by John at the

Jordan River (refer to Matthew 3:13-17). God the Father made Jesus into a sacrifice of propitiation for the sin of this world in order to make peace between human beings and Himself. Jesus was the incarnation of God's righteousness.

Jesus took away all the sins of this world by receiving baptism from John. Jesus became the alpha and the omega. This means that everyone can receive salvation from sin if he/she believes in the words that state that the Lord blotted out all the sins of the world, from the very beginning until the end.

God's righteousness that Jesus fulfilled allowed us to be at peace with God. It was made so that only a person who was at peace with God would be able to enter Heaven. Only after I started believing in the gospel of truth did I come to understand the verse, *"God set forth Jesus as a propitiation by His blood, through faith, to demonstrate His righteousness, because in His forbearance God had passed over the sins that were previously committed."* In the time of His forbearance, I came to understand and believe in God's righteousness through Jesus.

God's righteousness was fulfilled in **the past perfect tense**, which indicates that it had already been fulfilled. We received the remission of sins by faith in the true Word that says that Jesus eliminated all our sins by His baptism and blood. Even though our spirits have been forgiven of sin all at once, our fleshes still cannot help but commit sin. God referred to the sin we commit in this present world as 'sin committed previously.'

Why? God set up the baptism of Jesus as the starting point of salvation. Therefore, the remission of sins was fulfilled all at once through the righteousness of God, which Jesus Christ had fulfilled. The sins we commit with the flesh at this time are sins that have already been eliminated through the baptism of Jesus in God's view. All the sins of the world have already been forgiven in the sight of God. 'To pass over the sins previously committed' means 'to consider the wages of the sins to have already been paid.' All the sins of this world are sins that have already been washed away by the baptism the Lord received and His blood on the Cross.

Therefore, all the sins of mankind from the beginning of this world until the end, from the time of Adam until the last day of the earth and even the sins that people are currently committing are the sins 'previously committed' that Jesus had eliminated in the past. Those who believe in God's righteousness are without sin. This truth is that the previously committed sins have been passed over already. Even the sins we are committing at this very moment are also part of the sins previously committed and forgiven in God's view. People of this world are committing the sins that had been eliminated by God's Son, who was sent to this world to take away all the sins of the world. The sins we are committing right now are sins that our Lord had already eliminated. Do you understand what this means?

Jesus said that He had already blotted out the sins of this world by God's righteousness. One could misunderstand this if one doesn't really understand the meaning of this passage. In the Lord's perspective, the sins we human beings commit are sins that had already been put into judgment since He Himself got baptized at the Jordan River and was judged at the Cross. The reason God tells us not to worry about the sins is because Jesus came to this world and made people perfectly sanctified all at once.

This truth Paul talks about in this passages is very important to one who has been saved by believing in God's righteousness. However, people who have not been born again ignore God's righteousness and will go to hell. Brethren, you should listen and fully understand the word of God. Only then will it be good to the establishment of your faith and to the preaching of the gospel to another person. Do you know that God convicts the world of sin, righteousness, and of judgment in order to finally mention His righteousness? (John 16:8)

God set forth Jesus as a propitiation by His blood, through faith, to demonstrate His righteousness because in His forbearance, God had passed over the sins that were previously committed. Since God set forth Jesus as a propitiation, He teaches us that even the sins previously committed had already been eliminated. Therefore, we became righteous by believing in God's righteousness.

In verse 26 it is written, *"to demonstrate at the present time His righteousness, that He might be just and the justifier of the one who has faith in Jesus."* 'At the present time,' God allows us to have eternal life, and He doesn't want to condemn the world. 'At the present time,' when God sent Jesus Christ to 'demonstrate His righteousness', the Lord demonstrated God's righteousness by His baptism and blood. God made His only begotten Son come to this world to be baptized and crucified and thereby demonstrated to us His love and righteousness.

God fulfilled all His righteousness through Jesus. Every believer in God's righteousness is righteous. Our God fulfilled the righteous act of blotting out the sins of the world once and for all. Can we then believe in God's righteousness with our hearts? God says that we are righteous and without sin when we believe in His righteousness. Why? Isn't a believer in Jesus sinless since He has already done the righteous act of washing away all of our sins? A believer in God's righteousness is righteous because he/she possesses no sin. Because the Lord had blotted out all the sins we commit during our entire lives, we are able to believe in God's righteousness. Otherwise, we would never have been able to receive the righteousness of God.

There is only God's righteousness to boast about

Verses 27-31 state, *"Where is boasting then? It is excluded. By what law? Of works? No, but by the law of faith. Therefore we conclude that a man is justified by faith apart from the deeds of the law. Or is He the God of the Jews only? Is He not also the God of the Gentiles? Yes, of the Gentiles also, since there is one God who will justify the circumcised by faith and the uncircumcised through faith. Do we then make void the law through faith? Certainly not! On the contrary, we establish the law."*

Establishing the law means that we cannot be saved from sins by our deeds. We are weak and imperfect creatures, but God's righteousness made us perfect by His word. Believing in God's word of righteousness has saved us. Even after we are saved from sins, our Lord continues to speak to us, saying, "You are insufficient, but I made you sanctified. Therefore, you should draw near to God with His righteousness."

In verse 27, it is written, *"Where is boasting then? It is excluded. By what law? Of works? No, but by the law of faith."* One should know the law of God's righteousness that God has established and believe in this law of His righteousness. *"By what law? Of works? No, but by the law of faith."*

You should know that we are delivered from our sins only

when we believe in God's righteousness and cannot be saved by our own deeds. Romans chapter 3 talks about this part through Paul the Apostle. *"Will their unbelief make the faithfulness of God without effect? Certainly not!"* A believer in God's righteousness will stand fast, but one who doesn't believe in God's righteousness will fall.

Romans chapter 3 reveals God's righteousness clearly. You should keep in mind that God established the law of His righteousness to make those who believe in their own thoughts fall. God completely saved us from all sin. Therefore, we can be saved from all sin by believing in God's Word that reveals His righteousness. We come to inherit the Kingdom of God and have peace with Him by believing in His righteousness.

Those who don't believe in God's righteousness cannot have peace in their hearts. The question of whether one is blessed or cursed depends on whether one believes in God's righteousness or not. If one does not take in the words of God's righteousness, he/she will be judged according to the just condemnation of God's words. Salvation originates from God's love and then we receive salvation from our sins by believing in His righteousness. We praise our Lord who gave us this faith in God's righteousness. Let's give thanks for the fact that we have the same faith Paul the Apostle had! We praise the Lord.

We also praise and give thanks to Him for we have been delivered from all sin by believing in Jesus' baptism and His blood on the Cross. If it had not been for this salvation, the faith, or the church of God, we would have never been able to receive the remission of sins. We truly believed in God's righteousness with the heart, and confession was made into salvation with the mouth. We give thanks to God who saved us from all sin with His righteousness. ✉

Salvation from Sins Only by Faith

< Romans 3:1-31 >

"What advantage then has the Jew, or what is the profit of circumcision? Much in every way! Chiefly because to them were committed the oracles of God. For what if some did not believe? Will their unbelief make the faithfulness of God without effect? Certainly not! Indeed, let God be true but every man a liar. As it is written:

'That You may be justified in Your words,
And may overcome when You are judged.'

But if our unrighteousness demonstrates the righteousness of God, what shall we say? Is God unjust who inflicts wrath? (I speak as a man.) Certainly not! For then how will God judge the world? For if the truth of God has increased through my lie to His glory, why am I also still judged as a sinner? And why not say, 'Let us do evil that good may come'?—as we are slanderously reported and as some affirm that we say. Their condemnation is just. What then? Are we better than they? Not at all. For we have previously charged both Jews and Greeks that they are all under sin. As it is written:

'There is none righteous, no, not one;
There is none who understands;
There is none who seeks after God.
They have all turned aside;
They have together become unprofitable;
There is none who does good, no, not one.

Their throat is an open tomb;
With their tongues they have practiced deceit;
The poison of asps is under their lips;
Whose mouth is full of cursing and bitterness.
Their feet are swift to shed blood;
Destruction and misery are in their ways;
And the way of peace they have not known.
There is no fear of God before their eyes.'

Now we know that whatever the law says, it says to those who are under the law, that every mouth may be stopped, and all the world may become guilty before God. Therefore by the deeds of the law no flesh will be justified in His sight, for by the law is the knowledge of sin. But now the righteousness of God apart from the law is revealed, being witnessed by the Law and the Prophets, even the righteousness of God, through faith in Jesus Christ, to all and on all who believe. For there is no difference; for all have sinned and fall short of the glory of God, being justified freely by His grace through the redemption that is in Christ Jesus, whom God set forth as a propitiation by His blood, through faith, to demonstrate His righteousness, because in His forbearance God had passed over the sins that were previously committed, to demonstrate at the present time His righteousness, that He might be just and the justifier of the one who has faith in Jesus. Where is boasting then? It is excluded. By what law? Of works? No, but by the law of faith. Therefore we conclude that a man is justified by faith apart from the deeds of the law. Or is He the God of the Jews only? Is He not also the God of the Gentiles? Yes, of the Gentiles also, since there is one God who will justify the circumcised by faith and the uncircumcised through faith. Do we then make void the law

through faith? Certainly not! On the contrary, we establish the law."

People's unbelief cannot make the salvation of God without effect

The Apostle Paul says that the fulfillment of the law and the redemption of God's grace are not given to us through our deeds, but through faith. We are saved from our sins and become righteous through the salvation of God. *"What advantage then has the Jew, or what is the profit of circumcision? Much every way! Chiefly to them were committed the oracles of God. For what if some did not believe? Will their unbelief make the faithfulness of God without effect? Certainly not!" (Romans 3:1-4)*

The advantage of the Jew is that the word of God was committed to them. They lived while hearing His word from their ancestors. Because God committed them His word and it was handed down through them, they thought they were better than the Gentiles. However, the Bible says that God deserted the Jews because they did not believe Jesus who had delivered them from their sins.

Paul says, *"For what if some did not believe? Will their unbelief make the faithfulness of God without effect? Certainly not!"* People's unbelief can't make the salvation of God without effect. "The faithfulness of God" means "the sincerity of God." He means that God's sincerity and the salvation from sins cannot become invalid even though Jews do not believe it. The word of God's promise that He saves whoever believes is not canceled even if they may not believe it.

The Gentiles will believe if the Jews do not believe. God

says that whoever believes will be saved from sins. Therefore, God deserted the Jews because they did not believe that the word of truth was accomplished according to God's promise, even if God committed them His word.

The Apostle Paul's assertion is as follows: God gave the gift of salvation to all humanities. God says that He promised it in the Old Testament and accomplished it by sending Jesus Christ, His only begotten Son, to the world. Some people believe the gospel of God, but others don't. So, whoever believes is blessed of being God's child, just as He promised. And the blessings of God are not canceled out no matter how many people do not believe.

Whoever believes the truth can receive His great love

Whoever hears the word of truth and believes in it can receive God's great love, but unbelievers claim that God is a liar. In fact, God accomplished His promise, yet unbelievers are excluded from God's salvation because they do not believe in the grace of the remission of sins.

Paul says, *"Will their unbelief make the faithfulness of God without effect? Certainly not!"* God promised once and faithfully gave the gift of His salvation and glory to all people.

What does the Bible say the gift of God is? The Bible says that God, the Father, sent His beloved Son and gave the grace to become His children to those who believe in the remission of sins through His Son. Even before the foundation of the world, He planed that He would give all human beings the glory of becoming His children and the salvation from sin through His righteousness. And He fulfilled this faithfully.

Therefore, believers are blessed according to God's word, but unbelievers are judged according to it.

It is very proper for unbelievers to go to hell. God established a law so that we can be saved by the faith in His Word. He also says that the faithfulness of God will never be without effect, even though people do not believe. We are blessed by accepting the faithfulness of God's salvation. God says, *"Let God be true but every man a liar. As it is written: 'That You may be justified in Your words, and may overcome when You are judged'"* (Romans 3:4).

Every man is a liar. God is true. Why? Because God says, *"As it is written: 'That You may be justified in Your words, and may overcome when You are judged.'"* God says that He promises in advance and blesses those who will be blessed and curses those who will be cursed. It is just for God to bless believers and curse unbelievers. God says, *"Let God be true but every man a liar."*

"That You may be justified in Your words, and may overcome when You are judged." He says that He will save people according to His Word. The Word was made into flesh, dwelt among us and saved us. Therefore, the Lord is justified through His words.

The Lord defeated Satan with the written word of God. The Lord is just and sincere before Himself, Satan and all spiritual beings because He accomplished what He promised. However, human beings are not sincere. Their behaviors change promptly when they are at a disadvantage. On the contrary, God has never broken His promises. So the Apostle Paul says that our faiths should be based on God's word.

Our unrighteousness demonstrates the righteousness of God

Romans 3:5 states, *"But if our unrighteousness demonstrates the righteousness of God, what shall we say? Is God unrighteous who inflicts wrath? (I speak as a man.)"* All human beings are unrighteous, but what shall we say if their unrighteousness demonstrates the righteousness of God's salvation? What shall we say if our sins demonstrate the righteousness of God?

The righteousness of God is revealed even more because of our sins and unrighteousness. God is really sincere. He is the Lord of salvation, the Savior and the true God who promised to save us with His word and accomplished what He promised. What shall we say if the righteousness of God is revealed because of our weaknesses? Our infirmities reveal God's righteousness more because we sin until we die.

How do we know that God is the Lord of love? We can know it from our infirmities. God's love is revealed through us because we sin until the last day of our lives. The Lord says that He blotted out the sins of the world once and for all. God's love would be imperfect if He loved only good people who didn't sin. It is out of His true love that God accepts and deals with us sinners who can never be loved.

We human beings are unrighteous and betray God. We don't believe in Him and have no lovely side in front of God. Sinners are those who only do evil, but Jesus, who saved us from all our sins and iniquities, has fulfilled God's love to us.

God says that it was through His righteousness and love that He sent us His only begotten Son to save us from Satan's darkness and curses, when human beings sinned and were destined to go to hell under Satan's deception. It is the love and grace of God.

"But if our unrighteousness demonstrates the righteousness of God, what shall we say?" says the Apostle Paul. The thoughts of believers and those of unbelievers are divided at this passage. Unbelievers try to be good in order to enter the Kingdom of Heaven and to be blessed by God. But Paul makes a contrary comment, saying, *"But if our unrighteousness demonstrates the righteousness of God, what shall we say?"* Paul says that we human beings cannot do God's righteousness but only commit sin before Him, and that our evilness comes to demonstrate God's true love. Yes, it is true. All human beings are wicked and cannot be righteous, but the Lord saved them from all their sins.

We are saved by the righteousness of God

The Apostle Paul says that human beings cannot be righteous and are caught in the snare of sins. The Lord saved such sinners from their sins and loved them. We are in need of His perfect love because we cannot avoid sinning everyday. We were saved only by Jesus' absolute love, His free grace, and the gift of salvation through Jesus Christ.

The Apostle Paul says that his being saved is owed to God's righteousness. What God did to save all sinners from their sins shows His righteousness. Paul says that believing in the gospel saved him. The righteousness of God is revealed in the gospel of the water and the Spirit. Our salvation depends on the righteous act God had done for us. Therefore, sinners are saved from all their sins by faith. Those who are not born again think that they should be good so that they may enter the Kingdom of Heaven.

Paul does not mean that we may do evil things on purpose, but people wind up going to hell because they try to do good deeds without receiving the righteousness of God. They must repent to be converted and believe in the salvation God gave them in order to escape from going to hell.

Who can do good deeds in front of God? There is none. Then how can a sinner be delivered from all his/her sins? He/she must change his/her own thoughts. The Apostle Paul says that he was saved by faith. But what do people think? People think that they can be saved by doing good things. That's why they cannot be delivered. Those who are saved from their sins by believing in Jesus and have the perfect remission of sins, boast only of God's righteousness and let it be exalted.

However, those who are not born again, though they believe in Jesus, think that they can enter the Kingdom of Heaven by doing good deeds, and will go to hell if they don't do good deeds. Their faiths are wrong. The faith of the Apostle Paul is the same as that of the born again. Those who are not born again, though they think they believe in Jesus, have wrong faiths because they try to add their deeds onto their faiths. We are not saved by adding our virtuous deeds onto our faiths, but by believing in the righteousness of God: the baptism of Jesus and His death on the Cross.

The righteous cannot sin on purpose

"But if our unrighteousness demonstrates the righteousness of God, what shall we say?" The Bible says that our unrighteousness demonstrates only the righteousness of God and His love. The Bible also says, *"For if the truth of God*

has increased through my lie to His glory, why am I also still judged as a sinner? And why not say, 'Let us do evil that good may come'?—as we are slanderously reported and as some affirm that we say. Their condemnation is just" (Romans 3:7-8). Unbelievers' names are written in the Book of Judgment and they will be cast into the lake of fire. So, they must repent to be converted and believe the salvation accomplished by the water and the blood.

The Apostle Paul says, *"Is God unjust who inflicts wrath? (I speak as a man.) Certainly not."* People refute, saying, "Isn't it unjust for God to inflict wrath on unbelievers and send them to hell just because they don't believe that Jesus already saved them from their sins?" But Paul says, "Is God unjust who inflicts wrath? It is fair for unbelievers to go to hell because they don't believe the truth. God is not unjust."

Romans 3:7 states, *"For if the truth of God has increased through my lie to His glory, why am I also still judged as a sinner?"* Then people may say, "What? Will you sin on purpose because you have the remission of sins? You will lie more because you are saved by the righteousness of God. Will you sin more on purpose?" But the Bible says that they act in such ways with evil hearts, neither knowing God's salvation nor believing in His love.

Therefore, Paul says that the truthfulness of God has abounded to His glory, owing to our sinfulness and lies. But people confuted against Paul with their own thoughts, saying, "You may commit more sins if you believe that you are saved by faith without deeds." It is not true that people sin only by the will to sin. They cannot avoid sinning because they were born as sinners. It is natural for an apple tree to bring forth apples. The Bible says that it is also natural for a human being who is born sinful to continue sinning. The Lord saved such sinners with His righteousness, and they can be delivered only by accepting the salvation of the Lord.

"And why not say, 'Let us do evil that good may come' —*as we are slanderously reported and as some affirm that we say. Their condemnation is just"(Romans 3:8).* Those who are under the deception of false teachers while assuming they believe in Jesus think in this way. The Epistle to Romans was written by the Apostle Paul about 2,000 years ago. Many people at that time thought this way, just as today's unbelievers do. False believers think just as the unbelievers at the time of Paul did, saying, 'Will you purposely sin more if you have the remission of sins, are sinless, and know that your future sins are forgiven?'

Unbelievers act according to the faithless thoughts of the flesh. They cannot enter the truth of God's salvation because of their false thoughts of the flesh. Of course, even the righteous still sin after they received the remission of sins, but there is a limit. The Bible says that sinners continue sinning because they don't realize they are committing a sin and don't know it to be a sin before they are born again of water and the Spirit. However, the Bible says that the righteous cannot sin recklessly because they are under God's reign.

Some people told the Apostle Paul, "Don't you do evil things so that good may come because God saved you from all your sins? You'd better do more evil deeds for the righteousness of God to be revealed more." Paul says that their damnation is just. He means that it is right for them to be judged and go to hell. Why? Because they do not depend on faith, but on their deeds.

The righteousness of God never becomes invalid

The Apostle Paul says, *"For what if some did not believe? Will their unbelief make the faithfulness of God without effect?"* Will their unbelief make the salvation of God without effect just because they don't believe in God's salvation? People are saved if they believe, but they lose the grace of the remission of sins if they don't believe. The righteousness of God stands fast. Do you understand? Those who go to hell volunteer to go to hell because they chose not to believe. The works of God and the grace of salvation from sin never become invalid. They stand fast.

The salvation of the Lord has no relation with human efforts, based on the deeds of the law. It is in relation only to believers. Believers are saved according to God's truth, but unbelievers will go to hell because they are not saved by rejecting His truth. God sent *"a stumbling stone and a rock of offense" (Isaiah 8:14).* Whoever believes in Jesus is made righteous and has eternal life, however wicked he/she may be. Whoever doesn't believe in Jesus will go to hell because of the wages of sin, however good he/she may be. Jesus is a stone of stumbling and a rock of offense to those who don't believe in the forgiveness of sins.

There is no righteous person who has sin

The Apostle Paul talks about the faith to salvation to those who pretend to be good, so people regard Romans as the word of God that tells about faith. Some people wonder about those who identify themselves as the righteous. In fact, those whose sins are forgiven by Jesus are righteous because all their sins are forgiven. "Jesus is faithful" means "He faithfully saved sinners from their sins." Some people say that they are 'delivered' sinners, but there cannot be such people before God. How can a person still be a sinner after he/she has been delivered from sin? We are saved if Jesus saved us and are sinners if Jesus did not save us. There is no "middle" in salvation.

Is there a righteous person who has sin? There is no righteous person who has sin. The person is a sinner if he/she has sin, but righteous and sinless if he/she believes in Jesus. How can we settle the problem of daily and future sins? People think that they are inevitable sinners because they sin everyday and will sin until they die. However, we are made righteous by believing in the gospel that says Jesus took away the sins of the world, including future sins, at the Jordan River and was crucified.

"A righteous person who has sin" does not make any sense. Is it reasonable to think that a person is still in debt though he/she already paid his/her debts? Let's suppose that there once was a man who had a lot of money, but his son fell into a bad habit of buying candies on credit at all the stores of the town everyday as he grew up. However, his rich father had paid enough money that exceeded his son's life long debts to every store in advance, he could never be a debtor even though he enjoyed eating candies everyday without paying money until he die.

The Lord saved us with the righteousness of taking our sins onto Him once and for all in the Jordan River. He perfectly saved all of us. Therefore, we can never become sinners again, however weak we may be. God says that we are made righteous if we don't deny what He did.

People can neither believe the gospel nor be born again with carnal minds

Christians who identify themselves as 'delivered' sinners think with carnal minds. To be spiritually minded is to believe in God's word. The carnal mind is a human mind. It's human wisdom. The flesh cannot help sinning, but we can become righteous by believing in the baptism and the Cross of Jesus. The Bible says that we can never become righteous and sanctified by trying not to sin.

Can one enter the Kingdom of Heaven by becoming a holy person who never sins again after believing in Jesus? Or is it possible only by the salvation once for all? Are sinners actually made to be righteous by the grace of the remission of sins? It is impossible for you to be righteous with your carnal mind. The flesh never can become righteous. The flesh always wants something to eat whenever it feels hungry.

It is impossible for the flesh to be sanctified because the flesh has lusts and desires. Because of that, we are made righteous only by believing in the water and the blood of Jesus. Can we enter the Kingdom of Heaven by not sinning anymore and cleansing ourselves as pure as snow? It is prideful thinking for a human being, who has the lusts and passions of the flesh, to become sanctified by avoiding to sin. It is impossible.

People can neither believe in the gospel nor be born again because they think about faith with carnal minds. Jesus said, *"That which is born of the flesh is flesh, and that which is born of the Spirit is spirit" (John 3:6).*

It is impossible to become righteous with a carnal mind. You may also think it is impossible because you will sin tomorrow, even though how thoroughly you repent and believe in Jesus until today. You may think, 'How can I say I am without sin when I continue sinning even now?' Is it possible for you to become righteous if you think carnally, as the flesh does? It is impossible to become sanctified with the flesh.

However, God can make us righteous

However, God can perfectly save us even if a human being can't. God can cleanse our consciences and make us confess that we are righteous and that He is our Father and our Savior. You have to know that faith begins from believing in the true word with your heart. It begins with the word of the truth. We are made righteous by believing in the true word with our hearts. We can never be made righteous by the deeds of the flesh.

However, those who are not born again cannot free themselves from their own thoughts because they are locked in their thoughts. They can never say they are righteous because they think with carnal minds. On the contrary, faith by which we can say we are righteous begins with knowing the truth of God's word. If you really want to be born again, you can surely be born again only by hearing the true word through a concretely born again person because the Spirit in the born again saint pleases to work with the truth and *"searches all things, yes, the deep things of God" (1 Corinthians 2:10)*. People can be born again when they hear the word of God through the righteous because the Spirit dwells within the righteous, who have been born again. I want you to bear it in mind. You have to meet the righteous, who are born again, if you want to receive the grace of being born again.

Abraham begot Ishmael and Isaac. Ishmael was born of a bondwoman. Ishmael was already 14 years old when Isaac was born. Ishmael persecuted Isaac, who was born by a freewoman. Who actually had the right of succession? Isaac, who was born by the freewoman Sarah, had the right of succession.

Isaac had the right of succession and was approved even though Ishmael was older and stronger in the flesh than Isaac was. Why? Isaac was born after the word of God. Faith that is established by human thought is like a sandcastle. People can be born again only when they learn the truth of God's word and believe it.

"What then? Are we better than they? Not at all. For we have previously charged both Jews and Greeks that they are all under sin. As it is written: 'There is none righteous, no, not one'" (Romans 3:9-10). What do these passages mean? Do the passages indicate the state of human beings before being born again or after being born again? We were all sinners before we were born again. "There is none righteous" was the state of human beings before Jesus blotted out all the sins of the world. One can never become sanctified without believing in Jesus.

The word "gradual sanctification" came from idol worshippers of the heathen religions. The Bible says, *"There is none righteous, no, not one."* How can one become sanctified by training oneself? A human being cannot become righteous by himself/herself. There is no one who will become righteous or who became righteous by oneself. There is no one who is sinless by his/her efforts. It is possible only by the faith in God's word. The Bible says, *"There is none who understands; there is none who seeks after God" (Romans 3:11).*

They have all turned aside

"They have all turned aside; they have together become

unprofitable" (Romans 3:12). Is a human being useful in front of God? A human being is useless before God. All those who are not born again yet are useless in front of God. Don't they point fingers at heaven while fighting and cursing against God, resenting Him for not sending rain even thought they are all created by Him?

"They have all turned aside; they have together become unprofitable," said God. How can a person who has sin in his/her heart glorify God? How can sinners, who cannot settle their problems of sin, praise the Lord? How can a sinner praise the Lord? Sinners cannot give glory to God.

Praise ministry prevails these days. Sinners used to write the lyrics to gospel songs, quoting the Scriptures in Revelations. *"Blessing and honor and glory and power be to Him who sits on the throne, and to the Lamb, forever and ever!" (Revelation 5:13)* The Lord is worthy to be praised of course, but only the righteous can praise God. Do you think that God accepts the praises of sinners with joy? Sinners' praises are like Cain's offering. Their praises are vain and are sung toward an empty sky, even though they think they praise the Lord. Why? Because God does not rejoice over them. God never hears sinners' prayers (Isaiah 59:1-2).

The Bible says that they have all turned aside and they have together become unprofitable. The words *"they have all turned aside"* means that they believed their own thoughts, rejecting God's word. The true judgment is made by the word of God. Only God judges. Humans cannot judge. The words "they have all turned aside" means that they turned to their own thoughts. They always say things such as, "I think in this way and believe like this." Those who don't abandon their thoughts give way to their thoughts, so they don't return to the word of God.

Those who are not born again think they are their own judges. It is not important to them what is written in the word of God. They cling to their own thoughts and judge what they agree to be true or false, saying, "I think like this and believe in this way. That is not the same as what I'm thinking." How can they find the truth? God says all human beings have turned aside to their own thoughts. We must not turn aside to our own thoughts. We must instead return to the Lord. We have to be saved in the just way. We have to be judged in front of the true word. Then what is righteousness?

We must be born again by the word of God

Righteousness is the word of God, which is the truth. The word of God is the canon, which refers to a 'measuring rod.' We must know that the word of God is a criterion or a benchmark. *"In the beginning was the Word" (John 1:1).* Who was with God, the Father and the Holy Spirit? He is God, the Word. The Word is God. Jesus Christ, our Savior and King of kings, is the Word, our God.

It is written that the Word was with God in the beginning. Who was with God? The Word. So the Word is Jesus, our Savior and God. The Savior is God. An exact representation of His nature is the Word. So the word of God is different from our own thoughts because the Word is God. It is very ignorant for a human being to try to understand the word of God with his/her own carnal thoughts.

Therefore, God can use a person who stands fast in His word and in faith. The person who stands fast in the word of God is faithful and useful before God, and God blesses such a person.

Can one do what is good? The Word, who is God, says there is none righteous, no, not one. However, some think, 'There seems to be a person who does good.' In fact people play the hypocrite in front of God. We must know that we have no side of righteousness before we are born again.

All human beings rebel against God. They are cheating each other and even God while pretending to be holy, good and merciful. It is to challenge God for them to pretend to be good. Only God is good. It is to be against God and rebel against His truth to pretend to be good without being born again and believing in His love and righteousness.

Do you think only serious sinners are judged by God? Whoever is not born again, even if he/she a Christian, cannot escape God's wrath. Therefore, abandon your hypocritical way of life and hear the word of God. Be born again. Then you can escape the judgment of God.

Have you ever seen an evil person who is not full of the obsession to be good among those who are not born again? People are full of the obsession to be good. Who taught this? Satan. A human being originally can never be good. A human being can lead a good life when all his/her sins are blotted out in front of God. Then does God tell us to do evil things on purpose? No. God tells us to receive the remission of sins because we were already infected by sin before we were born and were destined to go to hell. God wants all of us to receive His true word so that we may be saved.

Satan always speaks a lie through unbelievers

"There throat is an open tomb; with their tongues they have practiced deceit; the poison of asps is under their lips;

whose mouth is full of cursing and bitterness. Their feet are swift to shed blood; destruction and misery are in their ways; and the way of peace they have not known. There is no fear of God before their eyes" (Romans 3:13-18).

"With their tongues they have practiced deceit." All people are good at deceiving. God says about Satan, *"When he speaks a lie, he speaks from his own resources" (John 8:44).* All those who are not born again say, "I really tell the truth. It is true," but their sayings are all lies.

Those who emphasize that their sayings are right are liars. Have you ever seen swindlers say, "I am a liar and a swindler," when they try to cheat others? They speak as if everything they say is true. They can convincingly say, "Let me tell you something. If you invest your money in this, you can make big money. If you invest one million dollars, you can make as much as the principal soon and you will make ten million dollars in a couple of years. It is a fantastic investment. Do you want to invest?' Those who aren't born again always deceive with their tongues.

When Satan speaks a lie, he speaks from his own resources. A preacher who is not born again always tells a lie. He/she claims one can be rich if one offers a large amount of tithes. Is there any passage in the Bible that says one can become rich if he/she becomes an elder? Why do people try to become elders? They try to be elders because they are led to believe that if they become elders, God will give them earthly blessings. They are deceived because they believe that they can have the grace of wealth if they become elders. They are caught in the snare of deceit.

Have you ever become an elder by being deceived by such a lie? Many people have lived like beggars after becoming elders. I know many of them around me. False prophets who are not born again appoint the rich as elders of their churches. Why? Because they want the elders to make big contributions to their churches. Sometimes they appoint people with no money as elders because they want to make them their blind followers.

The common saying, "One will be blessed with wealth if he/she becomes a elder," is a lie. There is no mention of this in the Bible. The Bible says God's servants would rather be persecuted rather than have the grace of riches. The Lord says, *"But seek first the kingdom of God and His righteousness, and all these things shall be added to you" (Matthew 6:33).*

"The poison of asps is under their lips," states the Bible. Human beings really have the poison of asps. What do those who are not born again say to the righteous? They curse the righteous and speak like asps. The Bible says, *"Their feet are swift to shed blood; destruction and misery are in their ways; and the way of peace have they not known. There is no fear of God before their eyes."*

What is the purpose of the law?

The passage, *"As it is written,"* means that it is the quotation from the Old Testament. The Apostle Paul quoted the Old Testament many times. He said, *"Their feet are swift to shed blood; destruction and misery are in their ways; and the way of peace have they not known. There is no fear of God before their eyes."* I feel pity for those who go to hell without knowing the way of being born again.

Romans 3:19 states, *"Now we know that whatever the law says, it says to those who are under the law, that every mouth may be stopped, and all the world may become guilty before*

God." God inflicts wrath according to the law. The reason Paul says, *"it says to those who are under the law,"* is because God gave the law to those who are not born again, who don't know sin and who don't consider sin as a sin, in order to enlighten sinners, who can never keep the law, on their real existence. God did not give us the law to make us keep it. Then does God say that He destroyed the law? No. He gave us the law through Moses to give us the knowledge of our sins. He did not give us the law to make us keep it. The law of God has a role of teaching us how sinful we are.

Nobody can be righteous by the deeds of the law

Romans 3:20 states, *"Therefore by the deeds of the law no flesh will be justified in His sight, for by the law is the knowledge of sin."* Born again Christians know that no flesh will be justified by the deeds of the law. The Apostle Paul and all the servants of God say, "No flesh will be justified by the deeds of the law." There is no one who keeps the law and who will keep it in the future. Therefore, we must confess that we can never become justified by the deeds of the law. Our deeds cannot make us righteous.

The Apostle Paul knew and believed this. Can we be justified by keeping the law? Can the law justify us? When you read the Scriptures, do you think it is right to believe that our flesh changes to be justified and enter into the Kingdom of Heaven by doing good deeds after believing in Jesus? No, this is not true. It's a lie. The fact that one enters the Kingdom of God by gradually transforming to be justified is a lie. All the people who are not born again are under the law because they think they must keep God's word with their own deeds. It makes them try to keep the law and pray for forgiveness daily. It's due to their fastening the first button in the wrong way. The law gives us the knowledge of being sinners. Sinners' efforts to keep the law is due to their ignorance and their own thoughts, which are against the salvation of the truth and are out of the flesh. It is a wrongly oriented faith.

The Doctrine of Sanctification, which says that we incrementally change to be justified, is also found in other secular religions in the world. Buddhism has a similar doctrine, the doctrine of Nirvana as the Christian doctrine of gradual sanctification. Many people say that their flesh can be sanctified more and more and they can eventually enter the Kingdom of Heaven. But the truth is that the Lord sanctified our spirits once and for all.

Even the righteous cannot become sanctified by the flesh. Those who don't have the Spirit cannot become sanctified. The more they try to do good deeds, the more serious a sinner they become. It's because they have sin in their hearts. Something dirty frequently comes out of them and makes them dirty, however hard they may try to outwardly cleanse themselves, because they are full of sin inwardly. It is the real existence of a sinner.

This state of being is opposite to those who have the remission of all sins. They can lead clean lives even though they cannot help sinning with their fleshes. Sinners who are born infected with sin spread sin all their lives because sin comes out of them against their wills. They have no choice but to get a healing shot that can eliminate their sins once and for all. The shot is of the gospel of God's truth. They can be delivered from their sins by hearing the word of the remission of sins. I want you to hear the word of being born again and receive the remission of sins.

Who can completely live by the law? Who can perfectly live according to the law even if he/she is born again? Nobody. In Romans, it is written, *"By the law is the knowledge of sin."* It's so simple. Adam and Eve were deceived by Satan in the time of innocence and were sold under sin. The sin was handed over to their descendants who did not know God's word. They did not know that they were born sinners even though they inherited sin.

After the time of Abraham and Jacob, the Israelites forgot about the faith and their sinful existence though their ancestor Abraham was made righteous by faith. So God gave them His law to let them have the knowledge of sin and wanted them to receive the remission of sins by believing in His promise. Do you believe this?

But now the righteousness of God apart from the law is manifested

Romans 3:21 states, *"But now the righteousness of God apart from the law is revealed, Being witnessed by the Law and the prophets."* The Apostle Paul says that the righteousness of God, apart from the law, is revealed. The words, *"Being witnessed by the Law and the prophets,"* indicate the Old Testament. The gospel of the water and the Spirit is the righteousness of God, which was revealed through the sacrificial system. The gospel reveals the righteousness that leads us to receive the remission of sins through the sin offering.

Romans 3:22 states, *"Even the righteousness of God, through faith in Jesus Christ, to all and on all who believe. For there is no difference."* Our faiths are in our hearts. The author and finisher of faith is Jesus Christ. Hebrews 12:2 states, *"Looking unto Jesus, the author and finisher of our faith."* The author and finisher of faith is Jesus and we believe in the true Word, which is God. We must learn and believe in the true words of the Bible from the born again servants in order to be saved from all our sins and to live by faith. We must believe in Jesus with our hearts.

God says, *"Even the righteousness of God, through faith in Jesus Christ, to all and on all who believe. For there is no difference."* Therefore, we are made righteous by believing in the true word with our hearts and have the confirmation of perfect salvation by confessing with our mouths. We cannot be saved by our own deeds, but by faith. We give thanks to only the Lord and the church of God.

Do you happen to be bound by your deeds though all your sins have been blotted out? You are righteous regardless of your flesh's weakness if you believe in God with your heart. The Holy Spirit testifies the word of God in your heart saying, "You are righteous," because He leads us to understand the true word when we hear the word. Were you saved by faith after hearing God's word?

"Even the righteousness of God, through faith in Jesus Christ, to all and on all who believe. For there is no difference." Whoever learns and believes in the word of God, which is the truth, can be saved from all his/her sins.

Jesus washed away all sins from the beginning to the end of the world

Romans 3:23-25 states, *"For all have sinned and fall short of the glory of God, being justified freely by His grace through the redemption that is in Christ Jesus, whom God set forth as a propitiation by His blood, through faith, to demonstrate His righteousness, because in His forbearance God had passed over the sins that were previously committed."*

The Bible says that all have sinned and fallen short of the glory of God. We received the forgiveness of sins and became justified freely by His grace and love while sinners go to hell. We reached the glory of God and became justified. God set forth Jesus to be a propitiation by His blood through faith.

Verses 25 and 26 state, *"Whom God set forth as a propitiation by His blood, through faith, to demonstrate His righteousness, because in His forbearance God had passed over the sins that were previously committed, to demonstrate at the present time His righteousness, that He might be just and the justifier of the one who has faith in Jesus."* Here, the words, *"set forth,"* mean that God sent His Son Jesus to be a propitiation for the remission of sins for the whole universe.

Jesus took away all the sins of the world by His baptism. Jesus is the Alpha and the Omega. Let's think about the beginning and the end of the world. God delivered us by the faith that washed away all our sins from the beginning to the end of the world. God set forth Jesus to be a propitiation through the faith in the truth. It was not until I believed in the gospel that I realized the words, *"to demonstrate His righteousness, because in His forbearance God had passed over the sins that were previously committed."*

All our sins are eliminated when we believe in the word that says Jesus washed away all our sins by His baptism and blood. We received the remission of sins once and for all, but our flesh still continues to sin. The flesh sins due to our weakness. However, the Bible states, *"God had passed over the sins that were previously committed."* Sins that the flesh commits even now and in future are sins that were previously committed from God's point of view.

Why? God made the baptism of Jesus the cardinal starting point of our salvation. Therefore, the present sins of the flesh are sins that are past, in God's perspective, because the remission of sins was accomplished by Jesus Christ once and for all. The present sins are sins that were already blotted out. The words, *"God had passed over the sins that were previously committed,"* mean that "He had already paid the wages of sins of the world." All the sins of the world were already forgiven through the baptism and the Cross of Jesus.

Therefore, God already blotted out all the sins committed from the beginning to the end of the world. So all sins are previously committed in God's eyes. People in the world are committing sins that were already blotted out by the Son of God. Jesus already washed away the sins that would be committed in the year 2002 about 2,000 years ago. Do you understand this?

God already blotted out the world's sins, including your and my sins. Do you see what this means? You may be confused when you preach the gospel to other people if you don't understand. The words, *"God had passed over the sins that were previously committed,"* mean that God overlooks all sins because He had already eliminated them about 2,000 years ago. The sins of all human beings were already judged because Jesus was baptized in the Jordan River and was crucified. God passes over all sins because Jesus was sent to the world and perfectly justified all human beings once and for all. Therefore, God does not charge the blame on the sins that are committed by all the people in the world and were already blotted out by

Him, but on their unbelief in the baptism and the Cross of Jesus.

Do you understand what the Apostle Paul means? It is very important to us who are saved. Those who are not born again will go to hell because they ignore it. We must hear and have the right knowledge of the word. It will be very helpful to your faith and to your preaching of the gospel to other people.

Where is boasting then?

The Bible says, *"To demonstrate His righteousness, because in His forbearance God had passed over the sins that were previously committed."* God teaches us that the sins of the past were already blotted out because God set forth Jesus to be a propitiation. Therefore, we are made righteous by faith.

Verse 26 states, *"To demonstrate at the present time His righteousness, that He might be just and the justifier of the one who has faith in Jesus."* "At this present time" God gave the world everlasting life so that the world would not perish. At this present time, God sent Jesus Christ to demonstrate His righteousness and accomplished what He promised. The Lord demonstrated His righteousness. God sent His only begotten Son and let Him be baptized and crucified to show us His love through the salvation of the truth.

The Lord came to sinners as their Savior. *"To demonstrate at the present time His righteousness, that He might be just and the justifier of the one who has faith in Jesus."* God is righteous and eliminated the sins of the world once and for all. We believe in Jesus with our hearts, so we have no sin. Those who believe in Jesus truthfully are without sin because He washed them away and even saved them from their future sins. Believing in what Jesus did with our hearts saves us. Our deeds are not included, not even 0.1%, in the faith in His salvation

Romans 3:27-31 states, *"Where is boasting then? It is excluded. By what law? Of works? No, but the law of faith. Therefore we conclude that a man is justified by faith apart from the deeds of the law. Or is He the God of the Jews only? Is He not also the God of the Gentiles? Yes, of the Gentiles also, since there is one God who will justify the circumcised by faith and uncircumcised through faith. Do we then made void the law through faith? Certainly not! On the contrary, we establish the law."*

The words, *"We establish the law,"* mean that we cannot be saved by our deeds. We are imperfect and weak and had to go to hell before the law. However, the word of God made us righteous and perfect because we were saved by His word. The Lord tells us that our flesh is still imperfect even after we are saved from all our sins, but He perfectly delivered us from all our sins. We can draw near to God by believing that Jesus saved us.

"Where is boasting then? It is excluded. By what law? Of works? No, but by the law of faith." We must know the law that God established and that the law is everlasting in His Kingdom. *"By what law? Of works? No, but by the law of faith,"* says God. Do you comprehend this? God saved us from all the sins of the world. We are saved when we believe according to the truth. We have to remember that the works of the law cannot save us.

God talks about the law of faith through the Apostle Paul in Romans chapter 3. God says, *"Will their unbelief make the faithfulness of God without effect?"* (Romans 3:3) Believers stand fast by faith, but unbelievers tumble down. Those who do not have the complete faith in the gospel of the truth will go to hell, even if they think they believe in Jesus.

God perfectly saved all of us from all sins

God established the law of God so that those who believe according to their own thoughts may stumble at the law of faith. God perfectly saved all of us from our sins. Romans chapter 3 talks about the law of faith. We are saved by believing in the true word. We inherit the Kingdom of Heaven and have peace by faith. Unbelievers cannot have peace. Instead, they go to hell. What is the reason for it? First, they are judged according to the law of God's truth because they did not receive the word of God's truth. Salvation comes from God's love and we are saved by knowing the truth and by believing what the Lord did with our hearts. Do you understand?

I praise the Lord who gives us this faith and His church on the earth. I give thanks to the Lord who gives us the truth, the faith and the word, which the Apostle Paul had, and who revealed the secret of the remission of sins to His church. I praise Him from the bottom of my heart.

We thank the Lord because He saved us through His baptism and the death on the Cross. We have no choice but to go to hell without this faith and His church. We were sinners, who could never be saved by nature, but we believed to righteousness with our hearts. We become His children who believe unto righteous with the heart and are made unto salvation with the mouth confession (Romans 10:10). ⊠

Do You Thank God for The Lord?

< Romans 3:10-31 >
"As it is written:
'There is none righteous, no, not one;
There is none who understands;
There is none who seeks after God.
They have all turned aside;
They have together become unprofitable;
There is none who does good, no, not one.
Their throat is an open tomb;
With their tongues they have practiced deceit;
The poison of asps is under their lips;
Whose mouth is full of cursing and bitterness.
Their feet are swift to shed blood;
Destruction and misery are in their ways;
And the way of peace they have not known.
There is no fear of God before their eyes.
Now we know that whatever the law says, it says to those who are under the law, that every mouth may be stopped, and all the world may become guilty before God. Therefore by the deeds of the law no flesh will be justified in His sight, for by the law is the knowledge of sin. But now the righteousness of God apart from the law is revealed, being witnessed by the Law and the Prophets, even the righteousness of God, through faith in Jesus Christ, to all and on all who believe. For there is no difference; for all have sinned and fall short of the glory of God, being

justified freely by His grace through the redemption that is in Christ Jesus, whom God set forth as a propitiation by His blood, through faith, to demonstrate His righteousness, because in His forbearance God had passed over the sins that were previously committed, to demonstrate at the present time His righteousness, that He might be just and the justifier of the one who has faith in Jesus. Where is boasting then? It is excluded. By what law? Of works? No, but by the law of faith. Therefore we conclude that a man is justified by faith apart from the deeds of the law. Or is He the God of the Jews only? Is He not also the God of the Gentiles? Yes, of the Gentiles also, since there is one God who will justify the circumcised by faith and the uncircumcised through faith. Do we then make void the law through faith? Certainly not! On the contrary, we establish the law."

Human beings have nothing to boast with the flesh

Romans 3:10-12 states, *"There is none righteous, no, not one; there is none who understands; there is none who seeks after God. They have all turned aside; they have together become unprofitable; there is none that does good, no, not one."* We are all full of sins because of the flesh in front of God. Can one become righteous by oneself with the flesh? Can there be righteous fleshes by nature before God? A human being can never become righteous with the flesh. The flesh can never be righteous without being delivered from sins through Jesus Christ.

Those whose sins are blotted out have nothing to boast with their fleshes. We whose sins are blotted out also cannot but turn aside with our flesh and have no ability to do good. We cannot say we lead good lives except when we serve the Lord and do spiritual work. Just as Jesus said, *"That which is born of the flesh is flesh, and that which is born of the Spirit is spirit" (John 3:6),* the flesh only wants to satisfy its lust while the spirit desires to walk by the Spirit. The flesh can never be transformed into the spirit.

All human beings are born sinful, live under sin, die in vain and are eventually cast into the lake of fire in hell. They wouldn't have had hope if God hadn't sent His only begotten Son to the world to save them from all their sins. If there is any hope for us, it is just because God gave us a true hope. If it were not for God, we would have neither righteousness nor hope. It is true when we investigate the fate of every individual including you and me in the world.

Even though we are called as "the lords of all creation, we are destined to be born sinful, regardless of our wills, live in vain and go to hell. How transient we are! We usually identify human being's ephemeral life with that a dayfly that is born and lives all its life in a day and dies and goes back to dust in vain. We have no hope without Jesus. The only necessary things human beings do in their lives is to be born, eat, drink, die and go to hell, however famous they may be or how great their exploits may have been. We live in vain and disappear in vain and are destined to receive the eternal judgment.

However, God gave us the law to give us the knowledge of sin and then freely made us righteous by His grace through the remission of sins in Jesus Christ. He sent His only begotten Son Jesus, who took all our sins and was crucified, to be a propitiation to those who believe in the baptism and the blood of Jesus. God set forth Jesus to be a propitiation for us and made us righteous.

How can those who have the remission of sins become righteous? Do we, who have the remission of sins, have the righteousness of the flesh? Do we have any side to boast before God? We have nothing to boast with the flesh. Because of God, the Lord, we are delighted and give thanks to Him, for we have the remission of sins, the confirmation of salvation and everlasting lives.

We who have the remission of sins are nothing without God. Does the flesh of a human being have something to boast? Is the flesh righteous at all? Do we have anything to boast in the 70-80 years of our lives? A human being has nothing righteous. What do we have to boast before God? The flesh really does not have anything to boast. The flesh has nothing to boast before God, not even 0.1%.

The only thing that we can boast is the righteousness of God

What we boast is that the Lord saved us from our sins, as it is written, *"But now the righteousness of God apart from the law is revealed, being witnessed by the Law and the Prophets."* The Lord is our eternal life and Savior. He made us righteous. We are righteous because Jesus perfectly saved us. We have nothing to boast with the flesh or with the deeds of the law. We are thankful and praise the Lord for being baptized and for washing away all the sins of the world to fulfill all righteousness.

We come to have the righteousness of faith. The Lord saved all the people in the world from their sins without leaving one person out. The salvation of God makes us happy and gives us hope. It gives us a new power. We have nothing to boast but the Lord. Far from boasting our righteousness before God, we are shameful. Many people try to offer their efforts to God with the pride of their deeds and their own righteousness, but their self-righteous egos are like dirty cloths. They may have something to boast to each other or to themselves, but nothing before God.

The Lord is the perfect Savior to us. 'Jesus' means 'the Savior' and He is said to be Christ too. This means that the Savior who came in the likeness of men was God. We call Him "Jesus Christ." Jesus is our Savior and God. We give thanks to the Lord, praise Him, do righteous works before Him and have faithful lives because God completely saved us. Only believers in God can do righteous works.

We can work righteously without sin because the Lord took away all the sins of the world and became our Savior who saved us from all our sins. We cannot settle the problem of sin by ourselves. A human being can neither eliminate his/her sins nor keep God's righteousness by doing good deeds with the flesh.

God blotted out all our sins and we received the righteousness from God. We are righteous. Can we keep our righteousness by sanctifying our flesh with virtuous deeds on our part? If one could do so, he/she would be an elder brother/sister to Jesus. Jesus could never be the Savior to such a person. We have an instinct for keeping our own righteousness with the ability of our flesh and emotions without realizing it. The flesh acts on instinct. We instinctively struggle not to be in danger when we meet danger, want to eat a lot when we see delicious food, and want to play when we see something interesting.

We instinctively want to keep the righteousness of God with the flesh because the flesh acts on instinct. However, we cannot. Our being saved is not through our own righteousness. We can never be saved by keeping the law well, doing good deeds with the flesh or by our dedicating ourselves to God. Our exploits are not included in the righteousness of God, not even 0.1%. We are made righteous by believing that God came to the world in the likeness of men and received baptism from John the Baptist before He was crucified to fulfill all righteousness, which perfectly saved us from our sins.

The Lord who saved us is the perfect Savior

The Lord fulfilled all righteousness by taking away all the sins that human beings commit before they die, became the perfect Savior to them, and made us righteous. God made us perfect by fulfilling all righteousness. God enabled us to work spiritually. We have the right to work spiritually before God because we received His righteousness, becoming sinless even though our flesh continues to work carnally. However, those whose sins are not blotted out yet cannot work spiritually. They are not qualified to do so.

We are qualified to do the spiritual things by God. Now we can do the things of the Spirit. We can do the righteous work of God apart from the things of the flesh. How perfect it is that God became our Savior! God, who created all things as well as human beings, is revealed to us as the Lord of salvation because He came to the world and fulfilled all righteousness. In His relations with us, God became our Lord and Savior who saved us.

Salvation would be imperfect if someone who is weak and has no ability saved us. There would be a probability of failure sometime. On the contrary, the One who saved us is not such a person. He is God and the Creator who created all things. John 1:3 states, *"All things were made through Him, and without Him nothing was made that was made."* Who is Jesus? The Savior. Who is the Savior? He is God, the Creator. God perfectly saved us. Our salvation is perfect because He saved us. It lasts forever. However our salvation would be invalid if He was not the Creator, but rather, a person among creatures. It wouldn't last long, and its righteousness is like a filthy rag. If one wears perfect leather clothes, they will never be worn out, even if one plays soccer or slides on a slide. But if they weren't perfect clothes, they would become worn out at once.

The Lord who saved us from our sins is not imperfect. The Lord who saved us is God, who is perfect. The salvation of Jesus, who was baptized to bear all our sins, crucified, rose again from the dead and is sitting on the right hand of God, never becomes invalid, however weak believers' flesh may be. This is the salvation that God gave us.

Our own righteousness should be broken for us to live by faith

In the Bible, those who were full of their own righteousness lived through various hardships because God wanted to break their righteousness through those hardships. There are many passages like "However, high places were not taken away" in the records about the kings. It means that a human being himself/herself is not perfect in the flesh, but he/she is made righteous by believing in the Lord.

My beloved saints, our God perfectly saved us, no matter weak we may be. We will die if we live only for our own righteousness. But the Lord God completely saved us from sins.

He will rejoice over us if we live for the righteousness of the Lord, however weak we may be. Isaiah 53:5 states, *"But He was wounded for our transgressions, He was bruised for our iniquities."* God took away our iniquities once and for all. We don't need to be careful for fear that our righteousness should be broken.

Some people have personalities similar to glass-vessels. I know a sister who went to America. She was so noble; spoke carefully and never cursed, whenever I met her. She used to say, "Oh! Mr. bad man," to a strikingly wicked man even though she received the remission of sins. She received the remission of sins by believing in the baptism of Jesus and His blood on the Cross, even though she was full of her own righteousness. However, after she received the remission of sins, she was still full of her own righteousness, so she was extremely careful in trying not to express herself for fear that her righteousness would be broken. There are many people who are like her. Does their righteousness last long? It will be broken soon.

Does your flesh have weaknesses even though you are saved? Yes. Do you live a perfectly good life? We can live perfectly after the remission of sins only when we walk with the Spirit. Only righteous works are qualified to be good in front of God. We are praiseworthy when we work and walk with the Spirit. We have nothing to be applauded with the flesh. Some people among the saints who have the remission of sins try to keep their righteousness for fear of it being broken.

However, the Lord does not rejoice over them. Human righteousness will be broken anyway. It would be better to be broken soon. It would be broken anyway after 10 or 20 years. Therefore, the outward man would be better off being broken now so that the inward man can live by faith. People try not to break their righteousness, even though it will break anyway.

The Lord became our Savior. How perfect our Savior is! The Lord God has become our Savior. He saved both you and me. Do you become a sinner again because of the infirmities of your flesh? No. God fulfilled all righteousness. Our righteousness is broken many times after we are born again of the water and the Spirit. Our evil is revealed many times as we follow the Lord. It is revealed while trying to hide itself, in the case of an introvert and it is revealed to other people in the case of an extrovert. When our righteousness is revealed, only our righteousness is broken while the righteousness of the Lord stands fast.

That which is born of the flesh is flesh, and that which is born of the Spirit is spirit

I want you to believe that the Lord God became our perfect Savior. Therefore, we must live by faith. God wants our own righteousness to be broken and He is pleased with it. John 3:6 states, *"That which is born of the flesh is flesh, and that which is born of the Spirit is spirit."* The flesh cannot become the spirit. In Buddhism, there is "the doctrine of emancipation from worldly existence." It insists that the flesh can become a spirit. The flesh can never become a spirit. No, it cannot. Who can do it? Come on. Nobody can do it.

Sung-chul, a very famous Korean monk in contemporary Buddhism, died some years ago. He sought after the truth by meditating while facing a wall for almost 2 decades. He neither lay down to sleep for a decade to achieve spiritual enlightenment. He even slept sitting for those 10 years, and he tried to have only a good mind, defeating evil thoughts, adultery, fornication, murder, theft, wickedness, pride, and foolishness that came up from within him. Many people thought that he was a living Buddha. However, he himself knew that he could not extinguish the lusts of his flesh at all, so he left a piece of a Nirvana poem when he was about to die, after cultivating his mind for almost 2 decades in the heart of mountains:

"For I have deceived many men and women during my lifetime, My sins are greater than the highest mountain. I will fall into the endless hell, And my lamentation will be divided into ten thousands ways. A piece of red sun goes down behind the blue mountains."

All the religious people of the world admired his sublime personality and seemingly profound teachings. However, he himself actually said that he would go to hell.

The flesh can never be the spirit, but our souls become God's children when we are born again by believing in His salvation. We just became the new creatures by the grace of God who resurrected us in His righteousness. A human being cannot be renewed by his/her own efforts.

Ministers, monks, and Catholic fathers who participate in prison ministry advise prisoners to live a virtuous life for the rest of their lives. However, the flesh never changes. God wants us to abandon our own righteousness and firmly believe that the Lord is our Savior. Believe in the baptism and the Cross of Jesus. Then, you will have the great faith in salvation.

Now God looks for believers

The Lord became a propitiation to us. He was baptized to

take away all things that separated God the Father from human beings. He was crucified to pay the wages of our sin, was judged in our place, and saved us from all sins. God became a propitiation to us.

He says, *"God set forth as a propitiation by His blood, through faith, to demonstrate His righteousness, because in His forbearance God had passed over the sins that were previously committed, to demonstrate at the present time His righteousness, that He might be just and the justifier of the one who has faith in Jesus" (Romans 3:25-26).*

God came to the world and fulfilled all righteousness. Everybody in the world is sinless. Nobody goes to hell if he/she just believes in the perfect salvation of God. He/she goes to hell due to his/her unbelief. One can be saved if he/she forsakes his/her own righteousness and hypocrisy and accepts God as the Savior by believing in Jesus' baptism and death on the Cross. We live in a state of no sin from God's viewpoint because He took all the sins of the world onto Him and eliminated them.

I believe in God. So do you. He is the Savior. We have no sin. The Lord God perfectly saved us. The only problem left for us is how we spend the rest of our lives. How should we live? We should walk with the Spirit. We have no reason to worry about eliminating our sins. The words, *"God had passed over the sins that were previously committed,"* means that God does not condemn us for our sins. We have no sin and nothing to be judged because God already saved us from our sins by receiving baptism from John the Baptist to take them away and by being crucified. Therefore, God does not condemn us for our sins. He looks for those who believe this truth with the heart.

The Bible says that there is none righteous, but we are

made righteous by the faith in God. God says, *"There is none righteous, no, not one; There is none who understands; There is none who seeks after God. They have all turned aside; They have together become unprofitable; There is none who does good, no, not one. Their throat is an open tomb; With their tongues they have practiced deceit; The poison of asps is under their lips; Whose mouth is full of cursing and bitterness. Their feet are swift to shed blood; Destruction and misery are in their ways; And the way of peace they have not known. There is no fear of God before their eyes"* (Romans 3:10-18).

God came to the world and took away all the sins of those who do every kind of evils while living this world and have no righteousness and became unprofitable in the Jordan River. Do you believe it?

Now, God looks for people who believe that He saved them from all their sins. The eyes of the lord are upon the righteous. He encourages us, the righteous. He takes care of us, is always with us, keeps us and works with us. God entrusted us with righteous works. Jesus will grieve more than we do if we grieve at the evils of our flesh. "Why do you grieve at your sins when I already saved you from all your sins."

What we have to do now is to believe in God, walk with the Spirit and preach the gospel to harvest souls. Those are the things we have to do now. Do you believe this? Do not show off your own righteousness or try to establish it either, comparing your righteousness with others to show it off. Do not slander the person who is not righteous by him/herself. In fact, there is no righteous human being by nature.

We give thanks to the Lord who saved us through His baptism and the Cross

We have nothing to boast before God except His love, which saved us perfectly. All we have to do is to boast of God's salvation, praise it, glorify Him, and preach the gospel of the water and the Spirit. We don't need to worry about sin and going to hell. *"There is therefore now no condemnation to those who are in Christ Jesus" (Romans 8:1).* Never. Do you see it? One goes to hell if he/she does not unite with the fact that the Lord saved him/her with His righteous act. However, one does not need to worry about going to hell if he/she believes it.

The Lord God saved us from all sins with the baptism and the blood of Jesus. How thankful we are! *"Therefore we conclude that a man is justified by faith apart from the deeds of the law. Or is He the God of the Jews only? Is He not also the God of the Gentiles? Yes, of the Gentiles also" (Romans 3:28-29).*

God is not only the God of the Jews, but also the God of the Gentiles. He is God to all human beings. The Lord God saved us from our sins. In order to do so, He came to the world, was baptized to bear all our sins, and was crucified to be judged for all the sins. Therefore, He became the God and the Savior of all human beings. This is the conclusion of Romans chapter 3. The Apostle Paul believed this. We believe this too.

The Apostle Paul does not only talk about the weakness of the flesh, but also about the righteousness of God apart from the law. We cannot be saved by the deeds of the law. By what can we be delivered? By the faith in God's salvation. The Lord God became a propitiation to us and passed over the sins that were previously committed. Therefore, unbelievers will be judged for the sin of being against the Holy Spirit. He doesn't judge the sins that were committed by the weakness of the flesh because there is no sin in the world.

Therefore, we must believe in the Lord God. There is no condemnation or judgment to believers. God is the God of believers, so we must spend the rest of our lives by walking with the Spirit. We can always do the things of the Spirit because all our sins were forgiven already, even though our flesh wants to live lustfully. The Lord God is the God of both the Jews and the Gentiles. He is also the God of both of believers and unbelievers. This means that God wants all human beings to be saved from their sins. He can become the Savior of unbelievers. He has already become the God of believers.

I give thanks to the Lord God from the bottom of the heart. How miserable I would have been if the Lord God had not been, if He had not come to this world in the likeness of a human flesh, and if He had not been baptized in the Jordan River to take away all our sins. If He did not become our perfect Savior, we would be sinners again after receiving the remission of sins because we are weak until the day we die. I give thanks to the Lord God. ⊠

CHAPTER

4

You can download Rev. Paul C. Jong's Christian Books on iPhone, iPad, or Blackberry by going to Amazon's Kindle e-bookstore (www.amazon.com).

Introduction to Romans Chapter 4

In Romans 4:6-8 Paul talks about the blessed people before God. A person who has been truly blessed in front of God is one whose lawless deeds are forgiven and whose sins are covered. So Paul declares, *"Blessed is the man to whom the Lord shall not impute sin" (Romans 4:8).*

Then Paul introduces Abraham as being a blessed person. Using Abraham as a typical person in the Bible, Paul explains what the true and blessed faith is. Abraham would have something to boast about if his own works had justified him, but in reality, it wasn't like that. The righteousness of God he obtained was possible only by believing in God's words.

The Bible indicates that the faith by which one can become righteous and blessed is the naïve faith in God's words just like the faith of Abraham. In this chapter, Paul the Apostle talks about how one can obtain God's righteousness in one's heart by believing in His words.

There is no one who never sin at all while living on earth. Moreover, we people commit as much sin as a thick cloud covering the sky. In Isaiah, it is written that our sins and transgressions are like thick clouds (Isaiah 44:22). So, there is no one among all of mankind who can escape from God's judgment without believing in the righteousness of Jesus Christ.

The baptism Jesus received and His blood on the Cross fulfilled God's righteousness. Everyone commits sins; both the born again and the non-born again commit sins with their flesh without exception. Moreover, we commit sins that we are not even aware of and therefore, we were destined to be judged for those sins.

One should keep in mind that if a person has even the slightest bit of sin, he/she has to die in front of God's justice. It was said in the Bible that the wages of sin is death (Romans 6:23), and we should therefore understand and believe in God's law. We must pay the price of the sins we have committed with our minds and deeds, and only when we have paid off all the wages of sin will the problem of sin be settled. On the other hand, no matter how hard we try, if we still don't pay the price of sin, the issue of the judgment of sin will not come to an end. What we should know is that even a person who believes in Jesus, yet has sin, will be judged of his/her own sins.

We live in this world that is flooded with all kinds of sins: big and small, perceived and unperceived, willingly and inevitably. We cannot but admit the fact that we should be condemned to death on account of our own sin according to God's law, *"The wages of sin is death."*

If one wishes to get all his/her sins covered, he/she should receive the remission of sin by believing in the righteousness of God, which comes of the water, the blood and the Holy Spirit. One who has obtained the remission of sin by believing in God's righteousness is able to and has proper qualifications to offer the sacrifice of praise to God continually for He has taken over all the sins by the baptism and the blood. Since our Lord had already taken over all the sins of the world, including my cloud-like sins, by His baptism, blood and resurrection, we therefore come to give thanks before the Lord who has given us eternal lives.

If Jesus Christ had not taken over all the sins at the Jordan River by getting baptized by John and dying on the Cross, we would have paid the wages of death by going to hell. How can we praise Him, if He hadn't blotted out all our sins completely? Would it be possible for us to praise God's name whenever we come before our Holy and Sacred God if our hearts were full of sin? Could we really offer the sacrifice of praise to His righteousness saying, "He has forgiven all our sins!" when we still had sin in our heart? No.

But now, we can praise Him in His righteousness. All of this has been possible because we believe in the gift of God's righteousness, which we have been clothed with.

Paul said that we have obtained the righteousness of God by believing in what God has done

"What then shall we say that Abraham our father has found according to the flesh? For if Abraham was justified by works, he has something to boast about, but not before God. For what does the Scripture say? 'Abraham believed God, and it was accounted to him for righteousness.' Now to him who works, the wages are not counted as grace but as debt. But to him who does not work but believes on Him who justifies the ungodly, his faith is accounted for righteousness" (Romans 4:1-5).

Here, Paul explains how to be justified by taking Abraham as an example. It is reasonable for one to receive his/her appropriate wage for his/her work. However, it is entirely God's gift and not the wage for our works that we were made to become righteous by being born again, without doing any good or living perfect lives before God.

Paul the Apostle said, *"Now to him who works, the wages are not counted as grace but as debt."* This talks about how a sinner obtained salvation from sin through the baptism of Jesus Christ and His sacrificial blood. This salvation was given as a blessed gift for the remission of sin to all who believe in God's righteousness.

The salvation of a sinner is the unconditional gift given by God's righteousness. One who has been born a sinner has no other choice than to sin, and he/she has no other choice than to confess to God that he/she is inevitably a sinner. The sins of such a sinner cannot disappear just because he/she diligently says prayers of repentance by believing some prevailing Christian doctrines.

A sinner cannot boast about his/her own righteousness before God. *"We are all like an unclean thing, and all our righteousnesses are like filthy rags"* *(Isaiah 64:6)*. So, a sinner has no other choice than to believe in God's righteousness, which was fulfilled by our Lord's baptism at the Jordan River and His atoning death on the Cross. Only then can one be forgiven for all one's sins by the faith in God's righteousness. There is nothing more a sinner can do in order to obtain God's righteousness. Your remission of sin can only be obtained by believing in God's righteousness.

All sinners are able to find His righteousness through Jesus Christ's baptism and His atoning blood on the Cross. Therefore, it is the faith in God's righteousness that makes it possible for a sinner to obtain salvation from sin. This is the truth. This is the gift of God's righteousness.

Paul the Apostle talks about how sinners obtain salvation from all sins

Paul explains this by using Abraham as a typical example. *"Now to him who works, the wages are not counted as grace but as debt."* Paul the Apostle is saying that one cannot obtain God's righteousness by doing a certain kind of lawful deed. The only way we can obtain God's righteousness is by believing in His righteous words of the spiritual circumcision.

God's righteousness is the truth that cannot be obtained by human efforts or deeds. The gift of God's righteousness was as follows: You and I were people who were destined to enter eternal destruction, but our Savior Jesus Christ took over all the sins through His baptism, given by John at the Jordan River. He then bore all of the sins on His back to the Cross, where He paid all the wages of sins with His blood. Jesus thereby fulfilled all of God's righteousness. All His righteous deeds had completed God's righteousness that saved sinners from eternal death.

Those who believe in the words of God can obtain Gods' righteousness!

Verse 5 states, *"But to him who does not work but believes on Him who justifies the ungodly, his faith is accounted for righteousness."*

In this part, Paul the Apostle explains the way to God's righteousness by using the 'ungodly' as an example. 'The ungodly' are those who are not only fearless of God, but also commit dissolute sins throughout their lives. God's words that say all people were born as 'masses of sin' are certainly right.

Moreover, it is also right that the true nature of humankind is that they have no other choice than to sin until they receive God's fearful judgment. However, if God calls us, the ungodly, as sinless and accounts our faiths for righteousness, what else could make this possible except God's righteousness?

Our Lord speaks to us, the ungodly: The Lord Himself had to get baptized at the Jordan River by John the Baptist, the last High Priest of the Old Testament, to take over all the sins of the world. He also had to pay the wages of our sins with His atoning bloodshed at the Cross to fulfill His words, *"The wages of sin is death."* Do you believe that Jesus Christ paid off the wages of all our sins with God's righteousness, by the baptism He received and His blood on the Cross? God accounts the faith of those who believe in His righteousness for righteousness. This is not an obstinate insistence but a fact made up of the fair righteousness of God.

Therefore, to a person who believes in God's righteousness, God the Father says, "Right, you are my people. You do believe in My righteousness. Now you are My child. You are sinless. Why? Because I have made you sinless by taking over all your sins by My Son's baptism and His blood! He also paid the price of your sins with His bloodshed according to the words, *'the wages of sin is death.'* He rose again from the dead for you. He is therefore your Savior and God. Do you believe in this?"

"Yes, I am." Then He will continues, "I gave you My righteousness, completed by the righteous deeds of My Son. You have now become My child, I have adopted you with the water and blood of My Son."

All of mankind is ungodly before God. However, our Lord Jesus took over all the sins of the ungodly—both the sins we have already committed and the sins we will commit in the future—at once by the baptism John gave Him. Moreover, God clothed all those who believe in God's righteousness with His righteousness and thereby saved them from all their sins. *"For you are all sons of God through faith in Christ Jesus. For as many of you as were baptized into Christ have put on Christ" (Galatians 3:26-27).* Now the question is whether we truly believe in God's word with our hearts or not. We become righteous if we believe, but if we don't, we come to lose God's righteousness.

Even the ungodly in the sight of God...

Even to those who are ungodly before God, He promised that His righteousness would become theirs if they only believe that Jesus took over the sins of the world at once by getting baptized at the Jordan River. God actually gave His righteousness to every believer. Anyone who believes in God's righteousness receives salvation from all the sins of this world. Our Father God told those believers in His righteousness that they are His children. "Yes, now you are sinless. My Son Jesus saved you from all your sins. You are righteous. You have been saved from all yours sins."

Even if we are not ungodly, God seals His righteousness on us to confirm that we are righteous. God's righteousness is eternal. Lord Jesus has truly done the right job for all mankind. The people of this world were saved from all the sins of this world by God's righteousness. God accounts the souls of the ungodly as sinless by looking at their faiths in His righteousness. *"Blessed is the man to whom the Lord shall not impute sin,"* because he has acquired the blessing of God's righteousness by faith.

God asks us, "Are you godly?" Then, we admit the fact that we are ungodly in the sight of God. When we acknowledge this fact, we come to be thankful that Jesus got baptized for the sinners, shed His blood on the Cross, and that it was God's righteousness that took over the sins of the world; not our own efforts. However, if we think that we are people who can obey the law very well, we can never be as thankful nor have faith in His righteousness.

One who believes in God's righteousness that *"justifies the ungodly,"* he/she comes to obtain His righteousness as a gift. God's righteousness will be given as a gift those who believe in the redemption and judgment of Jesus Christ, but to those who do not believe in God's righteousness, all of God's blessing and grace will remain locked.

Even to a born-again righteous person, the righteousness of God that was established by Jesus is essential day in and day out, since even we who believe in God's righteousness are people who cannot help but sin everyday while living in this world. Therefore, we need to remind ourselves of the joyful news of God's righteousness every day that Jesus took over all the sins by His baptism and His blood on the Cross. Every time we hear the joyful news, it refreshes our souls and reinforces our hearts with overflowing strength. Do you now understand the passage, *"But to him who does not work but believes on Him who justifies the ungodly, his faith is accounted for righteousness"*? This Scripture talks to all the people in this world.

The Bible talks in detail about how one can obtain God's righteousness through Abraham's example. However, it was said that one *"who works"* confronts God, rather than to be thankful for God's salvation. One *"who works"* does not believe in God's righteousness and thus, is not thankful. What verse 4 says is that a person who tries to go to Heaven by doing good deeds for him/herself does not need God's righteousness.

Why? Because there is no righteousness of God to be found since he/she tries to wash his/her sins by doing good deeds and saying prayers of repentance everyday for him/herself. Such a person does not want to accept God's righteousness thoroughly because the person does not willingly cast aside his/her own seemingly virtuous deeds. Rather, through prayers of repentance, he/she tries to earn the salvation of his/her own soul while crying and fasting. Therefore, God's righteousness is given only to those who truly believe in His righteous words.

To him who works, the wages are not counted as gifts!

"But to him who does not work but believes on Him who justifies the ungodly, his faith is accounted for righteousness" *(Romans 4:5).*

Brethren, this scripture is related to a person who acknowledges God and who believes in God's words just like Abraham. We believe in the Lord of salvation who saved the ungodly. There are two kinds of Christian believers in this world. In verse 4, there comes one "who works," and such a person does not regard God's salvation as a gift, but as debt. Because such people want to be recognized for their virtuous deeds in front of God after believing in Jesus, they are apt to refuse the salvation of God's righteousness. What kind of your sacrifice, do you think, is needed in receiving God's righteousness?

If you walk before God by holding on to your good deeds, you just become a sinner by not having obtained the righteousness of God. Did you know that the Doctrine of Sanctification, which most Christians support, induces them to excessively do virtuous deeds, turning them into God's enemies by confronting the gift of God's righteousness? The Bible does not state that we can gradually obtain the righteousness of God. Nor does it say that we can get God's righteousness with our works.

Supporters of 'human works' teach that you can become sanctified through prayers of repentance. They say that you can be more righteous if you live clean and virtuous lives and that you can be saved if you live piously until you die, even though Jesus Christ has eliminated your sins.

However, God's righteousness is incompatible with human deeds. Those who confront God's righteousness become allies with the demon. Because such persons refuse the Lord's righteousness, they cannot receive the remission of sin before the Lord.

Brethren, we were 100% ungodly. However, the reality is that many people misunderstand God's righteousness and are therefore walking on the wrong path of faith. Since many people think that they are somewhat godly, they do not believe in God's righteousness. They believe that they can be forgiven for their daily and future sins by saying prayers of repentance on their own. These people believe that there is at least some amount of godliness in them, so they put forward their good deeds without seeking for and believing in God's righteousness.

What sort of person can become righteous? Those who are not good at doing repentance prayers can become righteous.

This doesn't mean that one does not need to say prayers of confession. I hope you will not misunderstand me about this part. I will later deal with the issue of 'the life of the righteous.' Those who confront God's righteousness think highly of doing certain virtuous deeds, making fasting prayers or living pious lives.

However, only those who know that their deeds are insufficient can become righteous from a sinner's state by receiving Jesus' gift of the remission of sin in their hearts. The only thing we must do is to believe in God's righteousness and know that there is nothing to boast about among our own righteousness. What we have to acknowledge before God is, "O, God! We have committed such sins. We are sinners who will continue to sin until we die." That's only thing we should honestly confess. And the only other thing we have to do is believe that Jesus Christ completely fulfilled His righteousness.

By believing in God's righteousness, every sinner can receive salvation from all his/her sins completely. We praise by the faith in the righteousness of Jesus Christ, for we who were to be perished in the midst of sin, obtained salvation from all sin.

Who is a truly blessed person?

Who is a blessed person before God? The Bible defines a blessed person as the following. *"Blessed are those whose lawless deeds are forgiven, and whose sins are covered."* Even if one has not been able to do any good deeds in the sight of God, has insufficiencies and infirmities, or has not been able to keep all or certain parts of God's law, God gave the blessing of the remission of sin for the lives of believers who have faith in

God's righteousness, which eliminated all of our sins by Jesus' baptism and blood on the Cross. These kinds of people believe in God's righteousness and are the most blessed before God, for they have received the special blessing before Him out of a countless number of people. We have obtained salvation from all our sins by believing in God's righteousness. We believe that God has said so. Do we have anything more to add to His words even if God has said so? No, we don't.

There are many people in this world who still try to obtain salvation by their good deeds, even though they confess that Jesus is their Savior.

Is there anything more to complement the truth of God's salvation from sin, which says that Jesus got baptized by John, shed blood on the Cross and resurrected after death? No, there isn't.

However, today's Christians are very much confused about the part on believing in God's righteousness. People know that they might obtain salvation by believing in Jesus. But on the other hand, they still think it to be essential for their salvation that they must become sanctified gradually, live virtuously, and keep the law with God's words once they start believing in Jesus. Like this, people are very confused.

Even if what they say seems similar to that of the righteous, it is far from the faith that knows and believes in God's righteousness. How can a person believe in the Lord well? It is possible only when we have the naïve faith in the words of water and the Holy Spirit that contains God's righteousness and thus, receives the salvation from all our sins. God's truth enables us to obtain salvation from all sins by our faith in His baptism and blood on the Cross, in which God's righteousness is purely revealed.

We should cast away the absurd Christian doctrines on gradual sanctification, unconditional election and nominal justification, or the false faiths that say one can eventually obtain salvation from sin by not eating pork, or keeping the Sabbaths. We should keep away from those who talk of this kind of nonsense. There are no conclusions or correct answers to their talks.

Brethren, is it the correct faith or not that we obtain salvation from sin by believing in God's righteousness, without having done anything virtuous? —Yes, that is the true faith.— What kind of works have we done to obtain God's righteousness? Have we done any good deeds before God? —No.— Are we perfect by ourselves even in our thoughts? —No, we aren't.— Then does this mean that we should live any way we like? —No.— Should we live virtuously by the law to be His children? —No.— It means that we should become true children of God only by believing in His righteousness, by obtaining the remission of sin, and by receiving the Holy Spirit as a gift through correct faith.

It is absolutely impossible for people to live good lives. However, even if a person does not work, if he/she still believes in the righteousness given by Jesus, then he/she is a blessed person who has been saved from all sin. Everyone is originally incapable of living a good life. Therefore, God sympathized with us and sent Jesus to this world, making Him get baptized by John the Baptist, so that He could take over the sins of the world. Jesus was then made to carry the sins over to the Cross and settle the problem of sin.

In Oriental proverbs, there is a saying, "One should sacrifice one's life for the good of others." When someone drowns after saving a person from drowning, they praise him/her for the sacrificial benevolence. Brethren, what this means is that even though it is natural to save a drowning person, we tend to think too highly of it.

Here is another old saying called, *'Ingwa-eungbo.'* It means that if a person leads a good life, then he/she will be blessed in the future, but punished if he/she behaves badly. Brethren, is there truly a person who freely gives up his life for another person? Even in the case of heterosexual love, men and women love and care for each other because it suits their taste. Like this, all people are basically egocentric.

Therefore, God says that there can be no virtue within humans and we should examine carefully whether or not we really rely on and believe in His righteousness, which has eliminated even our most wicked sins, though we have never truly done any kinds of virtues. We should obtain salvation from all our sins by believing in God's righteousness our God has given us.

You should obtain the remission of all the sins of the lawless deeds

What are the lawless deeds before God? All wrongdoings we have committed in the sight of God are lawless deeds.

How can you and I get our sins covered before God? Can a thick bulletproof vest cover our sins? Or can 1-meter thick iron armor, made of the strongest metal, cover our sins in the sight of God? Brethren, whenever we do good deeds, do they cover the wrongdoings and faults we have committed before God? No. Good deeds of mankind are nothing more than self-consolations. One cannot escape from the just judgment of God by comforting one's own conscience by doing good deeds.

"Blessed are those ...whose sins are covered." This is what was said in the Bible. Brethren, if we would like to get our sins covered before God, the only way to do so is to believe in God's righteousness by which He saved us. This righteousness of God includes Jesus Christ's coming to this world to get baptized, His taking over our sins, and His vicarious death on the Cross. This is because Jesus took over the sins of the world by getting baptized and because He received the judgment by His death on the Cross. This is God's righteousness. All sins get covered when one believes in His righteousness.

Even if a person tries to covers up his sins with his good deeds, it is of no use before God. It is only the righteous deeds of Jesus' baptism and blood that can cover the sins of you and I. We were to be judged, destroyed, and go to hell by receiving God's furious rages due to our sins, but Jesus came to this world and fulfilled God's righteousness for us by getting baptized by John the Baptist and dying on the Cross. You should believe in this. We can get our sins covered by the faith in God's righteousness. Why? Because God's righteousness has already made the just compensation for all the sins of the world through His baptism and bloodshed. You and I can get our sins covered by believing in this truth.

What kind of person is blessed? A person with this kind of faith is blessed. *"Blessed are those whose lawless deeds are forgiven, and whose sins are covered; blessed is the man to whom the Lord shall impute sin."* A person with this kind of faith is a happy and blessed one. Do you and I have this kind of faith? A truly blessed person is one who has taken God's words that Jesus Christ saved us by water and the Holy Spirit into his/her heart. One who receives Jesus Christ together with His water and the blood in his/her heart and dwells inside Jesus Christ is a truly blessed person.

By faith, we the believers in God's righteousness have received the amazing salvation, which does not contain even the slightest bit of human thought or virtue. Only a truly blessed person believes in this faith, keeps it in his/her heart and can preach the true gospel.

Brethren, don't ever try to become God's children or get saved from sin by adding certain virtuous deeds of your own to His grace! Are you virtuous? It is arrogance if one tries to be virtuous even though he/she really isn't and thinks that he/she can be. If a poor person receives a huge diamond from a billionaire as a gift, the only thing the poor person needs to do is say "Thanks." The same goes for God's righteousness.

Romans chapter 4 talked about people who were blessed by God. Such people have been saved from all sin by believing in the words of the gospel that contains God's righteousness.

I hope this blessing becomes yours. ✉

Those Who Received Heavenly Blessing by Faith

< Romans 4:1-8 >
"What then shall we say that Abraham our father has found according to the flesh? For if Abraham was justified by works, he has something to boast about, but not before God. For what does the Scripture say? 'Abraham believed in God, and it was accounted to him for righteousness.' Now to him who works, the wages are not counted as grace but as debt. But to him who does not work but believes on Him who justifies the ungodly, his faith is accounted for righteousness, just as David also describes the blessedness of the man to whom God imputes righteousness apart from works. 'Blessed are those whose lawless deeds are forgiven, and whose sins are covered; blessed is the man to whom the Lord shall not impute sin.'"

Blessed are those whose sins have been blotted out

I give thanks to the Lord for having saved many souls these days. The Bible talks about blessed people in Romans chapter 4, so I would like to talk about those who have been blessed.

"Just as David also describes the blessedness of the man to whom God imputes righteousness apart from works. 'Blessed are those whose lawless deeds are forgiven, and whose sins are covered; blessed is the man to whom the Lord

shall not impute sin'" (Romans 4:6-8). The Bible talks about those people who have been blessed before God. Truly blessed are those whose sins are blotted out before God and to whom the Lord will not impute sin.

Before we go deeper into the Scriptures, let's examine our present state as it is. The Bible talks about the blessed people who have received the remission of their sins. Let's then think about whether we also deserve to be blessed or not.

There is not a single person in this world who doesn't sin. Mankind commits as much sin as a thick cloud just as it is written in Isaiah 44:22. Nobody is able to avoid God's judgment without the grace of Jesus Christ.

We were delivered from our sins and from God's judgment by Jesus' baptism and blood on the Cross, through which the Lord gave us the remission of sins. Furthermore, we are now able to live because of the sacrifice Jesus Christ offered. Could there possibly be one who never commits sin in this world throughout his/her whole life? Whether one is a person who has received the remission of sin or not, one sins throughout his/her life. Since we continually commit sins without even realizing it, we are destined to receive judgment due to the sins.

I believe in the fact that a person who possesses even the slightest amount of sin will go to hell. Why? Because the Bible says that the wages of sin is death (Romans 6:23). The wages of sin, whatever it may be, should be paid and the sins are forgiven only after one has paid the price. Sin only brings judgment.

We live amidst all sorts of sin, both grave and small, such as sins due to ignorance, sins committed with knowledge, and sins caused by infirmities. Strictly speaking, we cannot help but to admit our sins before God, even if we have good excuses to give Him. Do you agree with this concept? It is not right for us to refuse admitting our sins even though all our sins have been forgiven. Everyone must admit the things that should be admitted.

Only the righteous can praise the Lord

The righteous, whose sins and iniquities have already been forgiven and covered, are sinless and give thanks to God. We cannot but thank God every hour and minute, whenever we come forth before Him, for the Lord took away all our sins, even though our sins are as much as a thick cloud. We give thanks to the Lord who took away all our sins by being baptized by John the Baptist at the Jordan River, and received the judgment on the Cross in our place.

If the Lord had neither taken all our sins onto Him through His baptism nor had been crucified and died to pay the wages of sin, could we impudently call Him the Father? How could we praise the Lord? How could we praise the name of God and give thanks to His gift of salvation and glorify Him? All these are due to the gift of God's grace.

We, as the saints, can praise the Lord and give thanks to him at this time because our sins have already been blotted out. Through Christ's sacrifice and the fact that the Lord took away all our sins, including the sins as small as a whit, we can praise the Lord.

Though we have been forgiven for our sins, we cannot become perfect by our deeds while living on this earth. All of us are weak, but we, as the righteous, praise the Lord who paid the wages of all the sins of sinners with His grace. Are you in the darkness? No matter what kinds of darkness may exist, if we acknowledge even the smallest bit of sin before God, if we confess that we have sinned before God, and if we believe in the Lord who took away all these sins, the truth of the Lord will allow us to praise and give thanks to Him. We become the saints who cannot help praising Jesus Christ because of His grace and forgiveness of sins. Moreover, we become the worshipers to God after receiving the grace of the remission of sin in our hearts.

If we are made righteous without works, it is the gift of God

"What then shall we say that Abraham our father has found according to the flesh? For if Abraham was justified by works, he has something to boast about, but not before God. For what does the Scripture say? 'Abraham believed in God, and it was accounted to him for righteousness.' Now to him who works, the wages are not counted as grace but as debt. But to him who does not work but believes on Him who justifies the ungodly, his faith is accounted for righteousness" (Romans 4:1-5).

Human sin is expiated only after its wages are paid. Are you sure that your conscience is cleansed? Regardless of what kinds of sins they may be, our consciences can be cleansed only after the wages of sin are paid. We, sinners, had no other choice but to die, but the Lord died for our sins. Therefore, sinners were made to be righteous by being saved.

In Romans chapter 4, Paul said that sinners were saved by Jesus Christ, who took all the sins of the world onto Him at the Jordan River and was crucified to be judged for their sins, using Abraham, the ancestor of faith who believed in God's word, as an example. The Bible says that Abraham became righteous because he believed in God. He was not saved by his own deeds, but by the faith in God's word. Therefore, God accounted him to be righteous. Abraham obtained salvation by believing in God's words and became the father of all those who believe. He became righteous by believing in the covenant of God.

What is the salvation from sin and the grace of God that were bestowed on us sinners? Let's think about this to make the point clear. *"Now to him who works, the wages are not counted as grace but as debt" (Romans 4:4).* This verse talks about the salvation of God, which saved us from all sins. It talks about the remission of sins. *"Now to him who works, the wages are not counted as grace but as debt."* If a man receives wages for his work, will he regard his wages as grace or as a debt? Paul the Apostle explains salvation, using Abraham as an example. It is natural for a man who worked to receive the wages for his work in return. However, if we are made to be as righteous as the saints, even if we didn't lead perfect lives, it is through God's gift, not through our own efforts.

"Now to him who works, the wages are not counted as grace but as debt" (Romans 4:4). The salvation through the forgiveness of sins is due to the Lord's baptism and bloodshed of sacrifice. Salvation was made possible through grace and the gift of the remission of sins. Mankind cannot restrain from sinning, so they are forced to admit that they have sinned. They cannot wash away their sins, no matter what doctrines they may believe, or however hard they may pray for their sins.

The only way for sinners to wash away their sins is to believe in the salvation that says the Lord took the sins of the world onto Him by being baptized by John the Baptist at the Jordan River, and was crucified to receive the vicarious judgment for the sins. Sinners don't have the qualifications to pay for their own sins with any kind of sacrifice made on their own. All that sinners are able to do is to believe in the salvation through the forgiveness of sins. The only thing they can rely on is God's grace.

By receiving baptism at the Jordan River, Jesus took away all our sins in the most suitable way, and by sacrificing Himself on the Cross, sinners were saved from all their sins. This includes the small sins we commit due to our weaknesses under Satan's deceptions and the sins as big as a high mountain. Therefore, sinners received salvation by the faith in the baptism and the blood of Jesus Christ. Through God's free gift of salvation, we who were sinners are now righteous.

The remission of sin is given only by grace and gift

Paul the Apostle talks about how a sinner is saved from all his/her sins. *"Now to him who works, the wages are not accounted as grace but as debt."* He explains the grace of salvation by comparing it to the labors in this world. If a sinner, after having worked before God, says that he/she obtained salvation from his/her sins, it is not out of God's gift but out of his/her works instead. The remission of sins is given only by grace and as a gift. None of our deeds are included in the grace of God. Was the salvation from sin that we received God's gift to us, or not? Yes, it was. We had no other choice but to perish because of our sins. However, Jesus Christ, our Savior, took all our sins onto Him by getting baptized by John the Baptist at Jordan River.

We were saved from our sins by believing in the fact that Jesus Christ paid the wages of death and died for us. He sanctified us by taking away all our sins through His baptism and saved us from all our sins by bearing the sins to the crucifixion. All these are out of the grace of Jesus' salvation. Our being delivered was made possible through God's grace. It's a gift. It's free of charge. Sinners were saved by God's love toward sinners. Jesus took away all our sins through His baptism and saved sinners from all the sins in the world and from all the judgments of God by being crucified.

"But to him who does not work, but believes in Jesus Christ who justifies the ungodly, his faith is accounted for righteousness" (Romans 4:5). Before, we talked about the person who works. The phrase, *"But to him who does not work"* refers to those who don't perform any virtuous deeds for the purpose of becoming righteous. Paul continues with the rest of the verse by saying, *"but believes in Jesus Christ who justifies the ungodly, his faith is accounted for righteousness."*

He uses the ungodly as an example to explain God's righteousness. What does it mean to be ungodly? An 'ungodly' person is one who doesn't stand in awe of God and just leads a loose life until his/her last breath, which is the exact opposite of being godly. This word indicates one who sins before God until the day he/she dies. It is true that people are born full of sin. Furthermore, it was the true nature of humans to be destined to receive God's judgment due to their sins.

However, it is written, *"But to him who does not work, but believes in Jesus Christ who justifies the ungodly, his faith is accounted for righteousness."* Here, the phrase *"But to him who does not work"* means "although he is not godly." Are we godly before God? —No, we are not.—

The Lord says to us, the ungodly, "You are without sin and you are righteous." The Lord took away the wages of all our sins and paid for them. Do you believe that Jesus has already paid the wages of sins absolutely? To the believer, his/her faith is accounted for righteousness. "You are right. You really believe in it. You are my righteous people. You have no sin because I blotted them out when I was baptized by John the Baptist and by being judged for all your sins on the Cross!"

God took away all the ungodly sins of this world by Jesus' baptism, although all of mankind is ungodly. God sent His Only begotten Son and took away the sins by His baptism and He was crucified in place of the ungodly. God fulfilled both the laws that said that the wages of sin is death and the law of God's love at the same time. He saved all sinners from their sins.

God says, "Yes, you are sinless. My Son saved you. You have been saved," to those who believe that Jesus took away all the sins of this world at the Jordan River through His righteous act on behalf of sinners. Therefore, they are made righteous even if they haven't been godly. God says that they are His sinless people, although they are ungodly when He sees their faith in the salvation of the Lord. Blessed is the person to whom the Lord will not impute sin.

God asks us if we are godly. *"But to him who does not work, but believes in Him who justifies the ungodly, his faith is accounted for righteousness."* Do we do good deeds? We can't do good but are only apt to sin. Nevertheless God Himself saved us with the gift of salvation. We believe in the salvation of the Lord, namely, the baptism and blood of Jesus!

We must live by the faith in the salvation of the Lord

We come to praise the Lord and give thanks for His gift of

love and grace of salvation from sins, knowing how willingly He paid all the wages of the sins of us, the ungodly. We cannot thank Him enough for His paying the wages of our sins through His baptism and the Cross, when we admit we are ungodly before God. However, we can't give thanks for God's grace if we think we are godly.

To the person who believes in Jesus Christ, who justifies the ungodly, his/her faith is accounted for righteousness. Those who believe in the redemption and judgment of Jesus, which makes them righteous, receive the gifts of God. Nobody is godly before God because they make many mistakes while trying to live godly.

The fact that humans cannot help sinning proves their ungodliness. Therefore, I live by the faith in God's salvation, although I am ungodly. To live by faith does not mean to live as one pleases. There is a certain way to live by faith for one who has become righteous by faith.

Every single day, the gospel of the salvation of Jesus is needed by the born again saints. Why? Because their deeds are not godly on the earth and they cannot help but to sin all their lives. Everybody should hear the good news that says Jesus took away all the sins of the world through His baptism. The righteous must hear and recall the gospel every single day. Then, their spirits can live and be repeatedly strengthened like a spring. *"But to him who does not work, but believes in Jesus Christ who justifies the ungodly, his faith is accounted for righteousness."* For whom is this message? This message is designed for all the people in this world, including you and me.

The Bible tells us in detail how Abraham was made righteous. To the person who works, God' salvation isn't appreciated and he/she will reject it instead. Such a person doesn't give thanks for the gospel. First of all, what verse 4 describes is a person who works, that is, tries to do virtuous deeds, to enter the Kingdom of Heaven. This kind of a person never gives thanks for Jesus' sacrifice. Why not? Because he/she works and does many virtuous deeds while offering the prayers of repentance to be forgiven of his/ser daily sins, and thus he/she think his/her own exploits have worked somehow in receiving the forgiveness of hi/her sins, he/she is not thankful for His absolute grace, which is this gospel. Therefore, the person cannot truly receive the gift of God's salvation.

The Bible says, *"But to him who does not work, but believes in Jesus Christ who justifies the ungodly, his faith is accounted for righteousness (Romans 4:5)."* This means that the Lord perfectly saved those who were ungodly and whose sins could not be forgiven by their own deeds. It also shows us that God's grace is revealed to the righteous, who were saved by receiving the remission of sins.

But the person who works doesn't consider His grace as grace

Romans 4:5 is applicable to one who acknowledges God and believes in His words, just as Abraham did. We believe in the Lord who saved the ungodly. There are two kinds of people among Christians: those who still work to be forgiven for their sins and those who have been delivered absolutely from their sins. As it is written in verses 4 and 5, *"He who works"* and *"does not consider the wages as grace,"* rejects the grace of the remission of sins because he comes to God with works after believing in Jesus.

People cannot but remain sinners because they offer their deeds to God. The Doctrine of Justification is a Christian doctrine that states that a believer can and should be incrementally sanctified little by little until the day he/she dies, and thus it leads believers to reject the gift of the remission of sins and to fight against God. The Bible doesn't say that a person becomes righteous incrementally. Those who try to be sanctified incrementally by praying for the forgiveness of sins, by doing good, and by cleansing his/her dirtiness are the ones who work. These are the people who deserve to go to hell as Satan's servants. They cannot be accounted for righteousness because they reject the grace of the Lord.

None of us is godly. However, so many people are heading for and believing in the wrong direction at this moment. They believe that their actual sins are forgiven when they repent daily, knowing that Jesus washed away all their past sins. They do this because they think they are a bit godly. They show off their goodness and cleanliness before Jesus. In the end, they come short of the remission of sins, the gift of God.

Who is blessed?

The saints who are delivered from all their sins became righteous by having faith in Jesus. The answer to the question of what kind of person can become righteous is this: A person who knows his/her infirmities well and is not able to offer repentance prayers for his/her sins is apt to become righteous by faith among many others. Only those who aren't good at doing good deeds, making prayers, performing godliness, and who are poor in spirit will receive the gift of the remission of sins from Jesus. They will be made righteous. These people have not done good things before God.

The only thing they have done is to frankly admit their sins, saying, "I have sinned. I am a sinner who has no other choice but to go to hell when I die." Then Jesus Christ gives him/her the gift of complete salvation He had accomplished. Believing in the fact that the Lord was baptized by John the Baptist in the Jordan River to take away all their sins and was crucified, truly enables sinners to be saved from all the sins in their hearts. They were clothed with the blessing of becoming God's children. It is God's gift for sinners to be saved from all their sins before Him. I give thanks to the Lord, Jesus Christ, for having been delivered from being perished.

In verse 6, Paul the Apostle describes the man blessed by God *"apart from works."* He clarifies the following three parts concerning "to work." First, *"He who works,"* then *"He does not work"* and lastly *"without works."* The Bible says, *"Just as David also describes the blessedness of the man to whom God imputes righteousness apart from works, blessed are those whose lawless deeds are forgiven, and whose sins are covered; blessed is the man to whom the Lord shall not impute sin"* (Romans 4:6-8). "To have been imputed by the Lord" does not mean that God accounts a person as sinless, even though he/she is with sin, but He truly meant that the person actually has no sin.

God tells us about the blessedness of mankind. People who have been forgiven for all their sins are happy, aren't they? Nobody is happier than us. Nobody is happier than a person who has received the remission of sins. It means that whoever has sin, even as small as a whit, will be judged by God, and can never be happy at all. However, the righteous are happy because they have the remission of sins. God says, *"Blessed is the man to whom the Lord will not impute sin"* (Romans 4:8).

"Whose sins are covered" means that the Lord blotted out the sins of all mankind. David also said, *"Blessed are those whose iniquities are forgiven."* Blessed are those whose sins are forgiven, although they sin everyday in this world. The righteous, who have received the remission of sins, have been saved from their lifelong sins through Jesus Christ. The righteous are truly happy.

Blessed are those whose sins are covered

Secondly, what kind of person is happy? *"Blessed are those whose sins are covered."* We always sin, but what it means to get one's sins covered is that Jesus took away all our sins by His baptism and crucifixion. Then will God the Father judge us? Have all the sins of sinners been covered? We will not be judged because Jesus took away all our sins, shed His blood on the Cross and died for us because we are in Him.

Blessed are those whose sins are covered. Death, which is the wages of sin, doesn't fall on us because Jesus took away all our sins by the baptism. Hallelujah! We are happy. Do we have sin? No. Those who neither know Jesus Christ, who came by water and blood, nor know that all the sins of the world were passed onto Him when He received baptism in the Jordan River, will always have sin even if they believe in Jesus fervently.

However, those who know about the truth of salvation and believe in it possess no sin. Blessed are those whose sins are covered. Blessed are they who have passed over all their sins to Jesus Christ at the time He was baptized by John the Baptist. Who is really happy in this world? Blessed are they who have the Savior for themselves, in spite of their weaknesses. Blessed are those who believe in Jesus, the Savior, who took away all their sins, including the smallest of sins, and who was crucified to be judged in their place.

Blessed is the person to whom the Lord will not impute sin

Blessed are those who believe in the truth of salvation and have the good Shepherd within themselves. Thirdly, David said, *"Blessed is the man to whom the Lord will not impute sin" (Romans 4:8).*

We who possess the remission of sins are righteous, even though we are weak. Our flesh is still weak even if we are righteous by faith. Did the Lord take away all our sins through His baptism? Does the Lord regard us as the ones to be judged? No. The Lord doesn't admit that we should be judged, although we are insufficient and weak. Why doesn't the Lord impute sin to us? Because He already paid the wages of sin and was judged for us. The Lord neither remembers the sins of the person who is made righteous by faith nor accounts the person to be judged.

Blessed is the person who is made righteous by faith. Blessed is the person who is born again of water and the Spirit (John 3:5). We usually seek after worldly things and lose His blessing, forgetting the fact that God saved and blessed us. We will be against God when we lose His grace. We must bear the grace of God in our minds. The salvation of God exists within believers.

The Holy Spirit of God dwells within those whose sins have been blotted out. Only the righteous will not be judged by God. Blessed are those who are not judged by God in this world and in the Kingdom of Heaven. Why? Because they are accounted to be righteous by God, received His love and became His children.

We are blessed by faith

Blessed are those who became the righteous by faith. Are the born again the blessed before God? —Yes.— Paul the Apostle said, *"Rejoice always, pray without ceasing, in everything give thanks" (1 Thessalonians 5:16-18)* because he was blessed by faith as a descendant of Abraham, the father of faith. We are the descendants of Abraham too. Abraham was saved by having faith in God's word, just as we do. God spoke to Abraham, *"Do not be afraid, Abram. I am your shield, your exceedingly great reward" (Genesis 15:1).*

But Abram said, "Lord GOD, what will You give me, seeing I go childless, and the heir of my house is Eliezer of Damascus?" Then Abram said, "Look, You have given me no offspring; indeed one born in my house is my heir!" And the word of the LORD came to him, saying, "This one shall not be your heir, but one who will come from your own body shall be your heir." Then He brought him outside and said, "Look now toward heaven, and count the stars if you are able to number them." And He said to him, "So shall your descendants be." "I believe it, Lord." Thus, Abraham believed in the words of God.

Can you believe in God's word like Abraham in this world? Doesn't it seem impossible for humans to do so? Abraham's wife was too old to bring forth a son. However, Abraham believed in God's word at a time where there was little hope. Therefore, Abraham was accounted to be righteous before God.

Jesus blotted out all our sins. Jesus took all our sins onto

Him by His baptism and was judged for us with His blood. We became the descendants of Abraham by receiving the remission of sins and God's salvation because we were so ungodly, while others did not believe. The Bible says, *"The foolishness of God is wiser than men, and the weakness of God is stronger than men" (1 Corinthians 1:25).* God turns those who believe in the gospel of God into His children through their faiths in the baptism of Jesus (the water) and His Cross (the blood). This may seem to be foolish to mankind, but the salvation of God and His wisdom of the remission of sins are as such. It may also seem foolish from a human point of view, but God saved sinners from all their sins with His free gift.

Jesus called one out of ten thousand people from the four corners of the world and blessed them and saved them and received praise through them. Were we blessed or not? —Yes, we were.— Don't forget it was not because of your works. We are blessed because we believed in the blessings God gave us, and because He gave us faith through His words. God made us His children by coming by water, blood and the Spirit (1 John 5:4-8), and because He gave us His love.

We are blessed even if we live with many weaknesses on the earth. I really give thanks to the Lord. He gave us those precious blessings, didn't impute sin, forgave all our iniquities and covered us, even when we, the ungodly, were not able to work for our sanctification. We have been blessed with salvation only through faith. ✉

CHAPTER

5

Introduction to Romans Chapter 5

The Doctrine of Justification is not the truth

Paul proclaims by faith in this chapter that only those who believe in God's righteousness "have peace with God." The reason for this is because Father God made Christ get baptized for us and even made Him shed blood on the Cross.

However, we often witness that most Christians today are unable to have peace with God because they do not have the slightest bit of knowledge on God's righteousness. This is the reality of those who believe in today's Christianity. Therefore, the Doctrine of Justification is not right before God.

Obtaining God's righteousness by having faith in it is more proper than to believe in the Doctrine of Justification. Father God did not say that He would call the believers in Jesus His people even though they possessed sin in their hearts. God does not accept sinners as His children. God is not such a Being. He is the Savior who never regards a person possessing sin in his/her heart as one of His people. The God we believe in is Almighty. Wouldn't the omnipotent and omniscient God know about anyone's false faith correctly? We should then know and believe that He does not call a Christian-sinner, who has a false faith, as one of His people.

Everyone should be truthful before God. The Doctrine of Justification, which people falsely know and believe in, is something that ridicules God. Therefore, we should believe in Jesus as our Savior after correctly understanding the truth about God's righteousness. Father God doesn't say it's all right for one to possess sin, regardless of the fact whether one believes in Jesus or not. He is a Being who definitely judges a sinner for his/her sin.

Therefore, in order for you to get your problems of sin solved, you need to know and believe in God's righteousness. God will see our faiths in Jesus' baptism and blood on the Cross and absolve our sins. Because we believe in God's righteousness, God calls us His people, embraces us and even blesses us. Father God acknowledges that our faiths in His righteousness are right.

God is not an earthly judge

The faith believing in God's righteousness is based on the faith of Abraham, who purely believed in God's words. Most Christians misunderstand about the Doctrine of Justification, and thus we need to have clear understanding of it at this point. You surely know that there is no such thing as a perfectly correct or right judgment made in any court in this world. You need to keep in mind that a judge of this world can always make mistakes in his/her decisions.

The reason for this is because all human judges are insufficient and even ignorant of God's righteousness, which is the absolute criterion of good and evil. Most Christians are apt to misunderstand God's righteousness that judges us "righteous by our faiths" (Romans chapter 5), because they think His judgment uses the same logic as a sentence passed onto a sinner by a judge.

The Doctrine of Justification is a doctrine of misjudgment. It is because this doctrine was created based on human thought.

People are good at making misjudgments because they are not almighty. Therefore, they falsely believe in God, who has actually made them righteous, with their thoughts based on the Doctrine of Justification. This leads them to believe that God says, "I regard you as sinless because you somehow believe in me."

However, God can never do something like this. People often believe that even though they possess sin, God still acknowledges them as His people because they somehow believe in Jesus. This is something based on their own thoughts and nothing more than a false faith, which is the result of having been deceived by a demon.

Therefore, they should rebuild their houses of faith on their faiths in God's righteousness. How could the holy and Almighty God judge one who possesses sin in his/her heart as sinless? Does God decide that those who possess sin in their hearts are sinless? Thinking and believing that something like this could be true is nothing more than one's own human thought. God is the God of truth and never misjudges. How could God, who is the Truth itself, make errors in His judgments just as humans do? This can never happen. God is the righteous God who judges those who believe in His righteousness as sinless, based on His righteousness.

Do you know about God's righteousness? Do you know and believe in His righteousness? This righteousness can fully be found in the words of the gospel of the water and the Spirit. In order to comprehend God's righteousness talked about in Romans, you should understand and believe in the gospel of water and the Spirit. You can never comprehend God's righteousness without doing so. Everyone should realize this truth. One who understands God's righteousness is one who correctly understands the truth that made him/her righteous.

We should all believe in God's righteousness that is revealed in the Bible, otherwise, your faiths will go astray based on false human judgments and thought. If you have had this kind of false faith so far, you should believe according to the words of God's righteousness from now on.

Most Christians have learned the Doctrine of Justification from theology and have thought it to be true until now. However, you should now return to the true faith by believing in God's righteousness. God's righteousness is clearly revealed through the faith in the baptism Jesus received from John and His blood on the Cross.

It is said that tribulation produces perseverance

It is written in Romans 5:3-4 that, *"And not only that, but we also glory in tribulations, knowing that tribulation produces perseverance; and perseverance, character; and character, hope."* All born-again Christians have the hope that God will surely save them from all kinds of tribulations. This hope produces perseverance and perseverance produces character. Therefore, the righteous, who believe in God's righteousness, rejoice even in times of tribulations.

Paul said that the faith in God's righteousness hopes for God's Kingdom and it does not disappoint the hope. What kind of hope does the righteous have? They have the hope by which they can enter and live in the Kingdom of God. Where does this kind of faith come from? It comes from believing in the righteousness of Jesus Christ through Father God's love.

The Lord is saying that we used to be ungodly

"For when we were still without strength, in due time Christ died for the ungodly" (Romans 5:6).

From the time before we were conceived, or when we were in our mother's wombs, or when we were born but did not know the Lord, we had no other choice than to commit sins throughout our lives till death and eventually end up in hell.

When our ancestors Adam and Eve had sinned, God promised to send us the Savior saying, *"He shall bruise your head, and you (the serpent) shall bruise His heel" (Genesis 3:15).* According to this promise, Jesus Christ came to this world, even before we sinned, and saved us from all our sins. He got baptized by John to take over the sins of the world, and blotted them out by shedding His blood on the Cross. He eliminated our sins by His resurrection from death. The Lord took over the sins of mankind and the sins of the ungodly, such as you and I, through His baptism and saved believers from all their sins by dying on the Cross.

Are we godly? A godly person is one who stands in awe of God and keeps him/herself away from sin. It was the perfect righteousness of God that allowed Jesus to be baptized for you and I, the ungodly, and was crucified and then resurrected. It was also God's love that saved us when we were still without strength.

Just like the Israelites' one-year's-worth of sins that were passed on to the sin offering by the imposition of the High Priest's hands in the Old Testament (Leviticus 16:20-21), Jesus Christ not only took over all the sins of mankind at once by getting baptized by John the Baptist, but He also went to the Cross to be crucified because He was carrying the sins of the world in the New Testament. God's righteousness refers to the fact that Jesus Christ washed away all the sins of sinners by getting baptized and shedding His blood.

Are you and I godly? Didn't the Lord come to save us sinners because we are ungodly? God knows very well that we are all ungodly. We are ungodly because we cannot help but to commit sins from the day we are born until we die. However, by getting baptized by John and shedding His blood on the Cross, Christ demonstrated His love for us when we were still sinners.

Jesus has changed our destiny

We should think about what kind of fate we as humans face, starting from the day of birth. What were our fates from the day we were born? We were destined to go to hell. Then how was it possible for you and I to be saved from this fate of going to hell? Our fates changed because we believed in God's righteousness. The truth that changed our fates is the gospel of the water and the Spirit. Our fates became blessed because we believed in Jesus Christ, who had completed God's righteousness.

You may know the famous verses of the following hymn, "♪Amazing grace! How sweet the sound, ♫That saved a wretch like me! ♫I once was lost, but now am found, ♫Was blind, but now I see.♪" God's mercy and righteousness is the truth that testifies our salvation. Anyone can get all the sin in his/her heart forgiven and enjoy heavenly peace when he/she knows and believes in God's righteousness. Now everyone in this world who still possesses sin in their hearts, even though they believe in Jesus should return to the gospel of the water and the Spirit in order to know God's righteousness.

In fact, Christians who do not know the gospel of the water and the Spirit are also unaware that their sins have been passed over to Jesus. Therefore, they are unable to obtain God's righteousness. Though they believe that Jesus came to this world and saved them from their sins by dying on the Cross, they are not sure of their salvation. Thus, they just feel relieved by vaguely conjecturing that God has probably chosen them before the creation of the world. In other words, they believe in Christianity only as if it were merely another religion in the world.

Verse 11 states, *"And not only that, but we also rejoice in God through our Lord Jesus Christ, through whom we have now received the reconciliation."* Who reconciled us, the sinners, with God? Jesus Christ reconciled us with the Father. How? By coming to this world Himself, getting baptized by John the Baptist at the age of 30, being crucified, then resurrecting from death, thereby completing the work that has fulfilled all of God's righteousness. Jesus became our Savior, for believers in God's righteousness, by coming to this world as the heavenly High Priest and taking over the sins of mankind. By getting baptized by John the Baptist, the earthly High Priest, shedding blood on the Cross and then resurrecting from death, Christ became our Savior.

Since Jesus Christ has already eliminated all of our sins, we were able to obtain God's righteousness through our faiths. Anyone who believes that Jesus has absolutely saved us from all our sins will rejoice in God. Anyone with even the slightest bit of sin in his/her heart is not a child of God.

You brethren probably already know that people of this world think the Doctrine of Justification and the Doctrine of Sanctification are true. Is it right if God rules that we are sinless if we only say that we believe in Jesus, even though we have sins in our hearts? Or is it even more correct to be referred to as God's people because we just identify ourselves as Christians?

We say, "Our Father, Who art in heaven, Hallowed be thy name," in the Lord's Prayer. This phrase means that those who possess sins in their hearts cannot possibly call God 'Our Father.' Should we still believe in the Doctrine of Justification? Can a person who is currently a sinner call the Lord his/her Savior? He/she may call to the Lord for a couple of years, but will eventually leave the Lord because he/she conscientiously feels ashamed to be a Christian. Therefore, you should know that the Doctrine of Justification will separate you from God's righteousness.

The Doctrine of Sanctification is also wrong. This doctrine says that we can gradually go through changes until we become perfectly holy at the last moment before we die and thus, we can meet God as a holy person. Do you think you can gradually become holy for yourself enough to meet God without your sins? No way. The truth tells us that one can only enter God's Kingdom by knowing and believing in God's righteousness.

Even though through one man sin entered the world!

Let's now read verse 12. *"Therefore, just as through one man sin entered the world, and death through sin, and thus death spread to all men, because all sinned."* Through whom did sin enter the hearts of all people and through how many people did sin enter the world? The Scripture says, *"Through one man sin entered the world."*

In other words, it is said that sin came to exist because of one man, Adam, and we are all his descendents. Then through whom did the sins of the world disappear? It can be said that it happened in the same way sin first entered the world.

The sins of mankind came to exist because a man did not believe in the law God had established. Even now, one who does not believe in God's words will remain sinful and end up in hell.

Therefore, we should know the following. We are not sinners due to our own sins, but due to our ancestors who possessed sin. You should know that the reason people sin is because they are weak and have sin in their hearts. The sin people commit are called iniquities. The reason they sin is because they are born into this world possessing sin. Because everyone is deficient and born into this world bearing sin, he/she cannot help but to commit sins.

We originally became sinners, the seeds of sin, because we inherited all the sins from our ancestors. However, you should know that anyone can become a holy and righteous being at once by believing in God's righteousness.

When did sin first start to exist in man?

"For until the law sin was in the world, but sin is not imputed when there is no law" (Romans 5:13). Was there sin before we came to know the law of God? Before we knew the God's law, we didn't understand what was condemned as a sinful act before God. God told us, "You shall have no other gods before Me, you shall not make for yourself a carved image—any likeness of anything that is in heaven above, or that is in the earth beneath, or that is in the water under the earth;

you shall not bow down to them nor serve them, you shall not take the name of the Lord your God in vain, and remember the Sabbath day, to keep it holy." Before recognizing such laws of God and the 613 clauses of commandments that tell us what we 'shall and shall not do,' we really didn't know of our sins.

Therefore, *"For until the law sin was in the world, but sin is not imputed when there is no law."* Because we Gentiles did not have the law and thus did not know it, we committed sins without being aware of it. Most Koreans have been praying to a rock, thinking it is Buddha, yet they still don't realize that they are serving a carved image. They didn't know that bowing to other gods was a sin before God.

However, before the law came about, sin already existed in the world. God gave us the law about 2,500 years after He created Adam. Even though God gave the law to the Israelites through Moses approximately 1,450 B.C., sin had already entered the world through one man, Adam, and came to exist in the hearts of all people from the beginning, even before the law came.

Jesus is the Savior of His people

Did Jesus Christ eliminate all the sins of the world by Himself alone? Yes. Here in verse 14, it is said that death reigned over those who had not sinned or committed offenses according to the likeness of Adam's transgression. Therefore, Adam was a type of Him who was to come. Mankind became sinners through one man. Likewise, Jesus Christ came to this world and saved us from all our sins through the gospel of the water and the Spirit.

Jesus became the Savior who saved His people from their

sins. There is only one Savior who saved us, descendents of Adam, from sin. *"Nor is there salvation in any other, for there is no other name under heaven given among men by which we must be saved" (Acts 4:12).* His name is Jesus Christ, our eternal Savior.

We must understand that we automatically became sinners through one man, Adam. Do you know that Jesus Christ is the Savior who eliminated the sins of the world at once? Do you believe that Jesus Christ is the Savior who blotted out all the sins of the world by His baptism and bloodshed on the Cross all at once? Do you believe that Jesus became the true Savior of all humanity by eliminating the sins of this world, just as Adam became the source all sins by committing one transgression?

Jesus came to this world to save all those who had become sinners due to the one man, Adam, and took over all the sins of mankind by getting baptized by John, receiving judgment for the sins on the Cross by shedding His blood, and fulfilling all of God's righteousness, which eliminated all our sins. He thereby became our perfect Savior.

We did not obtain salvation by believing in the Doctrine of Justification or the Doctrine of Sanctification after believing in Jesus. Jesus gave us eternal salvation at once. Jesus said that only those who have been born again of the water and the Spirit could enter and see God's Kingdom.

What is the fixed idea that exists in the bottom of the human conscience? It is the principle of causality. They think that deep down in their thoughts, their efforts and endeavors will work toward salvation somehow. However, everyone receives true salvation from sin only by having faith all at once when he/she believes in the gospel of the water and the Spirit. Moreover, Jesus came to this world and was crucified to save us from sin. He became the Savior of all those who believe in the true gospel.

Free yourself from the unreasonable thought that one can reach sanctification and eventually become righteous through prayers of repentance. In the Bible, one Man, Jesus Christ, came to this world, got baptized to take over all our sins and fulfilled all of our salvation through His atonement of sins on the Cross.

Jesus gave us the eternal remission of sin that was not like our offenses

Verse 15 states, *"But the free gift is not like the offense. For if by the one man's offense many died, much more the grace of God and the gift by the grace of the one Man, Jesus Christ, abounded too many."*

Have the sins of you and I been passed onto Jesus when He was baptized? They have. Jesus went to the Cross carrying the sins of the world and received judgment for those sins in our place.

God's salvation is a free gift and it is said to be different from the offense.

Jesus has saved us, who cannot help but to commit sins throughout our whole lives, through His baptism and blood on the Cross during His 33 years of life. Even after we obtain salvation by believing in the remission of sin that was fulfilled at once, our flesh may continue to sin because it is insufficient and fragile. Although our flesh still continues to sin, we can still obtain the eternal remission of sin if we believe in the fact that Jesus took over all our sins at once by getting baptized and that He has fulfilled all of God's righteousness by shedding His blood.

The gift of salvation of the remission of sin is not like Adam's offense. God's gift of the remission of sin is not granted daily, like the daily sins people commit. The truth of the remission of sin says that the Lord has already saved us from all our sins at once by getting baptized and shedding His blood about 2000 years ago.

God's gift of salvation that saved us from all our sins is the righteousness that was fulfilled at once by Jesus' baptism and blood on the Cross. The eternal remission of sins is not like the daily pardoning through prayers of repentance, which most Christians seek nowadays. This truth says that the Lord has foreseen that we would sin everyday and has therefore taken over all the sins of this world at once when He got baptized. Therefore, Father God fulfilled all of His righteousness by the Son's baptism and crucifixion. All of God's righteousness has been completed because Jesus got baptized, shed blood on the Cross and was resurrected.

Nowadays most Christians believe that their sins get remitted when they offer prayers of repentance. Is this really true? Certainly not. A person who thinks that he/she can get his/her sins atoned after murdering someone by offering prayers of repentance is wrong. This way of thinking is nothing more than human thought. In order to eliminate the sins on God's side, one always needs to pay the wages of the sin. In order to do so, God made His Son Jesus get baptized by John and He blotted out all the sins by shedding blood on the Cross. The sins of humanity can be washed away and eliminated by believing in Jesus' baptism and blood on the Cross; not by offering prayers of repentance.

Therefore, the Bible says, *"For if by the one man's offense many died, much more the grace of God and the gift by*

the grace of the one Man, Jesus Christ, abounded to many."
God's gift of salvation overflows. Just as water overflows
when the tap is left running all night, no matter what sins we
have committed, His salvation overflows enough to save us
from all our sins.

Jesus has taken over all the sins of the world by getting
baptized. Also, because God's salvation is much greater than
the iniquities we have committed, His salvation is in abundance
even after we have been saved. Is this clear?

Through the one Man, Jesus Christ

Verses 16 and 17 state, *"And the gift is not like that which
came through the one who sinned. For the judgment which
came from one offense resulted in condemnation, but the free
gift which came from many offenses resulted in justification.
For if by the one man's offense death reigned through the one,
much more those who receive abundance of grace and of the
gift of righteousness will reign in life through the One, Jesus
Christ."*

Death has reigned over all of humanity through one man's
offense. This indicates that a sin of one man, Adam, caused all
to be sinners and due to that sin, everyone needs to face God's
curse. Anyone who has sinned had to die and go to hell. In a
similar sense, God's righteousness reigns in life due to the One,
Jesus Christ. Those who have received the overflowing gift of
grace and righteousness are those who have been granted the
gift of salvation for their faiths in the gospel of the water and
the Spirit. They receive a much greater grace from God, and
will reign in life.

Verse 18 states, *"Therefore, as through one man's offense*

judgment came to all men, resulting in condemnation, even so through one Man's righteous act the free gift came to all men, resulting in justification of life."

Here, we need to ask a question and answer it: "Is it true to think that by one person's sin, we have all become sinners?" Have you become sinners from your own sins, or on account of your ancestor Adam's offense against God? If we all have become sinners due to Adam's offense, then those who believe in the righteous act Jesus Christ performed to save us from our sins, become righteous. If one believes in God's righteousness, does his/her sin truly get eliminated? —Yes.— He/she becomes sinless.

"Through Man's righteous act the free gift came to all men, resulting in justification of life." Receiving the free gift of God's righteousness does not mean that one has to offer prayers of repentance every day to reach sanctification, after somehow being saved by believing in Jesus. Never! Neither does it mean a so-called Christian doctrine of 'acquiring justification by faith' when Paul the Apostle talked about 'having been justified by faith.'

Most Christians have sin in their hearts because they only believe in Jesus' blood on the Cross. Therefore, they accept and support the Doctrine of Justification in order to hide the sins in their hearts, while comforting themselves, "Although there are sins in our hearts, He considers us to be sinless." However, this doctrine is preposterous and shall be cursed.

Verse 19 states, *"For as by one man's disobedience many were made sinners, so also by one Man's obedience many will be made righteous."*

Here appears one who disobeyed and another who obeyed. One was Adam, and the other One was mankind's Savior,

Jesus Christ. Adam's disobedience made all of mankind sinners, and therefore Jesus obeyed His Father's will to reconcile people with God by receiving baptism from John, dying on the Cross for the sins of the world, and resurrecting to save us from our sins. God the Father made all the believers in Jesus absolutely righteous through His righteousness.

Verse 20 states, *"Moreover the law entered that the offense might abound. But where sin abounded, grace abounded much more."*

It is said that the law entered to add to our iniquities. As a descendant of Adam, people are originally born with sin, yet they haven't known of sin even while sinning. Without the law, one does not realize a sin to be a sin at all, and only through God's law one came to see his/her sins. However, when we came to know the law, we started realizing our sins more and more. Even though people were originally full of sins, they didn't know about their sinfulness until they came to gradually realize their sinful deeds after receiving the law. Therefore the Bible states, *"The law entered that the offense might abound."*

"But where sin abounded, grace abounded much more." This means that through God's law, one realizes his/her sins and becomes His child by believing in His righteousness. Mankind can realize God's grace through the true gospel that contains God's righteousness only when they become aware of their shortcomings and sinfulness through the law. Those who are well aware of their sins before the law acknowledge that they are meant to end up in hell, and therefore, with greater gratitude, believe in Jesus, who has saved them through His baptism and death on the Cross. The more we realize our sinfulness through the law, the more grateful we become for

the establishment of such a great salvation by God's righteousness.

Verse 21 states, *"So that as sin reigned in death, even so grace might reign through righteousness to eternal life through Jesus Christ our Lord."*

It is said in the Bible that sin reigned in death. However, God's grace that consists of the water and blood of Jesus is of His righteousness. Because His righteousness has completely saved us from all our sins, we have become God's children.

The Doctrine of Sanctification and the Doctrine of Justification are nonsensical hypotheses that were made of human logic and created by those who ignore God's words. It is not too much to say that such doctrines are no more than the sophistries of philosopher-theologians, which can never be unraveled. God's truths are clear and solid.

We are saved from the sins of the world by believing in the fact that Jesus, who is God in the likeness of human flesh, has saved us from all our sins. Those who have faith in Him are saved. Do you believe in this? —Yes.—

If you believe in God's righteousness, you are saved. You are definitely delivered and saved from all your sins. If you insist that endlessly offering prayers of repentance and living a flawless life to reach sanctification can save you, then you are stubbornly persisting that you can be saved without Jesus. Jesus is the only gateway towards salvation, no matter what deceptions the Doctrine of Sanctification teaches about being able to be saved by one's own deeds and efforts, regardless of the truth.

Being unable to carry out even 0.1% of the law is the same as being unable to carry out 100%. God tells us that we are unable to obey even 0.1% of His laws. Those who think they are carrying out approximately 5% of the law and plan to raise it to 10% in the course of time are completely ignorant of their own abilities, and are standing against God's righteousness. Do not try to understand God's righteousness with your own conception and logic. His righteousness has saved us from our sins and awaits us to believe in it so that we can become His children.

God is almighty and merciful, so He has saved us with His righteousness at once. We give thanks to God for Jesus' baptism and blood on the Cross, which absolutely saved us from all our sins. ✉

Through One Man

< Romans 5:14 >
"Nevertheless death reigned from Adam to Moses, even over those who had not sinned according to the likeness of the transgression of Adam, who is a type of Him who was to come."

Sinners must have the knowledge of sin first of all

Today, I want to speak about the origin of sin. Do not think to yourself, "You speak of the same things everyday. Tell me about other things." I want you to listen carefully. The gospel is the most precious thing. If a saint whose sins are blotted out does not repeatedly hear the gospel to remind him/her of it everyday, he/she will die. How can he/she live without hearing the gospel of the water and the Spirit? The only way he/she can live is by hearing the gospel. Let's open the Bible and share the real meanings in it.

I thought, "What is most needed by sinners whose sins are not forgiven yet?" Then I came to know they needed the right knowledge of sin according to the word of God because they can only receive the forgiveness of sins when they know about sin. I believe that sinners need the knowledge of sin the most.

A human being sins so many times from the time he/she is born regardless of whether or not he/she wants to. He/she does not deeply think about the sin that dwells within him/her even though he/she is a sinner before God because he/she sins too many times as he/she grows up. To sin is as natural as an apple tree growing up, flowering and bearing apples with time. However, we must know that the wages of sin is death according to the law of God.

If one thinks and truly knows about the result of sin, he/she can be delivered from sin and God's judgment, and receive all His spiritual blessings. So what is most needed by a sinner is to know about the sin and the result of it, and to learn the truth of the remission of sins, which God gave.

How did sin enter the world?

Why does a human being sin? Why do I sin? The Bible talks about this in Romans 5:12 saying, *"Therefore, just as through one man sin entered the world, and death through sin, and thus death spread to all men, because all sinned."* What entered the world through sin? Death. People tend to think that death merely means that of the flesh. However, death here implicates the meaning of being spiritually separated from God. It also implies hell and God's judgment, along with the death of the flesh. Romans 5:12 shows us how human beings became sinners.

The Bible says, *"Therefore, just as through one man sin entered the world, and death through sin, and thus death spread to all men, because all sinned."* The word of God is the truth. Through one man sin entered the world, and death through sin.

We were born as the descendants of Adam. Then do we or don't we have sin as the descendants of Adam? —Yes, we have sin.— Are we born sinful? —Yes, because we are the descendants of Adam, who is our ancestor.—

Adam begot all humankind, however, Adam and Eve had

Free book request www.nlmission.com

sinned against God's word under Satan's deception when they were in the Garden of Eden. God told them not to eat the fruit from the tree of the knowledge of good and evil but rather, to have eternal life by eating fruit from the tree of life.

But they were deceived by Satan and forsook God's word and ate from the tree of the knowledge of good and evil. Adam and Eve sinned by forsaking God's word, which is the word of eternal life. After Adam and Eve sinned, Adam came to sleep with Eve, and all human beings came to born through Adam and Eve. We are their descendants. We did not only inherit their outward appearances, but also their sinful nature.

Therefore, the Bible says that a human being is a seed of sin. All the people of the world have inherited sin from Adam and Eve. The Bible says, *"Therefore, just as through one man sin entered the world, and death through sin, and thus death spread to all men, because all sinned."* So all human beings are born sinful.

However, people do not know they are born sinners. They do not have the knowledge of sin even though they were born sinful. A tree begins to bud by its seed and brings forth fruit, but people think it is strange for them to sin because they do not know that they are born as seeds of sin. It is the same principle for an apple tree to think, 'It is strange. Why do I have to bear apples?'

Thus, it is natural for a human being to sin. The thought that a human being can avoid sinning is completely false. It is natural for a human being who inherited sin to commit sins throughout his/her life and bear the fruits of sin, but he/she does not deeply think about being a sinner. What does God say? *"Therefore, just as through one man sin entered the world, and death through sin, and thus death spread to all men, because all sinned."*

We sin throughout our lives because we were born as sinners. Therefore, we deserve to be judged by God. You may think, 'Isn't it unjust for God to judge us when we have no choice but to have sin?' However, after receiving the remission of sins, you will come to know that God planned to do so in order to make us His children.

We all are the descendants of one man, Adam

Then, how come human beings, who are descendants of one man, Adam, have different skin colors? Are their seeds different? Why are there white, yellow, and black people? Some people think that when God created man from the dust on the ground and burnt him, God made a white man by taking him out too early from the kiln, a yellow man by taking him out right on time and a black man by taking him out too late.

You may also wonder why there are black, white, and yellow races, though all human beings were given sin through one man. The Bible clearly states that God made Adam in the beginning, when He created the heavens and the earth. "Adam" means man. God created a man. Why are there different races in the world if God created one man, Adam, and all the peoples of the world were born through him? We may ask why, so here is the answer.

Scientists say that a pigment in the skin called melanin comes out of the skin to protect it from sunburn. When the earth moves around the sun, those who live in areas with a lot of sunlight become black, those who live in areas with minimal sunlight become white, and those who live in areas that have adequate sunlight become yellow. However, our ancestor is still one man, Adam.

Scientists announced that melanin automatically comes out of the skin and protects it from sunburn. So, I came to understand this from that time. I knew that human beings were descendants of Adam, but I did not know about melanin. We have not only inherited the flesh, but also sin because we are the descendants of one man, Adam.

Do you know sin? Let us investigate whether human beings are sinners or not from when they are born into this world. *"Even so, every good tree bears good fruit, but a bad tree bears bad fruit. A good tree cannot bear bad fruit, nor can a bad tree bear good fruit" (Matthew 7:17-18).* God says that false prophets bear only false fruit and can never bear good fruit. We are evil trees originally because we were born sinful, so we cannot help bearing evil fruit because we were born as bad trees.

We have inherited sin through one man. We are bad trees if compared to trees. A human being, who was born a sinner, cannot but commit sins even if he/she wants to lead a good life and tries not to sin, just as a bad tree cannot bear good fruit. Do you understand? Human beings really want to live gentle, meek, and virtuous lives. However, a person who does not have the remission of sin and was born a sinner cannot live a righteous life. He/she cannot be good, even with endless efforts. Some alcoholics try not to drink so heavily, but in the end, they suffer from alcoholism and their families desert them in hospitals.

One day, I watched a program titled, "I want to know it" on TV. A man was confined in a mental hospital for 13 years. When a reporter asked him about his family, he said that they haven't returned to bring him home even though he was a fully recovered alcoholic and his doctor assured of his recovery. He came to know from the reporter that his family prevented him from leaving the hospital by bribing his doctor. He was outraged. His family deserted him because they were so tired of him. The reporter said that the patients in the hospital could not help drinking regardless of their will and they drank heavily so many times that nobody could cope with them.

Why can't a man control his drinking? He knows it is not good for his health and tries to quit; yet he repeatedly drinks. The reason for this is because he is an alcoholic already, but the original cause for this is that his mind is always empty. He drinks because he feels emptiness in his heart. One always feels pain and is unable to be good because he/she is with sin. So, he/she comes to be pessimistic and drinks again. He/she may think, 'I do not know why I'm doing this. I shouldn't be doing this.' And the more he/she feels betrayed by himself/herself, the more he/she drinks heavily in self-abandonment.

One cannot quit drinking however hard one tries not to drink. So, one feels disillusioned and drinks more and eventually, he/she is deserted in a confined hospital. A human being's speech and behavior are merely the expressions of his/her intrinsic nature. A human being is born a sinner and thus cannot help sinning, regardless of his/her will, throughout his/her life just as an apple tree buds, flowers and bears apples because it inherits an apple gene. People want to be good, but those who don't have the remission of sins cannot be good because they don't have the ability to be good. They think their sins aren't grave, so they hide themselves, and it only becomes serious when their sins are revealed.

It is natural, instinctive and proper for a sinner to sin because he/she is born as a mass of sin and inherits it by nature. It is absolutely natural for a human being to sin because he/she is born with the genetics of sin, just as it is natural for a red pepper plant to bear red peppers and for a jujube tree to bear jujubes. A human being cannot avoid sinning because he/she is born as a sinner. How can a human being live without sinning when he/she is born with sin?

Man is born with twelve kinds of evil thoughts

Jesus said in Mark chapter 7 that a human being is born with 12 kinds of evils, namely, adultery, fornication, murder, theft, covetousness, wickedness, deceit, lewdness, an evil eye, blasphemy, pride, and foolishness. We are born with a desire to steal. The thought of theft is included in the heredity of sin. Do you steal? Everyone steals. If he/she does not steal, it is because there are people watching him/her. However, when there is nobody around him/her and there is a tempting object around, the sin of theft comes out and makes him/her commit a sin by stealing it.

So human beings have made ethics and rules that should be kept. Human beings have made their own rules that indicate that it is not right to do harm to others. Rules are needed when many people live together in a society. We must live according to social norms. However, we steal when we are alone, escaping another's gaze.

There is none who does not steal. Everyone steals. A long time ago, I asked the congregation in a revival meeting to raise their hands if they have never sinned in their lives. A grandmother raised her hands and said, "I have never stolen anything." So I asked her if she had ever taken anything on her way home. Then she was flustered at the unexpected question and replied, saying, "I once saw a young pumpkin on my way home. I thought it would be delicious so I looked around and found that nobody was there. I pulled it up, hid it in my underskirt, put it in bean paste pot stew and ate it." She did not know that she committed a sin of theft.

However, God says it is a sin to take other's possessions without permission. God commanded, "You shall not steal" in the Law of Moses. Everybody has an experience of stealing something. A human being is good at murder and theft whenever he/she gets the chance. He/she steals livestock, such as rabbits and chickens from other people's homes. This is said to be theft. He/she even has no consciousness of sin even though he/she slays and steals. It is natural for him/her to do so because he/she inherited sin from the time of birth.

A human being inherited sin

A human being also inherited the sin of adultery from his/her parents. He/she is born with the lust of committing adultery. He/she is very certain to commit adultery when there aren't any people are around. People like dark places such as cafés and saloons. Those places are very popular to sinners. Why? Those are good places to show the heredity of sin.

Even gentlemen like those places. They are good fathers at home and men of high social standings, but they go to dark places that are full of sin. They go to the places in which they can show their sinful natures and bear sinful fruit. They meet together in those places and soon become like old friends after drinking a glass of alcohol. They become very close as soon as they meet because they have the same sinful attributes as each other. "Do you have this too? I have this." "So do I. You are my friend." "How old are you?" "Age does not matter." "Nice to meet you."

Men show their inherent sins each other whenever they

meet other sinners because they were born with the sinful attributes in the world. It is natural for them to sin. Why? Because they have sin in their hearts and were created to be like that by nature. It's abnormal for them not to sin. However, they refrain themselves from living sinful lives when they live in a society because each society has its own social norms. So, they play the hypocrite and put on other facades, acting according to the social norms their societies established. People live like this and regard those who don't as foolish and evil. A human being is inevitably born a sinner, as the Bible says, *"Through one man sin entered the world" (Romans 5:12)*.

It's right. A man may say, "I am not lewd. I am indifferent to a woman who wears a miniskirt." Is he really indifferent? He may pretend to be indifferent when there are so many people around him, but cannot refrain from committing the sin of lewdness when there is no one around him.

A bad tree bears evil fruit just as a good tree cannot bear evil fruit, and vice versa. A human being must know that he/she is a sinner. If one knows one's own sins, one can be saved from sin through Jesus. However he/she will be judged by God and go to hell if he/she pretends not to sin and tries to hide his/her sins without knowing his/her sins. Human beings are born as sinners. Therefore, they are corrupt trees that bear sinful fruits from the time of their births.

Therefore, those who develop their own sinful natures from their childhoods are good at sinning all their lives. Those who are late in developing their sinful natures begin to bear evil fruit even in the twilight years of their lives. There was a female minister in Taegu City, Korea. When she converted to Christianity in her youth, she pledged herself to remain single throughout her life in order to serve the Lord as a female minister. However, she broke her pledge and was married to a widower after turning 60 years old. She developed her sinful nature too late. She developed the heredity of adultery late.

Most people usually develop their sinful natures from their childhoods. These days, young people tend to develop their sinful natures from their childhoods. They feel a generation gap between them and the older generation. They are said to be the X-generation. By the way, we have learned from the word of God that we are born sinners and we are the beings who cannot but continue sinning all our lives. Do you admit it?

The law of leprosy

Second, God says, *"Therefore, just as through one man sin entered the world, and death through sin, and thus death spread to all men, because all sinned" (Romans 5:12).* Sin causes a human being to be judged by God. So a sinner must know himself/herself and have the remission of sins. How can he/she know himself/herself? How can all his/her sins be forgiven before God?

God taught Moses and Aaron how to examine the leprosy in Leviticus chapter 13. In the Old Testament Age, there were many lepers. I do not know much about leprosy, but I saw many lepers when I was young. One of my friends was also affected by leprosy.

God told Moses and Aaron to examine the leprosy and isolate lepers from the camp of Israel. God taught them how to examine each of the lepers. *"When a man has on the skin of his body a swelling, a scab, or a bright spot, and it becomes on the skin of his body like a leprous sore, then he shall be brought to*

Aaron the priest or to one of his sons the priests" (Leviticus 13:2). When the priest thought he had a skin disease after examining him, the priest isolated him for seven days. Then, the priest examined the skin again after seven days. When the sore did not spread out on the skin, the priest pronounced him as clean, saying, "You are clean. You may live in this camp."

If the swelling on the skin was white, and it turned the hair white, and there was a spot of raw flesh in the swelling, it was leprosy, then the priest would have pronounced him as unclean. Leviticus 13:9-11 states, *"When the leprous sore is on a person, then he shall be brought to the priest. And the priest shall examine him; and indeed if the swelling on the skin is white, and it has turned the hair white, and there is a spot of raw flesh in the swelling, it is an old leprosy on the skin of his body. The priest shall pronounce him unclean, and shall not isolate him, for he is unclean."* The priest isolated him from the camp of Israel.

It is the same in our country. There are isolated villages for lepers in Korea such as Flower Village or Sorok Island. A long time ago, on my way home riding in the car, my wife teased me to look around 'Flower Village' when she happened to see the sign for it on a superhighway. Then I thought, 'You do not know what 'The Flower Village' is.' I said to her, "Honey, do you mean you want to visit 'the town'?' She said, "Yes." However, she was astonished to hear that 'Flower Village' was a place where lepers lived and she never teased me to go to Flower Village again. Lepers are isolated from the society in isolated villages.

Here, what we have to pay attention to is that the priest pronounced someone was clean when the leprosy spread and covered all of his/her skin. Do you think this makes sense? The priest isolated the person when the leprosy spread just a little, and the priest told him to live in the camp of Israel when the plague of leprosy covered all his skin, from head to toe.

God told the priest how to classify leprosy. *"And if leprosy breaks out all over the skin, and the leprosy covers all the skin of the one who has the sore, from his head to his foot, wherever the priest looks" (Leviticus 13:12).* This was the way God told the priest to classify leprosy.

What the law of leprosy tells us....

It tells us this. People are born sinners with sinful attributes and sin all their lives, but some people only reveal a few of their sins. They sin with their hands once and with their feet the next and with their minds another time after long intervals, so they do not outwardly reveal their sins. Who would say it is serious when leprosy spreads on just one spot here and another small spot there? Nobody knows his/her syndrome of leprosy.

A human being is born a sinner because of the inheritance of sin. But he/she does not know that he/she is a sinner until he/she sins a countless number of times, though God pronounced him/her to be a sinner. He/she finally comes to know that he/she is a sinner in the world.

However, a person who thinks him/herself too virtuous, endures well and sins just a little does not know that he/she is a sinner. God told the priest to pronounce the person whose leprosy spread just a little to be unclean and to isolate him/her. Sinners are separated from God. Do you understand? God is holy. A person who thinks that he/she has sin as small as a whit cannot enter the Kingdom of Heaven.

Who can live in the Kingdom of Heaven? Only those whose sins spread over the entire body and realize that they are inevitable sinners can enter the Kingdom of Heaven. All their sins are forgiven by the faith in Jesus, and they will enter the Kingdom of Heaven to reign with God.

The Bible says that God pronounces the person whose sin spreads just a little to be unclean. God calls on the person who repeatedly sins, in spite of his/her will not to sin, and confesses that he/she is a whole sinner. Jesus said, *"I did not come to call the righteous, but sinners to repentance" (Matthew 9:13)*. God calls sinners and washes away all their sins. God has forgiven all their sins. God has already washed away their sins once and for all. Jesus took all their sins through His baptism, was judged on the Cross for them and made them righteous through His resurrection to take them to the Kingdom of Heaven.

We must know ourselves

We must know whether we are whole sinners or partial sinners. God pronounces a person to be clean when leprosy spreads all over the skin of the body. God made the law of leprosy like that. A person who knows that he/she is full of sin cannot but believe in the gospel of the water and the Spirit and receives the remission of sins when Jesus comes to him/her, saying that He washed away all his/her sins through His baptism and the Cross. However, a partial sinner who thinks that he/she is not full of sins casts ridicule on the gospel.

Would there be sin if Jesus had washed them all away? No. We can receive the remission of sins once and for all. Therefore, a sinner should know himself/herself. All his/her sins can be eliminated when he/she knows himself/herself.

People are apt to take only their small sins to God. "Lord, I have sinned. I did not want to, but he made me do it. Please forgive me just for this case, and I will not sin anymore." They take just small sins to God. Then God says, "You are unclean."

A human being has no righteousness in front of God. "To be or not to be absolutely depends on You, God. I am a sinner and am destined to go to hell. Please do as You please, but God, be merciful on me and please save me. Please save me if You are God. Then I will believe in You and I will live according to Your will." God saves a person who admits that he/she is full of sin.

A human inherited sin that has 12 kinds of evil thoughts

Let us take a look at Mark 7:20-23. *"What comes out of a man, that defiles a man. For from within, out of the heart of men, proceed evil thoughts, adulteries, fornications, murders, thefts, covetousness, wickedness, deceit, lewdness, an evil eye, blasphemy, pride, foolishness. All these evil things come from within and defile a man."* From within, out of the heart of a human being, proceed evil thoughts. A human being inherited sin natively. Do you understand? One has evil thoughts throughout life. There is no way for him/her to be delivered if all his/her sins are not forgiven once and for all.

A human being is born with these 12 kinds of evil thoughts: adulteries, fornications, murders, thefts, covetousness, wickedness, deceit, lasciviousness, an evil eye, blasphemy, pride and foolishness. So, he/she cannot but continue sinning all his/her life. A person whose sins are not forgiven lives sinfully even though he/she does not want to live like that. All things from a human being, such as thoughts and behaviors are sinful before God.

It is hypocritical for a sinner to be good. He/she only pretends to be virtuous. It is cheating God. A human being who is born sinful must know himself/herself to be saved. However if a person does not know himself/herself to be sinful, he/she feels distressed whenever he/she sins and says, "Ah, why do I do these things?" He/she is deceived by himself/herself.

A human being has evil thoughts. A man may think, 'Why do I do evil thoughts? No, I shouldn't have these thoughts. Why do I think unclean things? My teacher told me to do good.' He thinks like that because he does not know why he does certain things. He feels distressed because of his stealing and committing adulteries because he does not know that he inherited sin. Murders, adulteries, fornications, wickedness, deceit, lasciviousness, an evil eye, blasphemy, pride, and foolishness come out of him incessantly and in turn. So, he hates himself and comes to be ashamed without knowing why.

We are masses of sin and bear 12 kinds of evil fruits throughout our whole lives because we are born sinners, who inherited sin from our common ancestor Adam. Blessed are those who know that they are sinners.

A human being seeks Jesus, the Savior who saves him/her from all his/her sins, when he/she knows he/she is an unreliable sinner. It is the only way to being blessed by God. However, a human being does not seek the Savior if he/she does not know himself/herself. A person who knows himself/herself well comes to deny him/herself, forsakes his/her efforts, quits depending on human beings, seeks Jesus Christ who is God, the Savior and the Prophet, and is forgiven by the grace of Jesus Christ.

Sinners need to know themselves because those who know themselves can be blessed before God. One who does not know oneself cannot be blessed. Therefore, sinners have to know themselves as they are. Do you understand? Have you ever done evil things before you receiving the remission of sins? If you have, do you know why? You did evil things against your will because you inherited sin.

As through one man sin entered into the world, and death through sin

Death is inevitable to human beings because they have sin. A human being should seek Jesus and meet Him to be delivered from sin so that his/her sins can be blotted out. Then he/she can have everlasting life. Do you want to be delivered from all your sins?

"Nevertheless death reigned from Adam to Moses, even over those who had not sinned according to the likeness of the transgression of Adam, who is a type of Him who was to come. But the free gift is not like the offense. For if by the one man's offense many died, much more the grace of God and the gift by the grace of the one Man, Jesus Christ, abounded to many. And the gift is not like that which came through the one who sinned. For the judgment which came from one offense resulted in condemnation, but the free gift which came from many offenses resulted in justification. For if by the one man's offense death reigned through the one, much more those who receive abundance of grace and of the gift of righteousness will reign in life through the One, Jesus Christ.) Therefore, as through one man's offense judgment came to all men, resulting in condemnation, even so through one Man's righteous act the

free gift came to all men, resulting in justification of life. For as by one man's disobedience many were made sinners, so also by one Man's obedience many will be made righteous. Moreover the law entered that the offense might abound. But where sin abounded, grace abounded much more, so that as sin reigned in death, even so grace might reign through righteousness to eternal life through Jesus Christ our Lord" (Romans 5:14-21).

"Therefore, just as through one man sin entered the world, and death through sin, and thus death spread to all men, because all sinned" (Romans 5:12). Here, who is the one man? Adam. Eve too came out of the one man, Adam. So the Bible says, 'By one man.' God made one man in the beginning and through the one man sin entered the world. There were two persons in the Garden of Eden in sight of us, but, in fact, there was one man in sight of God. All human races have spread by one man, Adam.

The words, "Through one man sin entered the world," means that all the descendants of Adam became sinners because Adam had sinned. Death passed upon all humankind, because all have sinned. Death was sentenced to all human beings because of sin. God cannot forbear a person who is with sin.

God is omnipotent but cannot do two things: He can neither tell a lie nor let a person who has sin enter the Kingdom of Heaven. He executes His law as He promised. God certainly judges a person who has sin because God cannot tell a lie nor ignore the law He Himself established. All human beings have become sinners by one man, Adam, who fell and sinned in front of God. God's judgment and death spread to all of humankind because they were made sinners and born as the descendants of one man, Adam. Death came to spread to all of them as such.

When God created man in the beginning, there was no death. There were not only the tree of the knowledge of good and evil, but also the tree of life. God commanded Adam to eat the fruit from tree of life and live an eternal life. However, Adam was deceived by Satan and ate the fruit of the tree of the knowledge of good and evil that God commanded him not to eat and challenged God by forsaking His word, so death spread to all the people of the world due to sin. Death entered the world through one man, Adam.

Why did God give man the law?

If sin had not entered the world through Adam, death could not have spread to all human beings. Why does a human die? He/she dies because of sin. Sin entered the world through one man, and so death spread to all people. Until the law, sin was in the world, but human beings did not have the knowledge of sin until there was the law.

The law of God came down to all people through Moses. Even in the time of Adam and Noah, there was sin, but God had not established the law until the age of Moses. However, the Bible says that there was sin in the hearts of all the people who lived at that time.

Let us take a look at Romans 5:13. *"For until the law sin was in the world, but sin is not imputed when there is no law."* There was sin even when there was no law in the world. Therefore, all people had to die because they sinned before God. God gave them the law that consists of 613 kinds of commandments, which were to be kept before Him and among people, to give them the knowledge of sin. What did people come to know through the law of God? They felt that they were sinful in the sight of God and came to know they had sin. People realized that they couldn't keep the law of God.

So, they came to know their sins. The descendants of Adam and Eve knew they were sinners and that God only should forgive their sins. But they forgot with time that they came to become sinners and had inherited sin from their ancestor Adam. At that time, they came to know that they were sinners when they sinned, but they didn't know they were sinners when they didn't sin. But they were wrong. These days, many people still think that they become sinners if they sin, and that they do not become sinners if they do not sin. In fact, all people are sinners regardless of whether they sin or not because they have inherited sin from their birth.

Human beings are inevitable sinners before they are delivered from sins. So God gave them His law for the knowledge of sin. A person who knows God through His law and admits the law knows that he/she is a grave sinner. A human being becomes a serious sinner as soon as he/she fully knows the law of God.

Death spread to all men through one man

Romans 5:13-14 states, *"For until the law sin was in the world, but sin is not imputed when there is no law. Nevertheless death reigned from Adam to Moses, even over those who had not sinned according to the likeness of the transgression of Adam, who is a type of him who was to come."*

God says that all people became sinners by one man and death spread to them through one man. Death spread to all of them through sin. It was because of one man. Who is this one man? Adam. We commonly know it. But, many people do not know it. Even many Christians do not know it. They separate sin into the original sin and actual sins and they think that their actual sins can be forgiven daily through the prayers of repentance. They do not know that the reason they are judged and go to hell is because of Adam.

The descendants of Adam have no relation with God because of their sins no matter how hard they try to be good. God judges all of them because they are the descendants of Adam, however hard they may try to live good lives. They will be cast into the eternal fire of hell because of their common ancestor Adam.

Adam is a type of Him who was to come

It is written that Adam is a type of Him who was to come. All people became sinners and death came to them through one man. However all of humankind is made righteous through one Man, Jesus Christ just as all people became sinners by one man, Adam. This is the law of God.

People made religions because they did not know the law of God. They say that they should do good deeds to be saved while they believe in Jesus. How widely it spreads in the world and how often they tell lies! They teach people, saying, "You should be good as Christians." Our sins are never blotted out by works.

"Adam is a type of Him who was to come." Who is the Man who was to come for our salvation from sins? He is Jesus Christ. Jesus was sent to the world and lawfully took away the sins of the world by His baptism once and for all to make us righteous and was crucified to save us from judgment.

Sin entered the world because Satan deceived Adam, a creature. Sin entered the world through Adam. However Jesus Christ, the Savior, the Creator, and the King of kings who is almighty, was sent in the likeness of men to save humankind from their sins once and for all. He blotted out the sins of the world once and for all. He took the sins of the world on Him though His baptism once and for all and paid the wages of the sins by being crucified.

A human being receives new life and has redemption if he/she believes that Jesus was sent to blot out all sins, however grave his/her sins may be. God planned and decided to create the heavens and the earth in order to make us His children. He came to the world and perfectly fulfilled His promise. So we certainly have no sin. God has never made a mistake. Adam was a type of Him who was to come. I do not understand why people rely on their own works. Our salvation absolutely depends on Jesus. Human beings became sinners through one man, Adam, and were redeemed through one Man, Jesus.

The only thing we should do is to believe the salvation of the remission of sins. It is the only thing we should do. We have nothing to do but rejoice in the fact that Jesus blotted out all our sins. By the way, why do you compel other people to zealously do good deeds? Can people be delivered from their sins through their works? No. Salvation depends on only the faith in the remission of sins.

The free gift is not like the offense

Romans 5:14-16 states, *"Nevertheless death reigned from Adam to Moses, even over those who had not sinned according to the likeness of the transgression of Adam, who is a type of*

Him who was to come. But the free gift is not like the offense. For if by the one man's offense many died, much more the grace of God and the gift by the grace of the one Man, Jesus Christ, abounded to many. And the gift is not like that which came through the one who sinned. For the judgment which came from one offense resulted in condemnation, but the free gift which came from many offenses resulted in justification."

What do these passages mean? The Bible says, *"But the free gift is not like the offense."* The free gift refers to God's salvation. It means that all people who inherited sin through Adam were destined to go to hell, but their sins could be forgiven indiscriminately through the faith in Jesus, who blotted out all their sins. It also means that Jesus already blotted out all of our future sins.

A human being who is born as a descendant of Adam is a sinner even if he/she does not sin. Therefore, he/she cannot avoid going to hell even if he/she does not sin. Jesus came to the world and became our Savior. The free gift is that Jesus gave us excessive redemption to forgive the sins that people continue committing until the end of the world.

Therefore, the free gift of one Man is greater than one man's offense. If one commits a sin of being against God, then the sin alone is serious enough to make him/her judged by God and go to hell. However, the gift of the Lord, who already blotted out all our sins and transgressions, is greater than one man's offense.

It means that Jesus' love and the gift of the remission of sins are greater than the offenses of all human beings. The Lord sufficiently blotted out all the sins of the world. The love of Jesus, who saved us, and the gift of salvation are so abundant and bigger than an offense committed by one man. The Lord already blotted out the sins of fighting against God even though we are against Him with our flesh. Now the Lord wants us to believe that He already blotted out the sins of the world all at once. That's why He saved sinners from all their sins as the Lamb of God, who took away the sins of the world.

The theory, which says that our sins are blotted out when we believe in God, and not blotted out when we don't believe in God, is untrue. God blotted out even the sins of unbelievers because He loves all the people of the world, yet people do not want to receive God's love. Nobody is excluded from God's love and salvation. The salvation of God comes to those who believe in the truth of the gospel, which states that Jesus blotted out all our sins.

We are such weak beings. God counts those who believe Jesus blotted out all sins to be without sin. We still have many weaknesses in our flesh even after all our sins are forgiven. Many times, we fight against God and even try to throw away His righteousness when we do not agree with His will. But God says, "I love you and I saved you. I already blotted out the sins that you have committed until right now." "Oh! Is it true, Lord?" "Yes, I have blotted out all sins." "Thank you, Lord. I praise You. I cannot help praising You because You loved me so much that You blotted out even the sin of denying You."

Those who became sinners were made righteous and became the slaves of love. They yielded themselves to His love. They cannot help believing in Jesus because the Lord blotted out the sin of denying Him, even though they deny Him because of their weaknesses, just as Peter did. It makes them praise the Lord. So the Apostle Paul says that God's salvation is greater than one man's offense.

Jesus took away all the sins; the original sin that was inherited and the actual sins that are committed by our deeds to the end of the world. So, how great the love of God is! So, the Bible says implicatively, *"Behold! The Lamb of God who takes away the sin of the world!" (John 1:29)*

The righteous will reign in life through the One, Jesus Christ

The sins of the world cannot be forgiven through the prayers of repentance. Believers come to have no sin and receive salvation from all sins because the Lord had already eliminated out even the sins that will be committed in the future. Romans 5:17 states, *"For if by one man's offence death reigned through the one, much more those who receive abundance of grace and of the gift of righteousness will reign in life through the One, Jesus Christ."*

We are blessed with the grace. Who are those who receive the abundance of grace and the gift of righteousness? They are those who believe in the Lord and whose sins are forgiven by having faith in Him. We praise the Lord because we received the abundance of grace of the remission of sins. *"Those who receive abundance of grace and of the gift of righteousness will reign in life through the One, Jesus Christ."* We are kings who reign in life.

Only kings reign. We reign now. Who can fight against kings? We, who receive the abundance of grace and the gift of righteousness, reign everyday. We reign today and we will reign tomorrow. Whoever shows kindness to us kings are blessed and can be kings with us. However, whoever does not believe in the gospel of the truth that kings preach will go to hell.

There have been many kings who were saved in the world and there have been many people who went to hell because they were against the kings. They should have been kind to the kings, but they weren't. They could have been kings if they had the eyes and the heart of a truth seeker.

Do you reign? We brag with confidence of our being kings to the world. We announce that unbelievers will go to hell when they fight against us. Only kings can do this. We are real kings. Is there anyone who does not reign among the righteous? It is impudent for them not to reign as kings. A king has to reign as a king. "You have wrong thoughts. You will go to hell if you do not accept the truth." A king has to behave as a king. A king must be dignified and give the command to believe the truth to sinners.

A king can and has to judge, command and sentence unbelievers to hell who are against God's righteousness, however young the king may be. He/she has the power to sentence unbelievers to hell in front of God, but it does not mean that the king may abuse his/her power as he/she pleases. The Lord tells us to reign in the world. Therefore, let us reign and enter the Kingdom of Heaven.

However, some of the righteous are too meek to use their power. The Lord will rebuke them when He comes again. "You gave up your faith. Why did you behave as a slave? I made you a king." There are some people who act like slaves to the world. Does it make sense for a king to say, "sir," to his subject like that? However, some of the righteous speak like that even though it does not make sense to. They beg for pardon on their knees to the world even after God delivers them from sin. A king should be kingly.

I proclaimed the independent kingliness against the world as soon as I became a king. I believed that I became a king and behaved in kingly way, though I was young.

By the obedience of One Man, Jesus Christ

Romans 5:18-19 states, *"Therefore, as through one man's offense judgment came to all men, resulting in condemnation, even so through one Man's righteous act the free gift came to all men, resulting in justification of life. For as by one man's disobedience many were made sinners, so also by one Man's obedience many will be made righteous."*

"As through one man's offence judgment came to all men, resulting in condemnation." Here, condemnation means judgment. A person who is born as a descendant of Adam and who is not born again of the water and the Spirit, though he/she believes in Jesus, is judged. *"Through one Man's righteous act the free gift came to all men, resulting in justification of life."*

All people are made righteous by the one righteous act of Jesus, who was born of the Virgin Mary and was baptized in the Jordan River to bear all the sins of the world. He sacrificed His life by being crucified in their place to make them all righteous. By one Man's obedience to the will of God the Father, many were made righteous.

Strictly speaking, are all the people of the world sinners, or are they righteous if we observe from the standpoint of faith? All of them are righteous. Some people get angry and fight against me when I say so by faith. In fact, there is none who has sin from God's viewpoint. God sent His only begotten Son to the world and passed all the sins of the world onto Him and let Him be judged as the representative of all people.

People enter the Kingdom of Heaven or hell according to their faiths

God does not judge the world any more because He judged Jesus in the place of all people. However, some people believe this and others don't, even though the Son of God took away all sins and blotted them out by His obedience to the will of God. Believers enter the Kingdom of Heaven by believing in God's righteousness. God accounts them to be righteous and says, "You are righteous. You believe that I really blotted out all your sins. Come on. I have prepared the Kingdom of Heaven for you." They enter the Kingdom of Heaven sufficiently.

But some people do not believe in Him and reject the gospel, saying, "God, is it true? I cannot believe it. Is it true? I do not really understand." God will say, "Why do you make me angry? Believe in Me if you want to believe, but do not believe if you do not want to believe." "Is the gospel of the water and the Spirit true, Lord?" "I saved you." "I can't believe it. I can believe as much as 90%, but I doubt the last 10%."

Then God will say to them, "You do not believe it though I already saved you. Do according to your faith. I made up My mind to send those who have sin as the descendants of Adam to hell. I made the Kingdom of Heaven, too. Enter the Kingdom of Heaven if you want to, and go to hell if you want to be cast into the fire of hell." It depends on their faiths whether they enter the Kingdom of Heaven or hell.

Do you believe that Jesus saved you from all your sins with His baptism and blood that was shed on the Cross? It depends on your faith. There is no midpoint between the Kingdom of Heaven and hell. There is no such thing as "No" in front of God. There is only "Yes." God also never tells us

"No." God promised all things and fulfilled them all. He blotted out all the sins of sinners.

Where sin abounded, grace did much more abound

Let us take a look at Romans 5:20-21. *"Moreover the law entered that the offense might abound. But where sin abounded, grace abounded much more, so that as sin reigned in death, even so grace might reign through righteousness to eternal life through Jesus Christ our Lord."* Why did the law enter? To make the offense abound. Human beings have sin inevitably as the descendants of Adam by nature. But they didn't know their sinful nature, and thus God gave human beings the law to give them the knowledge of sin because the law commands them what to do and what not to do, and it becomes a sin not to obey the law with their thoughts and deeds.

The law entered that the offense might abound. God gave us the law to make us know that we are grave sinners and are masses of sin. However, where sin abounded, grace bounded much more. This means that a person who is born with sin as a descendant of Adam, but thinks him/herself to be a minor sinner has nothing to do with the fact that Jesus saved him/her.

However, one who thinks he/she has many weaknesses and cannot live according to God's word with the flesh gives thanks to the Lord who saved Him. The gospel that says the Lord took away the sins of the world all at once is a great gift to such a person. *"But where sin abounded, grace abounded much more."* The gift abounded, so grave sinners are made perfectly righteous. The minor sinners who think they are not full of sin will go to hell. Only grave sinners are made perfectly righteous.

So a person who knows that he/she is a grave sinner greatly praises the salvation of Jesus. There are few good-natured preachers among the gospel preachers in the world. *"Where sin abounded, grace abounded much more."* This does not mean that we may sin on purpose so that grace may abound much more.

The Apostle Paul says in Romans 6:1, *"What shall we say then? Shall we continue in sin that grace may abound?"* Paul means, "We are saved if we just believe in God's righteousness. The Lord already blotted out all our sins and abundantly saved sinners from all their sins. We are made righteous by believing with our hearts. We can be saved if we believe in what the Lord did. No matter how wicked we may be or how many times we may sin, we are made righteous without works by having faith in the truth."

We become righteous by faith. How wicked are our deeds? How many times do we sin? How many shortcomings do we have if God, who is sinless, looks at our deeds? I cannot but praise the Lord. Romans 5:20-21 states, *"Where sin abounded, grace abounded much more, so that as sin reigned in death, even so grace might reign through righteousness to eternal life through Jesus Christ our Lord."*

God gave us eternal lives through Jesus Christ. The righteousness of the Lord made us reign with Him. I praise the Lord, who abundantly saved sinners from all their sins. Thank You, Lord. ✉

You can download Rev. Paul C. Jong's Christian Books on iPhone, iPad, or Blackberry by going to Amazon's Kindle e-bookstore (www.amazon.com).

CHAPTER

6

Introduction to Romans Chapter 6

We must realize the secret of Jesus' baptism

Do you know and believe in the secret of the baptism Jesus received from John? I would like to tell you about this through Romans 6:1-4. *"What shall we say then? Shall we continue in sin that grace may abound? Certainly not! How shall we who died to sin live any longer in it? Or do you not know that as many of us as were baptized into Christ Jesus were baptized into His death? Therefore we were buried with Him through baptism into death, that just as Christ was raised from the dead by the glory of the Father, even so we also should walk in newness of life."*

In order to understand this Scripture and dig out the truth, we must first of all comprehend Paul's faith shown in Galatians 3:27 and have the same faith as him. He says, *"For as many of you as were baptized into Christ have put on Christ."* What does this Scripture mean? Now we can understand these words through Matthew 3:13-17.

Paul asks whether we would continue in sin for we have received the remission of sins once and for all through believing in God's righteousness. Paul's answer was no, and it is also the answer that those who truly believe in God's righteousness should have. This does not mean that the righteous never sin in the flesh. That is not true.

It also doesn't mean that because our sins have been forgiven, we should plan to sin even more. The righteous have already been baptized into His death. How shall those who have faith in His righteousness still dwell in sins? This cannot be true. Paul explains the reason in Galatians 3:27 saying, *"For as many of you as were baptized into Christ have put on Christ."*

In other words, Jesus took over all of our sins with His baptism and died on the Cross so that those who believed in Him could be "baptized into Christ" by faith. Therefore, we must possess this kind of faith.

We must possess a faith united with Jesus' baptism

We must possess a faith that is united with Jesus' baptism and His death. It is said, *"For as many of you as were baptized into Christ have put on Christ."* This Scripture means that when Jesus was baptized by John at the Jordan, He took over all of our sins at once. This also means that Jesus' death on the Cross was the atonement of all our sins because He had taken over all the sins of the world through His baptism. Understanding and believing in this truth is having the faith united with our Lord.

We were separated from God's righteousness because of our iniquities. Do you know that Jesus took over all our sins and transgressions when John baptized Him? Jesus took over all of our sins at once through His baptism and died on the Cross to pay the wages of the sins. We are the beings who cannot but commit sins before God all our lives. Therefore, we must possess faiths united with Christ by laying our foundations of faith on Jesus' baptism and His blood on the Cross. We will be united with Christ only when we believe that Jesus fulfilled God's righteousness through His baptism.

Who obeyed the will of the Father, the fulfillment of His righteousness? It was Jesus Christ Himself. Jesus fulfilled God's righteousness all at once. Jesus could only pay the wages of sin with His death by taking over all of our sins through the baptism He received from John. If we want to be united with Christ, we must have faith in His baptism that took over all our sins once and for all.

We must unite with our Lord and believe in Him because He became our eternal Savior through His baptism. The only option left for you now is whether you accept this truth or not. To be God's child by believing in His baptism and bloodshed on the Cross or to be doomed to eternal death in hell by rejecting the truth is absolutely up to you. Jesus was baptized so that our sins might be taken away (Matthew 3:13-15).

If we look at Matthew 3:15, we can find the "for thus" as a means of fulfilling all of God's righteousness. The phrase "for thus" is *"hoo'-tos gar"* in Greek, which means 'in this way,' 'most fitting,' or 'there is no other way besides this,' stating that His baptism was the surest way of handing over our sins. This word clarifies that Jesus irreversibly took the sins of humankind onto Him through the baptism He received from John.

When Jesus was baptized, our sins were handed over to Him. We must believe in the truth in Romans 6:5-11, that Jesus was baptized so that our sins might be done away with and that He died on the Cross in order to consequently save mankind.

In order for you to repay someone, you have to pay back the wages equivalent to your debt. In the same manner, we must know in what way and how much our Lord paid the wages in order to do away with our sins.

When Jesus was baptized He took over all of the sins

committed from when we were born to age 10, and then 10 to 20, 30, 40, 50, 60, 70, 80, 90, and the sins we would commit until our last dying breath. He took over all our sins through His baptism and paid for the wages. Jesus took over all of our iniquities at once, committed both consciously and unconsciously. Jesus was baptized in order to wash away our sins and He paid for the wages of the sins on the Cross. This is the truth contained in the gospel of the water and the Spirit, and what the Scriptures are talking about.

We can see here that most Christians try hard to accept Jesus as their Savior by establishing and supporting the Doctrine of Sanctification, because they don't understand the secret of "the baptism" Paul talked about. If Jesus had not come to earth and received "the baptism" that John gave Him, mankind's sins would have eternally remained. Therefore, we must not believe in such a false doctrine that teaches that our hearts and bodies can become sanctified as time goes by.

The only and eternal truth on this earth is that Jesus was baptized and took over all of our sins. Belief in the gospel of the water and the Spirit helps us overcome all the false doctrines and brings victory to those who believe. Therefore, we have to believe in this truth. Some Christians go to hell while having not been born again because they have not united with Jesus' baptism.

Have you ever seen an image of a heart pierced with a dagger? It shows the sacrificial love of God. God loved us so much that He saved us from all our sins with the gospel of the water and the Spirit. *"For God so loved the world that He gave His only begotten Son, that whoever believes in Him should not perish but have everlasting life" (John 3:16).*

You have to accept the love Jesus gave us by being

baptized and shedding all His blood on the Cross. Our hearts have to unite with the righteousness of God. We must live in union with Jesus. A faithful life in union with the righteousness of Christ is beautiful. Paul says decisively in Romans chapter 6 that we have to live by faith in union with God's righteousness.

Do we, like Paul says in Romans 7:25, serve the law of God with our minds, but the law of sin with our flesh? Do we? Yes, we do. That is why we, like Paul, always have to have hearts that are united with God's righteousness. What happens if we do not unite our hearts with our Lord's righteousness? Complete destruction.

Those who unite with God's righteousness live lives united with His church. If you believe in God's righteousness, you must unite with His church and His servants. The flesh always tries to serve the law of sin, so we must live by faith, repeatedly pondering on God's law of life. If we keep in mind and ruminate about God's righteousness everyday, we will be united with Him. That is why the Bible says that the beasts that chew the cud are pure (Leviticus 11:2-3).

Unite with God's righteousness. Do you feel a new strength soaring or not? Try uniting with God's righteousness now! Let's say you have had united your heart with Jesus' baptism. Then, do you still have sin in your hearts or not? —We do not.— Now Jesus Christ has died on the Cross. Believe this in your heart. Have you also united your heart to this fact? Then, have we died or not? —We are dead.— And has Christ risen from the dead? —Yes.— Then, we have risen from the dead too. When we unite our hearts with Christ, our sins are washed away; we are dead on the Cross together with Him and are raised from the dead with Christ.

However, what happens when we do not unite with

Christ? "What are you talking about? Oh yeah, you are talking about Jesus' baptism. You mean, in the Old Testament it was the laying of the hands on the offering, and in the New Testament it is the baptism Jesus received from John. Maybe that's right! But what is so great about this that everyone makes a fuss of it?"

Those who only believe in His baptism in theory do not have true faiths, so they leave Christ in the end. The theoretical faith, like the mere information students learn in school from teachers, is not enough to earn God's righteousness. But there are students who truly respect their teachers and try to learn the character and leadership of their teachers. We must not accept God's words as mere knowledge but embed it in our hearts, along with His character, love, mercy and righteous words. We must throw away our desires to learn only the knowledge when we are taught the word of God.

The minds of those who are already deeply united with God's word are determined to serve the Lord and have good fellowship with Him, and are not easily moved by situations. They only move with circumspection in order to achieve the Great Commission. But small things easily affect those who have not yet united their hearts with Him.

We must have our faiths united with our Lord's righteousness. We must not let our hearts be shaken by the small things of the world. Those who united their hearts with Christ were baptized into Jesus, died on the Cross with Him and rose again with Him in order to be saved from all their sins. We are not people of this secular world therefore we must believe. We have to unite with His righteousness to please Him, who called us the servants of His righteousness.

If you unite with God's righteousness, your hearts will

always be in peace and filled with joy because the Lord's power will be ours. We can live greatly blessed lives because God abundantly endows on us His blessings and divine power.

Let your heart unite with God's righteousness. Then you will be able to unite with God's servants, like me, have a strong faith in His word through mutual fellowship and serve His work vigorously. The Lord has washed away your sins even though your faith might be as small as a mustard seed. Stay united with Him, especially with His baptism, even though you are insufficient.

We thank God for giving us the faith united with the Lord through the baptism of Jesus and His blood on the Cross. We have to unite our hearts with the Lord from now on until the day we meet our Lord. We are weak by ourselves so we have to unite. Have you learned the faith to unite your heart with the righteousness Jesus had fulfilled? Did you acquire the faith united with Jesus' baptism? You must now possess the faith that is united with Jesus' baptism and bloodshed. Those who do not possess such faiths will fail in being saved and live unfaithful lives. Therefore, God's righteousness is essential to your life.

Uniting with the Lord brings the blessings of the remission of sins and living as God's children through the faith in God's righteousness. It is my earnest wish that God's righteousness becomes your righteousness. Jesus Christ is the Lord of your faith and God's righteousness. Believe! And obtain God's righteousness. Then, God's blessings will be with you.

We must not offer God only our devotion

Some Christians do not believe in God's righteousness and only praise the Lord, "♫O, God take what's mine and make it Thine, ♪My small devotion, my life, my sacrifice, ♫Although it small, I give my all to You, my King. ♪I will only live for you my Lord! ♫Oh, the Holy Spirit comes like fire." We must not become like such Christians. They come to praise everyday and continue to lay down their devotions before God, so God does not have any chance to do anything for them.

Humans are bothering God by being too devoted. God is tired of our blind devotions. They urge God to receive their "human" righteousness. They incessantly cry out to the Lord, "O, God! Accept our devotions!" while they are cleaning the floor, sweeping the doorway, praying, praising and even eating. It is tantalizing that most Christians today just tell Jesus to accept their devotions of the flesh while they do not know God's righteousness or believe in it. We must lay aside our devotions for a while and accept God's righteousness, which consists of the baptism of Jesus and His blood on the Cross.

Our devotions of the flesh do not have any effect before God. But humans still ask God to accept their devotions and forgive their sins in return. It is as foolish as a foul and poor beggar giving all of his belongings to a billionaire and asking to live in the lordly mansion in compensation for the worthless and dirty offerings. God does not want us to boast of our own righteousness. God wants us to have faith by believing in Jesus' baptism and His blood on the Cross.

Christianity is not the kind of religion men created in this world. Christianity is not like other worldly religions such as Buddhism, which requires one to continuously pray, bow and purify oneself. We should not have such faiths; bowing and praying for blessings to the founder of a worldly religion. We must not give our devotion and request His blessing in return, but instead, know and accept God's righteousness because He wants to give it to us.

We will receive the remission of sins when we believe in Jesus' baptism from John and His bloodshed on the Cross. Jesus was baptized to take over the sins of the world and died to blot out the sins once and for all. Therefore, He does not need to repeat his baptism and death.

Hebrews 10:18 states, *"Now where there is remission of these, there is no longer an offering for sin."* Jesus took all of our sins by being baptized and died once, fulfilling all of God's righteousness. Now our faiths in the baptism and blood of Christ have restored our relationship with God.

Paul speaks on, *"Therefore do not let sin reign in your mortal body, that you should obey it in its lusts" (Romans 6:12).* We will reign with Jesus Christ, who is our Lord and eternal King of kings. Sin shall not have dominion over you. The times when sin reigned over us are over. We must not follow the wicked greed or ambitions of our flesh. We can overcome all these things competently because God gave us His perfect righteousness.

Present your heart and body as instruments of God's righteousness

"And do not present your members as instruments of unrighteousness to sin, but present yourselves to God as being alive from the dead, and your members as instruments of righteousness to God" (Romans 6:13).

Paul tells of three important axioms for resisting sin. First of all, we shall not obey our mortal bodies in its lust. We must refuse what our old selves try to do in lust. Secondly, we must not present our members as instruments of sin. We must stop our members, which are our abilities, from being used as instruments of unrighteousness. Thirdly, we must present our members as instruments of God's righteousness.

Before we believed in Jesus, we presented our hands, feet, mouth, and eyes to sin. We became instruments of sin and followed wherever it led us. But now, we must decide to restrain from using our members as instruments of unrighteousness to sin. We must not let sin have dominion over us without any resistance. When the temptation of sin approaches, we must declare, "Sin, you have died in Christ." And we must confess that God is the Lord of all our existences.

In a life of faith, we should keep in mind both the things that should be done and should not be done. We must not present our members to sin, but present them to God. What we have to do is as important as what we should not do. If we do not present anything to God, it consequently means that we are presenting it to sin. For example, if we present our time to God, we will not have time to present it to sin. We must become enemies to sin and belong to one family with God.

We could say by chance, "I do not have the courage to win over sin." However Paul tells us in Romans 6:14 that we should not think that way: *"For sin shall not have dominion over you, for you are not under law but under grace."* If we are still under the dominion of sin, we will certainly sin again. But if we are under God's grace, it will hold us and give us victory. So the Psalms writer prays, *"Direct my steps by Your word, And let no iniquity have dominion over me" (Psalms 119:133).*

As long as we live on this earth, sin will find its way to us. Even after we have confessed that we have already died in Christ, sin will try to topple us down and rule us. If we try to be righteous for ourselves under the law, we cannot be freed from the dominion of sin. But we have to bear in mind that we have faith believing in God's righteousness. So sin cannot dominate over us. We have to know this, and shout this out.

All of you must believe in God's righteousness and confess it with your mouths. *"For with the heart one believes unto righteousness, and with the mouth confession is made unto salvation" (Romans 10:10).* It is truly important for you to believe in God's righteousness with your heart and confess it with your mouth.

Therefore, whenever sin tries to reign over us—every time anger tries to rule our minds, every time adulteries and lewdness try to deprave us, greed enters tempting us to deceive others in order to improve our lives, hatred and suspicion grows, or envy grips our heart,—we have to shout: "Jesus has taken all these sins!" We must shout with faith, "Sin! You cannot rule me. God, with His righteousness, saved me absolutely from all my sins, destruction, curses and from Satan."

The phrase, 'we live to God' means we live righteously because of our faiths in His righteousness. God's righteousness made those who believed in Jesus' baptism and blood, perfect. That is why we died unto sin and lived to God by the faith in His righteousness. There is nothing as important as knowing and confessing that we were spiritually resurrected by believing in God's righteousness.

Paul said that where sin abounded, grace abounded much more (Romans 5:20). Then people misunderstood him and said that one must continue to sin to win more grace. But Paul refuted them. Things are still pending after believing in His baptism and blood. The worldly sins will encircle us and try to take over our hearts.

However, whenever that happens, we can rely on God's righteousness and win over our weaknesses or distrust with faith. We can live as God's children, with whom He is well pleased. With such faiths, we were able to die to sin and live to God. We can live the rest of our lives believing in and pursuing God's righteousness, and will live forever in His Kingdom once we get there.

Romans 6:23 says, *"For the wages of sin is death, but the gift of God is eternal life in Christ Jesus our Lord."* Amen. Those who have confessed Christ as their Savior believe in the power of His baptism and the effect of the judgment of the Cross. Amen.

Hallelujah! Praise the Lord! ✉

The True Meaning of Jesus' Baptism

< Romans 6:1-8 >

"What shall we say then? Shall we continue in sin that grace may abound? Certainly not! How shall we who died to sin live any longer in it? Or do you not know that as many of us as were baptized into Christ Jesus were baptized into His death? Therefore we were buried with Him through baptism into death, that just as Christ was raised from the dead by the glory of the Father, even so we also should walk in newness of life. For if we have been united together in the likeness of His death, certainly we also shall be in the likeness of His resurrection, knowing this, that our old man was crucified with Him, that the body of sin might be done away with, that we should no longer be slaves of sin. For he who has died has been freed from sin. Now if we died with Christ, we believe that we shall also live with Him."

What does baptism mean?

We call John, who baptized Jesus, John the Baptist. Then what does baptism mean? "Baptism" is "βάφτισμα" in Greek. It means, "being immersed." And the most important meaning of baptism is "taking away sin and death."

The phrase "being immersed" implies death. All the sins of the world were transferred to Jesus when John the Baptist baptized Him and thus He took them all away and died on the Cross to pay the wages of all our sins. Jesus died in our place. Death means the result of sin because *"the wages of sin is death" (Romans 6:23).*

Baptism also means, "being washed." All our sins were washed away without leaving even a bit of sin because Jesus took all the sins of the world on His flesh through His baptism. All sins in the hearts of human beings were washed away because they were passed onto Jesus through the baptism.

Baptism has the same meaning as, "laying on of hands." "Laying on of hands," means, "pass to." The act of Jesus' receiving baptism from John the Baptist was to bear all the sins of the world. It was the eternal law of God's salvation that the priest laid his hands on the head of the sin offering to pass the sins of Israel to it on the tenth day of the seventh month.

Leviticus 16:21-22 states, *"Aaron shall lay both his hands on the head of the live goat, confess over it all the iniquities of the children of Israel, and all their transgressions, concerning all their sins, putting them on the head of the goat, and shall send it away into the wilderness by the hand of a suitable man. The goat shall bear on itself all their iniquities to an uninhabited land; and he shall release the goat in the wilderness."* When Aaron, the high priest, laid his hands on the head of the live goat, the goat took away all the sins of Israel and was slain for the people.

"Laying hands on the head of the sin offering" in the Old Testament stands for "the baptism" in the New Testament

The meaning of baptism is "being immersed." It includes

"being buried, being washed or passing to." People in the Old Testament brought goats or lambs without blemishes and laid their hands on the head of the offering to pass their sins onto it. This is similar to the act of baptism in the New Testament. The goat took away sins by "the laying on of hands" and was slain. Jesus was baptized by John the Baptist, who is the representative of all humankind, to take away all the sins of the world and was crucified.

Aaron, the high priest and Israel's representative, laid his hands on the head of the goat to pass the sins of Israelites to it, slew the goat, took its blood with his finger and put it on the horns of the altar of the burnt offering. Therefore, Luke said that John the Baptist, who was born in the family of Aaron, was the representative of all humankind, just as Aaron, the High Priest, was the representative of all Israelites.

The Bible says, *"Among those born of women there has not risen one greater than John the Baptist" (Matthew 11:11).* John the Baptist had the right to pass the sins of the world onto Jesus through baptism once and for all as the earthly high priest according to the eternal statute of God. John the Baptist was the last High Priest. When I say that John the Baptist was the High Priest, some people say, "Where is it written that John the Baptist was the High Priest in the Bible?" Isn't it written? The man who was begotten by Zacharias was John the Baptist. Priest Zacharias of the division of Priest Abijah, a grandson of Aaron the High Priest, was clearly a descendant of the family of Aaron.

The Bible talks about the divisions of the priests, who were the descendants of Aaron, in 1 Chronicles chapter 24. In the last days of David, there were lots of priests and they needed to be arranged. So, they were arranged by lots into 24 divisions according to 24 grandsons' families of Aaron. The eighth lot fell to Abijah. Each division served the sanctuary and the house of the Lord for 15 days. And Zacharias of the division of Priest Abijah was chosen by God as an on-duty priest of his division.

Luke 1:9 states, *"According to the custom of the priesthood, his lot fell to burn incense when he went into the temple of the Lord."* It shows us that John the Baptist was born in the family of Aaron the High Priest, and the last High Priest who would represent all human beings (Matthew 11:11, 3:13-17). Only a man who was born into the family of the High Priest could become a High Priest according to the law. Only lions can bear lion cubs. John the Baptist took over the high priesthood of Aaron, his ancestor.

The Apostles of Jesus testified the baptism of Jesus

All the Apostles, especially Paul, Peter, Matthew and John testified the baptism of Jesus. Let us take a look at the testimony of the Apostle Paul written in today's main passages. *"What shall we say then? Shall we continue in sin that grace may abound? Certainly not! How shall we who died to sin live any longer in it? Or do you not know that as many of us as were baptized into Christ Jesus were baptized into His death? Therefore we were buried with Him through baptism into death, that just as Christ was raised from the dead by the glory of the Father, even so we also should walk in newness of life. For if we have been united together in the likeness of His death, certainly we also shall be in the likeness of His resurrection, knowing this, that our old man was crucified with Him, that the body of sin might be done away with, that we should no longer be slaves of sin. For he who has died has been freed from sin.*

Now if we died with Christ, we believe that we shall also live with Him."

Galatians 3:27 also states, *"For as many of you as were baptized into Christ have put on Christ."* Let us see the testimony of Peter. 1 Peter 3:21 states, *"There is also an antitype which now saves us—baptism (not the removal of the filth of the flesh, but the answer of a good conscience toward God), through the resurrection of Jesus Christ."*

The Apostle John says in 1 John 5:5-8, *"Who is he who overcomes the world, but he who believes that Jesus is the Son of God? This is He who came by water and blood—Jesus Christ; not only by water, but by water and blood. And it is the Spirit who bears witness, because the Spirit is truth. For there are three that bear witness in heaven: the Father, the Word, and the Holy Spirit; and these three are one. And there are three that bear witness on earth: the Spirit, the water, and the blood; and these three agree as one."*

The testimony of Matthew is written in Matthew 3:13-17. *"Then Jesus came from Galilee to John at the Jordan to be baptized by him. And John tried to prevent Him, saying, 'I need to be baptized by You, and are You coming to me?' But Jesus answered and said to him, 'Permit it to be so now, for thus it is fitting for us to fulfill all righteousness.' Then he allowed Him. When He had been baptized, Jesus came up immediately from the water; and behold, the heavens were opened to Him, and He saw the Spirit of God descending like a dove and alighting upon Him. And suddenly a voice came from heaven, saying, 'This is My beloved Son, in whom I am well pleased.'"*

Jesus took away all the sins of the world by receiving baptism from John the Baptist. *"For thus it is fitting for us to fulfill all righteousness.*" Jesus took the sins of the world onto Him by receiving baptism from John the Baptist, which was in the most proper manner. God Himself testifies it. *"When He had been baptized, Jesus came up immediately from the water; and behold, the heavens were opened to Him, and He saw the Spirit of God descending like a dove and alighting upon Him. And suddenly a voice came from heaven, saying, 'This is My beloved Son, in whom I am well pleased."* Jesus took away all our sins through His baptism, testified the gospel of the water and the Spirit for three years, was crucified to death and rose again from the dead on the third day. He is now sitting on the right hand of God.

Jesus will come again to those who wait for Him without sin. Hebrews 9:28 states, *"So Christ was offered once to bear the sins of many. To those who eagerly wait for Him He will appear a second time, apart from sin, for salvation."* God Himself said, "This is My beloved Son, in whom I am well pleased," and the Holy Spirit testifies that the Man who took away all the sins of the world was Jesus, the Savior. However, people don't understand the Bible because their spiritual eyes are shut. Their spiritual eyes should be opened and they should be born again of water and the Spirit (John 3:5).

Therefore, they think that only Jesus alone ministered for the salvation of humankind. But in truth, Jesus was the Lamb of God and needed John the Baptist, who was the representative of all humankind and who could pass all the sins of the world to Him, because similarly, Aaron the High Priest laid his hands on the head of the sin offering (the live goat) and passed the sins of all Israelites onto it by laying his hands on the head of offering. Aaron then set them free from their sins by slaying the sin offering. So God sent His messenger before Jesus.

Who is John the Baptist?

John the Baptist is the messenger of God who is predicted in Malachi 3:1-3. The Lord needed the messenger, John the Baptist, who would represent all humankind. Jesus Christ, the Son of God, took away the eternal sins of all human beings through John the Baptist and was crucified as the wages of sin in the New Testament, while the sheep took away the sins of a limited period of time and was slain in the Old Testament. Therefore, Jesus saved all people from eternal sins.

Two big events happened before the birth of Jesus. One was that Mary conceived Jesus and the other was that John the Baptist was born in the division of Abijah. These two events happened in Divine Providence. It was the perfect play written by God. God sent John the Baptist to the world six months prior to Jesus and then sent His only begotten Son in order to set us free from warfare and pain. Do you understand? Let's look deeper into the Bible.

Let us look at Mathew 11:7-14, in which testifies John the Baptist. *"As they departed, Jesus began to say to the multitudes concerning John: 'What did you go out into the wilderness to see? A reed shaken by the wind? But what did you go out to see? A man clothed in soft garments? Indeed, those who wear soft clothing are in kings' houses. But what did you go out to see? A prophet? Yes, I say to you, and more than a prophet. For this is he of whom it is written: 'Behold, I send My messenger before Your face, Who will prepare Your way before You.' Assuredly, I say to you, among those born of women there has not risen one greater than John the Baptist; but he who is least in the kingdom of heaven is greater than he. And from the days of John the Baptist until now the kingdom of heaven suffers violence, and the violent take it by force. For all the prophets and the law prophesied until John. And if you are willing to receive it, he is Elijah who is to come."*

People went out to the wilderness to see John the Baptist, who cried out, *"Repent, for the kingdom of heaven is at hands!" (Matthew 3:2)* Jesus told them, *"What did you go out into the wilderness to see? A reed shaken by the wind? But what did you go out to see? A man clothed in soft garments? Indeed, those who wear soft clothing are in kings' houses. But what did you go out to see? A prophet? Yes, I say to you, and more than a prophet."*

In the age of the Old Testament, a king was no more powerful than a prophet. Kings obeyed what prophets said. Who was more powerful than all the kings and prophets in the Old Testament? He was John the Baptist. Jesus Himself testified it. Who was the representative of all humankind? Who was the representative of all human beings who have flesh, except for Jesus? He was John the Baptist. John the Baptist was the earthly High Priest of all humankind. He was appointed by the Lord Himself and sent to the world and played his role.

"But what did you go out to see? A prophet? Yes, I say to you, and more than a prophet. For this is he of whom it is written: 'Behold, I send My messenger before Your face, Who will prepare Your way before You.'"

Isaiah prophesied that the warfare in Jerusalem would come to an end. We can find that the prophecy was realized when John the Baptist said, *"Behold, the Lamb of God who takes away the sin of the world" (John 1:29).* John the Baptist testified that Jesus was the Son of God and took away all the sins of the world.

On the other hand, Jesus testified that John the Baptist was God chosen messenger who was to come. *Matthew 11:11 states, "Assuredly, I say to you, among those born of women there has not risen one greater than John the Baptist."* Has there risen one greater than John the Baptist among those who are born of women? No. What does *"among those born of women"* mean? It means "all the people in the world." The words, "among those born of women has not risen one greater than John the Baptist," means that John the Baptist was the representative of all the people in the world. He was a High Priest because he was born in the family of Aaron.

John the Baptist was the representative of all the people in the world

Can you believe that John the Baptist was the representative of all the people in the world and the High Priest who passed all our sins onto Jesus, knowing that God appointed Aaron and his descendants to minister the priesthood forever in the Old Testament?

Who was the representative of all humankind? And who was the representative of all the people who have flesh, except for only Jesus? He was John the Baptist, who baptized Jesus.

"Yes, I say to you, and more than a prophet. For this is he of whom it is written: 'Behold, I send My messenger before Your face, Who will prepare Your way before You.'"

And the man who testified, *"Behold, the Lamb of God who takes away the sin of the world" (John 1:29),* was John the Baptist.

Jesus said, *"And from the days of John the Baptist until now the kingdom of heaven suffers violence, and the violent take it by force. For all the prophets and the law prophesied until John" (Matthew 11:12-13).* This passage shows that Jesus took away all the sins of the world by receiving baptism from

John the Baptist and became the Savior to all humankind. It also shows that John the Baptist passed all the sins of the world onto Jesus. Jesus Himself said so. This means that John the Baptist passed the world's sins onto Jesus and whoever believes this fact is saved from all his/her sins and will enter the Kingdom of Heaven. Is this right or wrong? It's exactly right according to God's word, and thus we the preachers of the biblical truth can deliver it in a dignified manner. Whoever believes the truth will enter the Kingdom of Heaven.

John the Baptist passed the sins of the world onto Jesus as the last High Priest of the Old Testament

Zacharias, the father of John the Baptist, heard from an angel of the Lord. Let us examine the testimony of Zacharias to his son. Isn't the testimony of his father more than exact? Let us see his testimony sung in the form of a psalm. *"Now his father Zacharias was filled with the Holy Spirit, and prophesied, saying: 'Blessed is the Lord God of Israel, For He has visited and redeemed His people, And has raised up a horn of salvation for us In the house of His servant David, As He spoke by the mouth of His holy prophets, Who have been since the world began, That we should be saved from our enemies And from the hand of all who hate us, To perform the mercy promised to our fathers And to remember His holy covenant, The oath which He swore to our father Abraham: To grant us that we, Being delivered from the hand of our enemies, Might serve Him without fear, In holiness and righteousness before Him all the days of our life. And you, child, will be called the prophet of the Highest; For you will go before the face of the Lord to prepare His ways, To give knowledge of salvation to*

His people By the remission of their sins, Through the tender mercy of our God, With which the Dayspring from on high has visited us; To give light to those who sit in darkness and the shadow of death, To guide our feet into the way of peace.' So the child grew and became strong in spirit, and was in the deserts till the day of his manifestation to Israel" (Luke 1:67-80).

His father predicted what kind of prophet and priest John would become. Let us see what he predicted to his son. *"And you, child, will be called the prophet of the Highest; For you will go before the face of the Lord to prepare His ways, To give knowledge of salvation to His people By the remission of their sins, Through the tender mercy of our God, With which the Dayspring from on high has visited us; To give light to those who sit in darkness and the shadow of death, To guide our feet into the way of peace"* (Luke 1:76-79).

Here, the Bible clearly says, *"To give knowledge of salvation to His people by the remission of their sins."* Who gives us knowledge of salvation? Luke 1:76 indicates that he is John the Baptist. We come to know Jesus and believe in Him because John the Baptist testified that Jesus Christ saved sinners from their sins by receiving baptism from him to take away the sins, which was done in the most just and fair manner. John the Baptist *"came for a witness, to bear witness of the Light, that all through him might believe. He was not that Light, but was sent to bear witness of that Light"* (John 1:7-8).

We must be saved

We have to be redeemed by believing that Jesus saved all the people in the world through the most just and fair manner by receiving baptism from John the Baptist. The righteousness of God says that Jesus came to the world in the likeness of men, delivered sinners from all their sins in the most just and fair manner by being baptized by John the Baptist and was brought back to life after being crucified. The righteousness of God is hidden in the gospel of the water and the Spirit.

The righteousness of God that is revealed in the gospel teaches us that Jesus was sent in the likeness of men, was baptized, crucified, and rose again from the dead on the third day. We came to believe in Jesus through the testimony of John the Baptist and were saved from all our sins by believing in Jesus' righteousness. All people's sins were blotted out and they have eternal lives by the faith in Jesus through John the Baptist. They have received the Holy Spirit, who testifies us to be God's children, as a gift. ⊠

Present Your Members as Instruments of Righteousness

< Romans 6:12-19 >

"Therefore do not let sin reign in your mortal body, that you should obey it in its lusts. And do not present your members as instruments of unrighteousness to sin, but present yourselves to God as being alive from the dead, and your members as instruments of righteousness to God. For sin shall not have dominion over you, for you are not under law but under grace. What then? Shall we sin because we are not under law but under grace? Certainly not! Do you not know that to whom you present yourselves slaves to obey, you are that one's slaves whom you obey, whether of sin leading to death, or of obedience leading to righteousness? But God be thanked that though you were slaves of sin, yet you obeyed from the heart that form of doctrine to which you were delivered. And having been set free from sin, you became slaves of righteousness. I speak in human terms because of the weakness of your flesh. For just as you presented your members as slaves of uncleanness, and of lawlessness leading to more lawlessness, so now present your members as slaves of righteousness for holiness."

We cannot continue in sin for more grace

The Apostle Paul tells us how the righteous should live

after being saved from sins in Romans chapter 6. He clarifies 'the faith' again with Jesus' baptism. Our sins were forgiven once and for all through the faith in the baptism, the Cross and the resurrection of Jesus.

We cannot be full of God's righteousness and salvation without the baptism of Jesus. If Jesus had not taken away all our sins when He was baptized, we would not be able to say that we are righteous after receiving the remission of sins.

We can confidently say that we are righteous because all our sins were passed onto Jesus and because He was crucified and judged for all our sins. Romans chapter 6 teaches both of the salvation by faith and the practical lives of the righteous. He says, *"What shall we say then? Shall we continue in sin that grace may abound?" (Romans 6:1)* He says in the previous passages, *"But where sin abounded, grace abounded much more, so that as sin reigned in death, even so grace might reign through righteousness to eternal life through Jesus Christ our Lord" (Romans 5:20-21).* The sins of the world cannot exceed God's love and righteousness, however grave they may be. Our sins were forgiven by God's love and righteousness through the faith in the true word.

The Bible says that we cannot continue in sin that grace may abound even though we who live in the flesh have received the remission of all our sins. *"How shall we who died to sin live any longer in it? Or do you not know that as many of us as were baptized into Christ Jesus were baptized into His death? Therefore we are buried with Him through baptism into death" (Romans 6:2-4).*

We are buried with Jesus through baptism into death

Our old selves were crucified with Jesus. This means we are dead to sin. All our sins were passed onto Jesus and He died in our place. Therefore, the death of Jesus is our death to sin. *"Therefore we are buried with Him through baptism into death."* Our old selves of flesh were buried with Him through baptism into death.

The Lord took our sins on Him through His baptism and died on the Cross in the place of sinners. He was without sin by nature. However, He took all the sins of sinners onto Him and was judged in their place. Do you believe this? He Himself did not need to be judged, but we who were sinners were judged in Him, for we were baptized into Jesus Christ.

The Apostle Paul put a great emphasis on the baptism of Jesus. We also preach about the baptism of Jesus. It is not wrong to preach about His baptism from a faithful point of view. Jesus took away the sins of sinners through His baptism and died for them just as a sinner passed over his sins by laying his hands on the head of the offering and slaying it in the Old Testament age.

John the Baptist baptized Jesus, the Lamb of God. He took all the sins of the world onto Him when He was baptized as the sin offering. Therefore, His death was our deaths and all believers' deaths. All who were baptized into Jesus Christ were buried with Jesus Christ. Those who are not baptized into Jesus can neither be saved, believe, deny themselves nor overcome the world.

Only a person who believes in the baptism of Jesus Christ knows that he/she died on the Cross in Him. This person reigns and overcomes the world, denying himself/herself. He/she can rely on God's word and believe it. Only those, who believe that the baptism of Jesus is the indispensable method for Him to bear all the sins of the world, receive the remission of sins, that is, His perfect salvation.

The gist of the salvation through the remission of sins is the baptism and the blood of Jesus. If Jesus had not taken away the sins of sinners through His baptism, His death would have had nothing to do with our salvation. The kernel of salvation is the baptism of Jesus. All the sins of the world were passed onto Jesus when John the Baptist baptized Him.

We came to live with God and walk in newness of life

The Apostle Paul says, *"We were buried with Jesus through baptism into death" (Romans 6:4).* All those who were baptized into Jesus Christ have redemption by faith, were buried within Him and had new lives within Him. This faith is a great faith. The faith in His baptism is the faith that is established on solid ground.

"Therefore we were buried with Him through baptism into death, that just as Christ was raised from the dead by the glory of the Father, even so we also should walk in newness of life. For if we have been united together in the likeness of His death, certainly we also shall be in the likeness of His resurrection" (Romans 6:4-5). We can be united with God by the faith in Jesus' baptism.

Now those who believe in Jesus Christ can walk in newness of life. Our old selves who existed before being born again died, and we became renewed, and are now able to do new works, live in new ways and live by new faiths. A born again person does not live in the old lifestyle and way of thinking. The reason why we have to deny our old ways of thinking is because our old selves died on the Cross with Jesus Christ.

2 Corinthians 5:17 states, *"Old things have passed away; behold, all things have become new."* The Lord was baptized in the Jordan River to take away our sins, was crucified and rose again from the dead. Thus, He saved all sinners from their sins to make them walk in newness of life. Our old 'things' like misery, hardness, bitterness and wounded hearts have passed away. Now our new lives have begun. Being saved is the starting point of our new lives.

God told the people of Israel to keep Passover after they escaped from Egypt and entered the land of Canaan. The exodus from Egypt symbolizes being saved from sins. God told the people of Israel, *"Now the Lord spoke to Moses and Aaron in the land of Egypt, saying, 'This month shall be your beginning of months; it shall be the first month of the year to you. Speak to all the congregation of Israel, saying: 'On the tenth of this month every man shall take for himself a lamb, according to the house of his father, a lamb for a household. And if the household is too small for the lamb, let him and his neighbor next to his house take it according to the number of the persons; according to each man's need you shall make your count for the lamb. Your lamb shall be without blemish, a male of the first year. You may take it from the sheep or from the goats. Now you shall keep it until the fourteenth day of the same month. Then the whole assembly of the congregation of Israel shall kill it at twilight. And they shall take some of the blood and put it on the two doorposts and on the lintel of the houses where they eat it. Then they shall eat the flesh on that night; roasted in fire, with unleavened bread and with bitter herbs they shall eat it. Do not eat it raw, nor boiled at all with water, but roasted in fire—its head with its legs and its entrails. You shall let none of it remain until morning, and what remains of it until morning you shall burn with fire. And thus you shall eat it: with a belt on your waist, your sandals on your feet, and your staff in your hand. So you shall eat it in haste. It is the Lord's Passover"' (Exodus 12:1-11).* We must remember that God commanded them to eat the flesh of the lamb with unleavened bread and with bitter herbs in the Passover feast.

There are many bitter things to come after being saved from sins. Bitter herbs represent denying oneself. There is certainly hardship, yet we must remember that we are buried with Christ. *"For the death that He died, He died to sin once for all; but the life that He lives, He lives to God. Likewise you also, reckon yourselves to be dead indeed to sin; but alive to God in Christ Jesus" (Romans 6:10-11).*

This is the heart of being united to Jesus. We become united to Jesus by believing in His baptism, the Cross and resurrection, which He fulfilled. His ministry includes His birth, receiving baptism from John the Baptist, crucifixion, resurrection, ascension and His coming again to judge the dead. Believing in all those things is the true faith, that is, the faith in salvation, judgment, and the righteousness of God.

Romans 6:10 states, *"For the death that He died, He died to sin once for all."* Jesus did not wash away our sins at two separate intervals. Jesus blotted out the sins of the world all at once. Romans 6:10-11 states, *"But the life that He lives, He lives to God. Likewise you also, reckon yourselves to be dead indeed to sin, but alive to God in Christ Jesus our Lord."* We are indeed dead to sin but alive to God. Now, we are alive to

God. We have new lives and have become new creatures.

"Therefore do not let sin reign in your mortal body, that you should obey it in its lusts. And do not present your members as instruments of unrighteousness to sin, but present yourselves to God as being alive from the dead, and your members as instruments of righteousness to God. For sin shall not have dominion over you, for you are not under the law but under grace" (Romans 6:12-14).

"For sin shall not have dominion over you, for you are not under the law but under grace." We have no sin after being redeemed, no matter what weaknesses may be revealed in our lives. We certainly have weaknesses because we still live on in the flesh. However, sin will not have dominion over us. There is no condemnation to us because we received the remission of sins through the faith in the baptism of Jesus and in the judgment of sin through His blood, however weak we may be. Our iniquities are sins too.

It is true that sin cannot have dominion over us. God made the righteous not to be dominated by sin. The Lord cleanly washed away our sins through Jesus' baptism once and for all so that sin wouldn't have dominion over us, however weak we may be. He paid the wages of sin on the Cross. Believers are without sin because the Lord had paid off the wages of sin.

The righteous see that many weaknesses and iniquities are revealed in them, but sin cannot have dominion over them and there is no condemnation to them when they rely on the Lord by faith. Therefore, we can always walk in the newness of life.

Present your members as instruments of God's righteousness

The Lord has blessed the righteous to live new lives everyday. However, can they continue in sin? Certainly not. Romans 6:13 states, *"And do not present your members as instruments of unrighteousness to sin, but present yourselves to God as being alive from the dead, and your members as instruments of righteousness to God."*

"But God be thanked that you were slaves of sin." We were slaves of sin by nature and were good at sinning, but the Bible says, *"Yet you obeyed from the heart that form of doctrine to which you were delivered. And having been set free from sin, you became slaves of righteousness"* (Romans 6:17-18).

We who became righteous have been set free from sin and became slaves of God's righteousness, who can be righteous by grace. We have been completely set free from sin and have been able to be righteous. We became the righteous who can work for His righteousness.

But what should we do with our flesh after having redemption? How should we behave ourselves with the flesh after we are saved? The Bible says, *"Now present your members as slaves of righteousness for holiness"* (Romans 6:19). What does the flesh do though we are saved from sins? The flesh usually falls into sin even if we have no sin in our hearts. Therefore, we can escape from falling into sin when we present our flesh as slaves of righteousness. This also means that we should simply present our flesh to righteous works because we have been made righteous.

We need to exercise ourselves toward godliness

Are we sinless, though the flesh is so weak, after we are saved? It is certain that to those who believe in the baptism of Jesus, the Cross, the resurrection, the advent and the final judgment of Jesus, there is no sin. They are sinless. We only have to present our flesh to righteous works and our hearts also want to work righteousness. But the flesh is not good at working for His righteousness. So 1 Timothy 4:7 states, *"Exercise yourself toward godliness."* We have to exercise ourselves toward godliness.

It is not done in a short amount of time. When we give away gospel booklets to other people, we may be shameful if we meet familiar people. We may avoid them and come back home at first because we feel shameful. However, if we try to do it several times, thinking, 'My old self already died,' and then taking courage saying, "You will go to hell if you do not have redemption, so receive this booklet and read to have redemption!" When you act like that, you can present your flesh to righteousness.

Romans chapter 6 tells us to present our members as slaves of righteousness for holiness. We must present our members as slaves of righteousness. We must exercise it many times. It is not done in a short time. We must try again and again. We will come to know how interesting it is to attend church if we try to attend church. We must not think, "I believe it, but I would like to believe everything at home. I obviously know what my pastor will preach." Both the flesh and the heart should be at church. Faith grows in the heart only when we present our members as slaves of righteousness.

We must present our members to the work of

righteousness. Do you see what I am saying? We must not keep ourselves away from gathering together and meeting leaders. When you go to the market, you'd better drop in at church and open the door saying, "I'm dropping by on my way to market. What's up?" To drop by at church often is to present your member as a slave of righteousness.

Then a leader will say, "Sister, let me see, can you please clean this up?"
"O.K."
"And, please come back this evening."
"For what?"
"We will have Youth Fellowship this evening."
"O.K. I'll come back tonight."

We are busy in the world, but to where do we have to present our flesh first when the people of the world ask us to attend their meetings?

We must present ourselves to church. We have to attend church, though we are asked to dine with our company colleagues. We should not let our flesh be in a restaurant though our hearts are in church. If we make our flesh escape from the world and let it be in church, both our fleshes and hearts will get comfortable.

What do you think? If your flesh frequents some other carnal places, you will become enemies against God against your wills even though your heart wants to be united to the church.

We must exercise the flesh well with the Spirit

We must present our flesh as slaves of righteousness, but it doesn't mean that the flesh is perfect. We must present our members to righteous works again and again, though our flesh tends to do as it pleases. We usually go a familiar way. It depends on what we present our flesh as slaves of.

The Apostle Paul says, "Present your members as slaves of righteousness for holiness. Present your members as instruments of God's righteousness." It depends on how you tame your flesh. If you tame the flesh to go drink, the flesh automatically goes to drink. As a result, the flesh rushes to a bar while you are in church. If you sit in a bar, the heart feels pain. But if you sit in the church, the heart is comfortable though the flesh is painful.

The flesh also has personality. The flesh depends on how it is tamed by the heart. The flesh says, "I like alcohol," when we repeatedly drink. But the flesh says, "I hate it," when we don't drink. Why? Because the flesh is not tamed. It depends on how we tame the flesh, though the heart is sanctified. The Holy Spirit takes care of our hearts. The Holy Spirit still holds us even though we are out of church. However, we must present the flesh as slaves of righteousness for holiness. So attend church again and again anyway.

Those who are saved must exercise themselves toward godliness. The Bible tells us to obey the word of God and to be led by it. The reason why we should be led by the word of God is because we always like to do as our flesh pleases, thinking our flesh is ours. Because we go shopping, dancing and drinking as we please, it is so hard for us to sit and concentrate on the worship service in church. So, a leader must lead us. "You have a seat down here and listen to the word of God." "O.K."
We should be patient, though we get bored of hearing a sermon, thinking, 'I have to sit here with patience. Why am I so bored,

though I can sit down for 3 hours in a bar? Why can't I stand sitting here for even an hour? Just an hour has passed since I have heard the sermon! I have drunk for 5 hours in a bar and even played poker for 20 hours without taking a break."

It all depends on taming the flesh. The flesh that usually sits down in church hates to go to a bar. However, to a person who is well tamed in drinking, sitting down in church is like hell. I want you to endure for several days and then you can learn to endure. It is very hard until you tame your flesh. We must spend our time in church when we want to do other things with our time.

We spend our time in church, talking with leaders, brothers and sisters to be tamed. I am so comfortable in church and there is nothing that seduces me there. However, when I walk in the street, many things seduce me! There are many temptations such as clothes in the showcases of clothing stores. It takes me 2 hours to go home when I look around at all the things I want to see and I may go astray in the end.

I go to look at a strange thing if there is something strange over there. Later, I realize, 'When will I arrive at home? I want someone to lead me home.' Therefore, do not wander from place to place on your way home. We must go straight home after worship services, ride on the church bus and go straight to our destinations. If you think, 'Do not pick me up to go to church. I alone will go to church. I have two strong legs, so there is no reason for me to go to church by the church bus.' You may go astray by being tempted. You should be thankful that you could ride on the church bus to go to church and back home as soon as worship service is over, not having to worry about useless things. You're better off reading the Bible, offering prayers and going to bed as soon as you get home....

It would be better for you to live like this. A man may

think, 'I have a strong faith. I have no sin. I will prove something to myself. I will not drink even if I go to a bar. Where sin abounded, grace abounded much more. I am filled with grace.' If he thinks like that and goes to a bar, his friend will say, "Hey, have a drink."

"No, have you ever seen me drinking? I quit drinking."

"Have a drink anyway."

"No."

"Why don't you drink just a cup of wine?"

His friend pours wine into a glass and gives it to him. But he thinks, 'I'm drinking soda, though you tempt me to drink alcohol." Then he comes to recollect his having drank long ago and thinks, 'How delicious it will be. Why don't you offer me wine once more? I will have just one drink.' He quickly finishes the soda.

Then, his friend becomes aware that he wants to drink and pours wine into the empty glass.

"It is mild. You may drink it as a cocktail."

"No, I shouldn't. Don't you know that I believe in Jesus?" However, he finally drinks a glass of alcohol and his friend knows that he drinks well.

"Just drink today."

"O.K. I'll drink today, but you should believe in Jesus, O.K.? I have no sin though I drink. But do you have sin? You should be saved from your sins."

The important thing is where we yield the flesh

Human beings are like that. They are nothing peculiar. The important thing is where we present the flesh. Present your members as slaves of righteousness for holiness. Present your flesh to holiness because the flesh is not holy. I used drinking as an example here. But other things are the same as this. It depends on how we tame the flesh.

We are saved by faith in one breath and it is eternal, but the godliness of our hearts and flesh depend on where we present the flesh. We feel that the heart also becomes dirty when we present our flesh to dirtiness, though the heart is clean. Then, we come to forsake our faiths, go against the church, take the name of God in vain and go away from God's presence, being deceived by Satan. We come to be destroyed in the end.

Therefore, watch yourself lest you should be destroyed. You must be careful. How can we deal with our daily sins after we are saved from sins? *"Where sin abounded, grace abounded much more."* The Lord also thoroughly blotted out our daily sins so that we could never become a sinner again, though we may sin many times.

However, we may have a problem if the flesh is veered toward evil again and again. To where should we present our flesh? The flesh should go the designated way. I have spoken until now to make you understand this.

The flesh becomes holy just as the heart is holy, and it becomes the slave of righteousness before God when we present it as a slave of righteousness. We must center our lives on church after we are saved, if we don't know how to live after we are saved. The Bible says that church is like an inn. We drink water, eat spiritual food and continue in fellowship just as we would drink and talk to each other at an inn.

Church is the same as an inn. We continue in fellowship and talk with each other in the church, so we have to usually go to church anyway. A person who usually goes to church becomes a spiritual person and a person who usually doesn't go to the church cannot walk in the Spirit, however great of a faith he/she might have before. The person who usually comes to church automatically prospers spiritually, no matter how weak he/she may be. It is due to the spiritual fellowship after having redemption.

There is no place but the church for us to dwell in. I want you to come to God's church as many times as you can and continue in fellowship with His people. Drop in at the church, attend every worship service, listen to God's word and consult with the church leaders in whatever you plan to do.

We must center our lives on God's word and assemble ourselves together. Then, we can have success in the life of faith without failure. We can be used preciously and be blessed by the Lord. I want you to present your flesh and hearts as instruments of righteousness to God. ⊠

HAVE YOU TRULY BEEN BORN AGAIN OF WATER AND THE SPIRIT?

HAVE YOU TRULY BEEN BORN AGAIN OF WATER AND THE SPIRIT?

PAUL C. JONG

Among many Christian books written about being born again, this is the first book of our time to preach the gospel of the water and the Spirit in strict accordance with the Scriptures. Man can't enter the Kingdom of Heaven without being born again of water and the Spirit. To be born again means that a sinner is saved from all his lifelong sins by believing in the baptism of Jesus and His blood of the Cross. Let's believe in the gospel of the water and the Spirit and enter the Kingdom of Heaven as the righteous who have no sin.

RETURN TO THE GOSPEL OF THE WATER AND THE SPIRIT

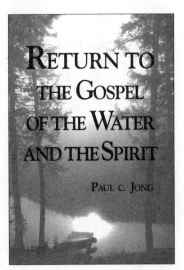

RETURN TO THE GOSPEL OF THE WATER AND THE SPIRIT

PAUL C. JONG

Let's return to the gospel of the water and the Spirit. Theology and doctrines themselves can't save us. However, many Christians still follow them, and consequently have not been born again yet. This book clearly tells us what mistakes theology and doctrines have made and how to believe in Jesus in the most proper way.

The Fail-safe Way for You to Receive the Holy Spirit

In Christianity, the most significantly discussed issue is salvation from sins and the indwelling of the Holy Spirit. However, few people have the exact knowledge of these two topics. Nevertheless, in reality people say that they believe in Jesus Christ while they are ignorant of true redemption and the Holy Spirit.

Do you know the true gospel that makes you receive the Holy Spirit? If you want to ask God for the indwelling of the Holy Spirit, then you must first know the gospel of the water and the Spirit and have faith in it. This book will certainly lead all Christians worldwide to receive the Holy Spirit through the remission of all their sins.

Our LORD Who Becomes the Righteousness of God (I) & (II)

The teachings in these books will satisfy the thirst in your heart. Today's Christians continue to live while not knowing the true solution to the personal sins that they are committing daily. Do you know what God's righteousness is? The author hopes that you will ask yourself this question and believe in God's righteousness, which is dealt in detail in these books.

The Doctrines of Predestination, Justification, and Incremental Sanctification are the major Christian doctrines, which brought only confusion and emptiness into the souls of believers. But, dear Christians, now is the time when you must continue in the Truth which you have learned and been assured of.

These books will provide your soul with a great understanding and lead it to peace. The author wants you to possess the blessing of knowing God's righteousness.

IS THE AGE OF THE ANTICHRIST, MARTYRDOM, RAPTURE AND THE MILLENNIAL KINGDOM COMING? (I)

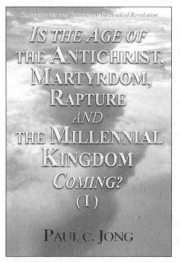

After the 9/11 terrorist attacks, traffic to "www.raptureready.com," an Internet site providing information on the end times, is reported to have increased to over 8 million hits, and according to a joint survey by CNN and TIME, over 59% of the Americans now believe in apocalyptic eschatology.

Responding to such demands of the time, the author provides a clear exposition of the key themes of the Book of Revelation, including the coming Antichrist, the martyrdom of the saints and their rapture, the Millennial Kingdom, and the New Heaven and Earth-all in the context of the whole Scripture and under the guidance of the Holy Spirit.

This book provides verse-by-verse commentaries on the Book of Revelation supplemented by the author's inspired sermons. Anyone who reads this book will come to grasp all the plans that God has in store for this world.

IS THE AGE OF THE ANTICHRIST, MARTYRDOM, RAPTURE AND THE MILLENNIAL KINGDOM COMING? (II)

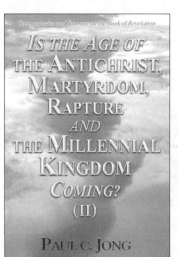

Most Christians today believe in the theory of pre-tribulation rapture. Because they believe in this false doctrine teaching them that they would be lifted before the coming of the Great Tribulation of seven years, they are leading idle religious lives steeped in complacency.

But the rapture of the saints will occur only after the plagues of the seven trumpets run their course until the sixth plague is all poured-that is, the rapture will happen after the Antichrist emerges amidst global chaos and the born-again saints are martyred, and when the seventh trumpet is blown. It is at this time that Jesus would descend from Heaven, and the resurrection and rapture of the born-again saints would occur (1 Thessalonians 4:16-17).

The righteous who were born again by believing in "the gospel of the water and the Spirit" will be resurrected and take part in the Rapture, and thus become heirs to the Millennial Kingdom and the eternal Kingdom of Heaven, but the sinners who were unable to participate in this first resurrection will face the great punishment of the seven bowls poured by God and be cast into the eternal fire of hell.

The TABERNACLE: A Detailed Portrait of Jesus Christ (I)

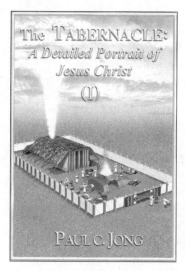

How can we find out the truth hidden in the Tabernacle? Only by knowing the gospel of the water and the Spirit, the real substance of the Tabernacle, can we correctly understand and know the answer to this question.

In fact, the blue, purple, and scarlet thread and the fine woven linen manifested in the gate of the Tabernacle's court show us the works of Jesus Christ in the New Testament's time that have saved the mankind. In this way, the Old Testament's Word of the Tabernacle and the Word of the New Testament are closely and definitely related to each other, like fine woven linen. But, unfortunately, this truth has been hidden for a long time to every truth seeker in Christianity.

Coming to this earth, Jesus Christ was baptized by John and shed His blood on the Cross. Without understanding and believing in the gospel of the water and the Spirit, none of us can ever find out the truth revealed in the Tabernacle. We must now learn this truth of the Tabernacle and believe in it. We all need to realize and believe in the truth manifested in the blue, purple, and scarlet thread and the fine woven linen of the gate of the Tabernacle's court.

The TABERNACLE: A Detailed Portrait of Jesus Christ (II)

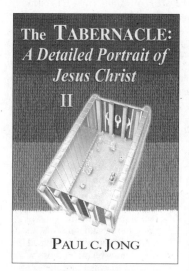

As God had commanded Moses to build the Tabernacle in the Old Testament, in the New Testament, God wants us to also build a Sanctuary in each of our hearts so that He may dwell in us. The material of faith with which we can build this Sanctuary in our hearts is the Word of the gospel of the water and the Spirit. With this gospel of the water and the Spirit, we must wash away all our sins and be cleansed. By telling us to build Him a Sanctuary, God is telling us to empty our hearts and believe in the gospel of the water and the Spirit. We must all cleanse our hearts by believing in the gospel of the water and the Spirit.

When we cleanse away all the sins of our hearts by believing in this gospel Truth, God then comes to dwell in them. It is by believing in this true gospel that you can build the holy Temples in your hearts. It is highly likely that until now, at least some of you have probably been offering your prayers of repentance to cleanse your hearts, trying to build the Temples by yourselves. But now is the time for you to abandon this false faith and be transformed by the renewing of your minds by believing in the gospel of the water and the Spirit.

The Elementary Principles of CHRIST

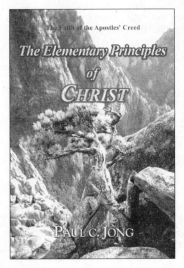

We must have the faith that the Apostles had and believe as they did, for their faith and beliefs came from the Holy Spirit. The Apostles believed in Jesus Christ, His Father, and the Holy Spirit as their God.

The Apostle Paul confessed that he died with Christ and was brought to new life with Him. He became an instrument of God by believing that he was baptized into Jesus Christ (Galatians 3:27). In God's gospel are found the baptism that Jesus received, the blood that He shed on the Cross, and the gift of the Holy Spirit that He has bestowed on everyone who believes in this true gospel of the water and the Spirit.

Do you know and believe in this original gospel? This is the very gospel that the Apostles had also believed. We, too, must therefore all believe in the gospel of the water and the Spirit.

The Gospel of Matthew (I), (II), (III), (IV), (V), (VI)

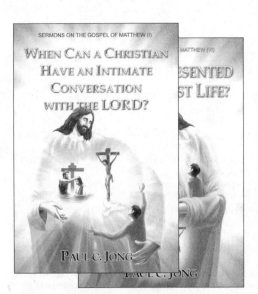

There are countless new Christians throughout the world, who have just been born again by believing in the gospel of the water and the Spirit that we have been spreading. We are indeed yearning to feed on the bread of life to them. But it is difficult for them to have fellowship with us in the true gospel, for they are all far away from us.

Therefore, to meet the spiritual needs of these people of Jesus Christ, the King of kings, The author proclaims that those who have received the remission of their sins by believing in the Word of Jesus Christ, must feed on His pure Word in order to defend their faith and sustain their spiritual lives. The sermons in these books have been prepared as new bread of life that will nourish the born-again to edify their spiritual growth.

Through His Church and servants, God will continue to provide you with this bread of life. May God's blessings be on all those who have been born again of water and the Spirit, who desires to have true spiritual fellowship with us in Jesus Christ.

The First Epistle of John (I) & (II)

He who believes that Jesus, who is God and the Savior, came by the gospel of the water and the Spirit to deliver all sinners from their sins, is saved from all his sins, and becomes a child of God the Father.

The First Epistle of John states that Jesus, who is God, came to us by the gospel of the water and the Spirit, and that He is the Son of God the Father. The Book, in other words, mostly emphasizes that Jesus is God (1 John 5:20), and concretely testifies the gospel of the water and the Spirit in chapter 5.

We must not hesitate to believe that Jesus Christ is God and to follow Him.

Sermons on Galatians: From Physical Circumcision to the Doctrine of Repentance (I) & (II)

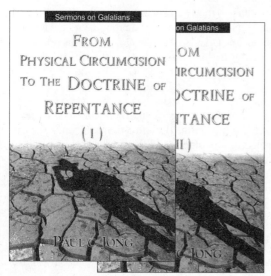

Today's Christianity has turned into merely a world religion. Most Christians nowadays live in a situation of being sinners because they haven't been born again by spiritual faith. It is because they have only relied on Christian doctrines without being aware of the gospel of the water and the Spirit until now.

Therefore, now is the time for you to know the spiritual fallacies of the circumcisionists and keep distance from such faith. You have to know the contradictoriness of the prayers of repentance. Now is the time for you to stand firmer than ever on the gospel of the water and the Spirit.

If you haven't believed in this true gospel so far, you have to believe in our Savior who came to us by the gospel of the water and the Spirit even now. Now, you have to be complete Christians with the faith of believing in the gospel Truth of the water and the Spirit.

The Love of God Revealed through Jesus, The Only Begotten Son (I), (II), (III)

It is written, "No one has seen God at any time. The only begotten Son, who is in the bosom of the Father, He has declared Him" (John 1:18).

How perfectly did Jesus reveal the love of God to us! How perfectly did Jesus deliver us! What perfect Truth of salvation is the gospel of the water and the Spirit! We have never regretted receiving our salvation through our faith in Jesus, who came by water and blood (1 John 5:6).

Now, we have become His sinless people. Whoever believes in the gospel of the water and the Spirit can receive the eternal remission of sins and earn eternal life.

Eat My Flesh And Drink My Blood

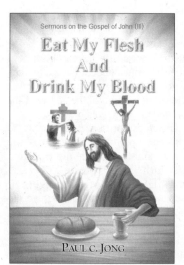

Until now, most Christians have not known the Truth, but only inherited religious acts. From the gospel to Holy Communion, today's Christianity maintains its orthodoxy not through the knowledge of the Truth, but by emphasizing only formal procedures and consecrated rites.

As a result, when today's Christians come across the bread and wine that signify the flesh and blood of Jesus during Communion, they are thankful only for the sacrifice of His blood, and they can't help but remain completely ignorant of the fact that Christ took upon Himself all their sins once and for all by being baptized by John the Baptist.

Therefore, I admonish all Christians throughout the whole world to learn, even from now on, what the flesh and blood of Jesus mean within the gospel of the water and the Spirit, to believe in it, and to thereby receive their salvation and also partake in Holy Communion with the right faith.

The Relationship Between the Ministry of JESUS and That of JOHN the BAPTIST Recorded in the Four Gospels

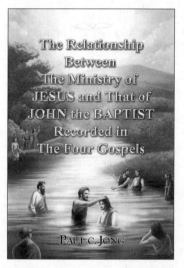

Do you perhaps think that it doesn't matter whether there needs to be the ministry of John the Baptist or not? You must believe according to the written Word of God. We must understand and believe in the ministry of John the Baptist within the frame of the ministry of Jesus Christ. John the Baptist in the New Testament was the prophet Elijah promised to be sent down to this earth according to the Book of Malachi chapter 4, verses 4-5. As the prophet Elijah to come, John the Baptist was born six months before Jesus, and he was the one who passed on the sins of this world at once by giving Jesus the baptism at the Jordan River at the age of thirty. Thus, we must become the recipients of God's blessing by knowing the ministry of John the Baptist and accepting the ministry of Jesus Christ.

THE WILL OF THE HOLY TRINITY FOR HUMAN BEINGS

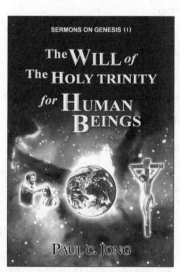

Through the Book of Genesis, God wants us to realize His good intentions toward us. Where is God's will for us revealed? It is revealed in the gospel Truth of the water and the Spirit that God accomplished through Jesus Christ. We must come into this good intention of God by faith, manifested in the gospel of the water and the Spirit. To do so, when we consider God's Word, we need to cast aside our existing carnal thoughts we have had, and believe in God's Word exactly as it is. All of us must throw away our mistaken knowledge accumulated until now, and open our spiritual eyes by placing our faith in the righteousness of God.

The Fall of Man and the Perfect Salvation of God

In the Book of Genesis, the purpose for which God created us is contained. When architects design a building or artists draw a painting, they first conceive the work that would be completed in their minds before they actually begin working on their project. Just like this, our God also had our salvation of mankind in His mind even before He created the heavens and the earth, and He made Adam and Eve with this purpose in mind. And God needed to explain to us the domain of Heaven, which is not seen by our eyes of the flesh, by drawing an analogy to the domain of the earth that we can all see and understand.

Even before the foundation of the world, God wanted to save mankind perfectly by giving the gospel of the water and the Spirit to everyone's heart. So although all human beings were made out of dust, they must learn and know the gospel Truth of the water and the Spirit to benefit their own souls. If people continue to live without knowing the dominion of Heaven, they will lose not only the things of the earth, but also everything that belongs to Heaven.

Heretics, Who Followed the Sins of Jeroboam (I) & (II)

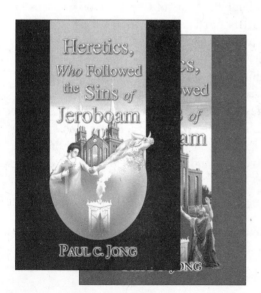

Christians today do not know what the gospel Truth of the water and the Spirit that the Lord has made and given us is. Thus, they continue to believe in the doctrines of Christianity and not the gospel of the water and the Spirit. For that reason, the fact of the matter is that despite their claim of having faith in Jesus, they continue to believe in and follow golden calves.

We must discern those that worship golden calves as God within Christianity. And by coming back before God of the Truth, we must offer the sacrifices of righteousness to God. The sacrifice that God receives with rejoice is the sacrifice of righteousness that people offer by faith after having received the remission of sin by having faith in the gospel of the water and the Spirit. Before God, you must seriously think about whether or not you are offering the sacrifice of God-given righteousness by the faith of believing in the gospel of the water and the Spirit.

The Lord's Prayer : Misinterpretations and Truth

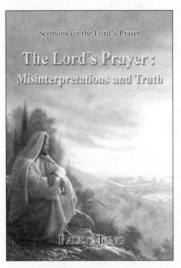

In order to interpret the Lord's Prayer correctly, we must first correctly understand the gospel of the water and the Spirit, which was spoken to us by the Lord. We have Truth in us when we not only know and understand the gospel of the water and the Spirit but also believe it with our hearts. The true gospel, which we believe in, has led us so far, so that we can lead truly faithful lives that the Lord wants from us in the Lord's Prayer.

Exegesis on the Book of ROMANS (I)

The righteousness of God is transparent. God's righteousness cannot be substituted by anything. That is because His righteousness is different from the righteousness of man. We need to know what God's righteousness is, and we need to believe in it.

God's righteousness is fundamentally different from human righteousness. The righteousness of mankind is like a filthy rag, but the righteousness of God is like a brilliant pearl shining forever. God's righteousness is the Truth that is absolutely needed by every sinner, transcending all ages.

HAVE YOU MET JESUS WITH THE GOSPEL OF THE WATER AND THE SPIRIT?

It is written, "No one has seen God at any time. The only begotten Son, who is in the bosom of the Father, He has declared Him" (John 1:18).

How perfectly did Jesus reveal the love of God to us! How perfectly did Jesus deliver us! What perfect Truth of salvation is the gospel of the water and the Spirit! We have never regretted receiving our salvation through our faith in Jesus, who came by water and blood (1 John 5:6).

Now, we have become His sinless people. Whoever believes in the gospel of the water and the Spirit can receive the eternal remission of sins and earn eternal life.

Sermons on the Gospel of Luke (I), (II), (III), (IV), (V), (VI), (VII)

It is Jesus Christ who moves the entire history of this world. Our Lord came to this earth to save all humans from the sins of the world, and He has become the bread of new life for those of us who believe in the gospel of the water and the Spirit. In fact, it was to give this new life to us, who were all destined to hell for our sins that our Lord came looking for you and me.

No More Chaos, Void or Darkness Now (I) & (II)

Although we may be powerless and because the Word of God has power, when the Word falls to the ground it bears fruit without fail. Further, because the Word of God is alive we can see for ourselves that it is the same today and tomorrow, and forever unchanging. Unlike the words of man, God's Word never changes, for it is ever faithful. When God speaks, He fulfills exactly according to His Words.

For the Word of God has power, so when God said, "Let there be light," there was light, and when He said, "Let there be a greater light and a lesser light," it was fulfilled just as He had commanded.

THE DIFFERENCE BETWEEN ABEL'S FAITH AND CAIN'S FAITH

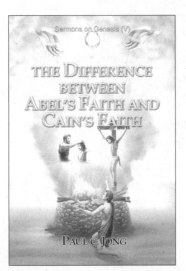

Whenever we stand before the presence of God to glorify Him, we should not approach Him through some religious rituals, but instead we have to approach Him by trusting in what He has done for us and thanking Him for His love. Only then does God accept our worship and pour the Holy Spirit on us abundantly.

FOR THE LOST SHEEP (I) & (II)

What God wants to do is to make us into His children by making us born again through the gospel of the water and the Spirit.

We humans are born as God's creations first, but if we receive the remission of sins by believing in the gospel of the water and the Spirit, we are born again as the children of God. This means that, after the Lord came and remitted all our sins, we who were blind could now obtain our sight.

WISDOM OF THE PRIMITIVE GOSPEL

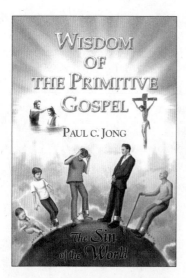

The primitive gospel is the Truth of salvation that's absolutely indispensable to everyone. Transcending all denominations, this primitive gospel will clearly teach every Christian how God's blessings could be bestowed on them. This true gospel will now fill your heart with God's overflowing love. And it will be the most precious gift to all your loved ones.

BE A GOSPEL WITNESS WHO SAVES
THE HUMAN RACE FROM DESTRUCTION

Mankind, who had eaten the fruit of the knowledge of good and evil, came to have the different standard for good and evil from God's. Then, which is correct, God's Word or our judgment? Our standard is always relative and selfish. Therefore we should cast away our own ideas and simply trust and follow God's Word focusing on "What does the Word of God say?" Ignoring God's Word and seeking self-righteousness is Cain's faith and religious belief. Abel put his faith in the Word of God he heard from his father, Adam, and offered the firstborn of his flock and of their fat. But self-conceited Cain brought an offering of the fruit of the ground to the Lord. God accepted Abel's offering but refused Cain's offering. It is God's lesson that faith in man-made religions cannot bring salvation.

THOSE WHO POSSESS ABRAHAM'S FAITH

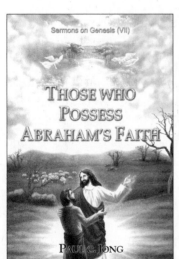

There are two kinds of righteousness in this world which are constantly in conflict and struggle with each another; these are the righteousness of God and the righteousness of man. Although God's righteousness faces many obstacles, it always prevails over the righteousness of man and leads us to the victorious way. That's because the Word of God is almighty. Because God's almighty power is with us, we are able to taste His blessings, for the Word of God has the power to reach our hearts, thoughts and souls, and brings all His blessings to us.

WHAT SHOULD WE STRIVE TO BELIEVE AND PREACH?

The Gospel of Mark testifies that Jesus Christ is the Son of God and God Himself. And it also testifies that He is our Savior. So we can see the writer of the Gospel of Mark bearing witness of Jesus forcefully, testifying that He is the very God and our Savior. This is why I would like to bear witness of this Jesus Christ who is manifested in the Gospel of Mark as much as possible based on the gospel of the water and the Spirit. What is obvious is that the core Truth of Christianity is found in the gospel of the water and the Spirit. Jesus said to Nicodemus, "Most assuredly, I say to you, unless one is born of water and the Spirit, he cannot enter the kingdom of God" (John 3:5).

FROM THIS CORRUPTED WORLD TO HEAVEN ABOVE

We must open our spiritual eyes and clearly see the wonders and beauty of this world. This is possible only when we escape from darkness through the Lord and live out our faith with the conviction that we have no sin. When you are born again through the gospel of the water and the Spirit and open your spiritual eyes, your life in this world will be more enjoyable than anyone else's life. So you must escape from darkness and dwell in the light, taking and enjoying everything the Lord has given you in your life, for the Word of God says, *"Let the hearts of those rejoice who seek the LORD!"* (Psalm 105:3).

THE BLESSING OF FAITH RECEIVED WITH THE HEART

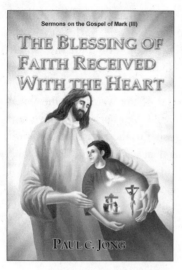

This special day of amnesty, when the remission of sins and the blessings of faith are received by believing in the gospel of the water and the Spirit with the heart, is found in no country in this world, but it is the greatest holiday that can be celebrated together with people from any country in the world. Today is the day you can receive the remission of sins, and it is the only common holiday celebrated together with God's people from all over the world.

The TABERNACLE (III): A Prefiguration of The Gospel of The Water and the Spirit

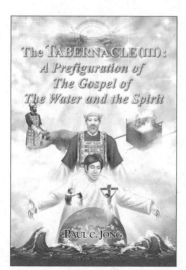

All Christians should stand firm in the faith of the gospel of the water and the Spirit. They will then understand the gospel of the water and the Spirit through the revelations which are manifested in the Tabernacle system as written in the Old Testament. They also can be sure of having received the remission of sins by faith. If you have as yet not possessed such faith, you need to strive to get it as soon as possible.

You should receive the remission of sins first if you want the Holy Spirit to abide in your heart. To do so, you need to put your faith in the righteousness of God fulfilled by the Lord. This is the only way the Holy Spirit can dwell in your heart.

WHAT GOD IS SAYING TO US THROUGH THE EPISTLE TO THE EPHESIANS

Today God has founded His Church on the faith of the believers in the gospel of the water and the Spirit. God's Church is the gathering of those who have been saved by believing in the gospel of the water and the Spirit. Therefore, if your hearts now have faith in the gospel of the water and the Spirit, you can then lead the true life of faith. Such a life of faith is possible only in God's Church. Furthermore, only such faith qualifies us to live forever in the Kingdom of the Lord. Through this faith we must receive the love of salvation and all the spiritual blessings of Heaven from God the Father, Jesus Christ and the Holy Spirit.

HOW CAN YOU STRENGTHEN YOUR FAITH?

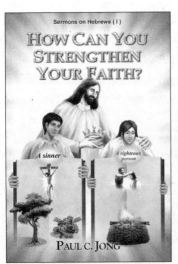

Every sinner must now believe in the genuine gospel. The God-given gospel of salvation is the gospel of the water and the Spirit that is manifested in the righteousness of God. The writer of the Book of Hebrews is trying to correct your misguided faith. Therefore, our faith needs to be deep rooted in the foundation of the gospel of the water and the Spirit. Those who are standing sure-footed on this absolute gospel Truth abide most certainly in the faith in the righteousness of Jesus Christ.

SERMONS FOR THOSE WHO HAVE BECOME OUR COWORKERS (I), (II), (III), (IV)

This book is a collection of sermons that have been written to direct our fellow coworkers and saints and to show them how to lead a life as a true servant of God. For this reason, these books are entitled *"Sermons for Those Who Have Become Our Coworkers."*

The author earnestly desires to share fellowship with coworkers within the faith, those who believe wholeheartedly in the righteousness of Christ, excluding personal interests. He does really desire this because he has met them by faith in the Lord's righteousness and they are also preaching it now.

ARE YOU NOW LIVING AS THE OBJECT OF GOD'S AFFECTION?

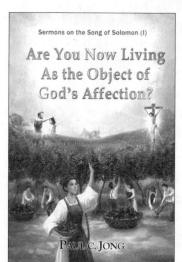

If you want to experience the Lord's love in your life always, listen closely to His voice. If you want to be loved by the Lord in your ministry, accept the God-given gospel of the water and the Spirit into your heart and then carry out the Lord's work. The Lord loves us precisely because we believe in and serve the gospel of the water and the Spirit. Our Lord cannot help but love whoever believes in His gospel of the water and the Spirit and serves Him faithfully to spread this gospel all over the world.

Paul C. Jong's Christian books have been translated into 76 major languages at this point: Afrikaans, Albanian, Arabic, Asante, Bengali, Bulgarian, Burmese, Cebuano, Chichewa, Chin, Chinese, Croatian, Czech, Danish, Dioula, Dutch, English, Fongbe, French, Georgian, German, Greek, Gujarati, Hebrew, Hindi, Hungarian, Indonesian, Iranian, Italian, Japanese, Javanese, Kannada, Khmer, Kirghiz, Kirundi, Kissi, Latvian, Luganda, Luo, Madi, Malagasy, Malayalam, Marathi, Mindat, Mizo, Mongolian, Nepali, Oriya, Polish, Portuguese, Punjabi, Romanian, Russian, Serbian, Shona, Slovak, Slovene, Spanish, Swahili, Swedish, Tagalog, Taiwanese, Tamil, Telugu, Thai, Turkish, Ukrainian, Urdu, Vietnamese, and Zou. They are also available now through our free e-book service.

E-book is digital book designed for you to feel a printed book on screen. You can read it easily on your PC monitor in your native language after downloading the viewer software and a text file. Feel free to visit our web site at http://www.nlmission.com or http://www.bjnewlife.org to download our e-books, and you will get the most remarkable Christian e-books absolutely for free.

And, would you like to take part in having our free Christian books known to more people worldwide? We would be very thankful if you link your website to ours so that many people get an opportunity to meet Jesus Christ through our inspired Christian books. Please visit our site at http://www.bjnewlife.org/english/about/take_banners.php to take our banners to your website. In addition, we would also be very grateful if you introduce our website to the webmasters around you for adding our link.

The New Life Mission
Contact: John Shin, General Secretary
E-mail: newlife@bjnewlife.org

Memo